PRISONS AND JAILS

A DETERRENT TO CRIME?

ISSN 1536-5190

PRISONS AND JAILS

A DETERRENT TO CRIME?

INFORMATION PLUS® REFERENCE SERIES
Formerly published by Information Plus, Wylie, Texas

GALE®

THOMSON

GALE™

Detroit • New York • San Diego • San Francisco • Cleveland • New Haven, Conn. • Waterville, Maine • London • Munich

Prisons and Jails: A Deterrent to Crime?
Miklos Laci

Project Editor
Ellice Engdahl

Editorial
Andrew Claps, Paula Cutcher-Jackson, Kathleen J. Edgar, Dana Ferguson, Debra Kirby, Prindle LaBarge, Elizabeth Manar, Sharon McGilvray, Charles B. Montney, Heather Price

Permissions
Ann Taylor

Product Design
Cynthia Baldwin

Composition and Electronic Prepress
Evi Seoud

Manufacturing
Keith Helmling

LIBRARY OF CONGRESS CATALOGING-IN-PUBLICATION DATA

ISBN 0-7876-5103-6 (set)
ISBN 0-7876-7344-7
ISSN 1536-5190

Printed in the United States of America
10 9 8 7 6 5 4 3 2 1

TABLE OF CONTENTS

This chapter outlines the history of the punishment of criminals, from ancient times until today, and discusses the accompanying changes in correctional philosophy. Also explored are the public's attitudes toward punishment and rehabilitation and the treatment of juveniles in the criminal justice system.

Operating prisons and jails is costly. Incarceration rates have been rising not just in proportion to population increase but as a percent of the resident population, putting pressure on federal, state, and local budgets. States bear the largest costs for prisons, local governments for jails. Attempts at controlling costs in various ways are in conflict with legislative initiatives to increase the time convicts spend behind bars.

Jails, locally operated facilities that hold individuals for varying purposes, face numerous issues. These include the growth of jail populations, the confinement of juveniles, the operation of community-based programs, the question of privatization, and the shift toward requiring inmates to pay for services and participate in work programs.

The rate of incarceration is increasing, resulting in overcrowded prisons, rapid construction of new prisons, and a reliance on private facilities and local jails to house prisoners. This chapter explores reasons for the increase in the incarceration rate as well as the controversy surrounding the privatization of prisons and the details of prison work programs.

This chapter provides a statistical breakdown of the state and federal prison populations, by race, ethnicity, age, gender, and type of crime for which people are imprisoned. Also discussed are inmates' educational attainment, their abuse in the past, and their children.

A large number of prison inmates report physical or mental impairments or injuries. These are compared to rates experienced by the general public. HIV/AIDS prevalence is much higher in prisons than in society at large and high among incarcerated women. The mental health of prisoners is discussed.

Juveniles pose special problems to the corrections system. They may be taken into custody for a range of reasons, from protection to punishment, and they may be placed in public or private facilities. Changing approaches to juvenile delinquency are traced. Trends in confining juveniles as adults are reported and the characteristics of juveniles in residential placement are explored.

The majority of the nation's offenders are not in prison but on probation or parole. This chapter presents demographic information about probationers and parolees and compares these two categories. A third of those on probation and nearly a half of parolees fail to complete their sentences successfully. The issues are explored.

Significant changes relating to the sentencing of offenders began in the 1980s under the concept of "truth-in-sentencing." The history of this policy is presented and illustrated using the federal system. Three-strikes laws are a special instance of sentencing guidelines. The consequences of these laws are presented. Also covered are alternative sentencing practices used by the courts.

This chapter deals with prison populations not covered in earlier chapters because of their unusual characteristics. These include military offenders, prisoners held in U.S. Territories and Commonwealths, jails in Indian Country, immigrants held in confinement by the federal government, and death row inmates. Where applicable, laws governing these populations are discussed.

PREFACE

Prisons and Jails: A Deterrent to Crime? is one of the latest volumes in the Information Plus Reference Series. The purpose of each volume of the series is to present the latest facts on a topic of pressing concern in modern American life. These topics include today's most controversial and most studied social issues: abortion, capital punishment, care for the elderly, crime, health care, the environment, immigration, minorities, social welfare, women, youth, and many more. Although written especially for the high school and undergraduate student, this series is an excellent resource for anyone in need of factual information on current affairs.

By presenting the facts, it is Gale's intention to provide its readers with everything they need to reach an informed opinion on current issues. To that end, there is a particular emphasis in this series on the presentation of scientific studies, surveys, and statistics. These data are generally presented in the form of tables, charts, and other graphics placed within the text of each book. Every graphic is directly referred to and carefully explained in the text. The source of each graphic is presented within the graphic itself. The data used in these graphics are drawn from the most reputable and reliable sources, in particular from the various branches of the U.S. government and from major independent polling organizations. Every effort has been made to secure the most recent information available. The reader should bear in mind that many major studies take years to conduct, and that additional years often pass before the data from these studies is made available to the public. Therefore, in many cases the most recent information available in 2003 dated from 2000 or 2001. Older statistics are sometimes presented as well if they are of particular interest and no more recent information exists.

Although statistics are a major focus of the Information Plus Reference Series, they are by no means its only content. Each book also presents the widely held positions and important ideas that shape how the book's subject is discussed in the United States. These positions are explained in detail and, where possible, in the words of their proponents. Some of the other material to be found in these books includes: historical background; descriptions of major events related to the subject; relevant laws and court cases; and examples of how these issues play out in American life. Some books also feature primary documents or have pro and con debate sections giving the words and opinions of prominent Americans on both sides of a controversial topic. All material is presented in an even-handed and unbiased manner; the reader will never be encouraged to accept one view of an issue over another.

HOW TO USE THIS BOOK

Crime is one of the big issues facing Americans today, but crime cannot be discussed in proper context without discussing the American system of prisons and jails. Much public funding is spent on the construction of new prisons and jails and the maintenance of old ones, but many people question the effectiveness of prisons and jails as a deterrent to crime. Is the purpose of institutions such as prisons and jails to rehabilitate criminals or to punish them? Are certain races or ethnicities more prevalent in the prison population than others? Does juvenile incarceration work? What should day-to-day life be like for those in prisons and jails? What rights do prisoners give up and what rights do they retain? These and other basic questions are discussed in this volume.

Prisons and Jails: A Deterrent to Crime? consists of eleven chapters and three appendices. Each of the chapters is devoted to a particular aspect of prisons and jails in the United States. For a summary of the information covered in each chapter, please see the synopses provided in the Table of Contents at the front of the book. Chapters generally begin with an overview of the basic facts and background information on the chapter's topic, then proceed to examine subtopics of particular interest. For example, Chapter 7, Juvenile Confinement, begins with a discussion of exactly how America defines a "juvenile" as that term relates to criminals. It then examines changing approaches to juvenile delinquency, trends in juvenile arrests, juveniles held in jails and prisons, and juveniles in residential placement facilities. Readers can find their way through a chapter by looking for the section and sub-section headings, which are clearly set off from the text. They can also refer to the book's extensive index if they already know what they are looking for.

Statistical Information

The tables and figures featured throughout *Prisons and Jails: A Deterrent to Crime?* will be of particular use to the reader in learning about this issue. These tables and figures represent an extensive collection of the most recent and important statistics on prisons and jails and related issues—for example, graphics in the book cover the number of people in jail or prison in the United States, characteristics of those incarcerated, and the amount of money spent on the prison system. Gale believes that making this information available to the reader is the most important way in which we fulfill the goal of this book: to help readers to understand the issues and controversies surrounding prisons and jails in the United States and to reach their own conclusions.

Each table or figure has a unique identifier appearing above it for ease of identification and reference. Titles for the tables and figures explain their purpose. At the end of each table or figure, the original source of the data is provided.

In order to help readers understand these often complicated statistics, all tables and figures are explained in the text. References in the text direct the reader to the relevant statistics. Furthermore, the contents of all tables and figures are fully indexed. Please see the opening section of the index at the back of this volume for a description of how to find tables and figures within it.

Appendices

In addition to the main body text and images, *Prisons and Jails: A Deterrent to Crime?* has three appendices. The first is the Important Names and Addresses directory. Here the reader will find contact information for a number of government and private organizations that can provide further information on the American prison and jail system. The second appendix is the Resources section, which can also assist the reader in conducting his or her own research. In this section, the author and editors of *Prisons and Jails: A Deterrent to Crime?* describe some of the sources that were most useful during the compilation of this book. The final appendix is the detailed Index, which facilitates reader access to specific topics in this book.

ADVISORY BOARD CONTRIBUTIONS

The staff of Information Plus would like to extend their heartfelt appreciation to the Information Plus Advisory Board. This dedicated group of media professionals provides feedback on the series on an ongoing basis. Their comments allow the editorial staff who work on the project to make the series better and more user-friendly. Our top priorities are to produce the highest-quality and most useful books possible, and the Advisory Board's contributions to this process are invaluable.

The members of the Information Plus Advisory Board are:

- Kathleen R. Bonn, Librarian, Newbury Park High School, Newbury Park, California
- Madelyn Garner, Librarian, San Jacinto College—North Campus, Houston, Texas
- Anne Oxenrider, Media Specialist, Dundee High School, Dundee, Michigan
- Charles R. Rodgers, Director of Libraries, Pasco-Hernando Community College, Dade City, Florida
- James N. Zitzelsberger, Library Media Department Chairman, Oshkosh West High School, Oshkosh, Wisconsin

COMMENTS AND SUGGESTIONS

The editors of the Information Plus Reference Series welcome your feedback on *Prisons and Jails: A Deterrent to Crime?* Please direct all correspondence to:

Editors

Information Plus Reference Series

27500 Drake Rd.

Farmington Hills, MI 48331-3535

ACKNOWLEDGMENTS

The editors wish to thank the copyright holders of material included in this volume and the permissions managers of book and magazine publishing companies for assisting us in securing reproduction rights. We are also grateful to the staffs of the Detroit Public Library, the Library of Congress, the University of Detroit Mercy Library, Wayne State University Purdy/Kresge Library Complex, and the University of Michigan Libraries for making their resources available to us.

Following is a list of the copyright holders who have granted us permission to reproduce material in Information Plus: Prisons and Jails: A Deterrent to Crime? Every effort has been made to trace copyright, but if omissions have been made, please let us know.

For more detailed source citations, please see the sources listed under each individual table and figure.

Centers for Disease Control and Prevention: Table 6.2

Central Intelligence Agency: Table 10.2

Executive Office of the President: Figure 2.1

Federal Bureau of Investigation: Table 3.4

Federal Bureau of Prisons: Table 5.5

National Center for Juvenile Justice: Table 7.4, Table 7.9, Table 7.10

National Institute of Corrections: Table 3.12, Table 11.1

National Institute of Justice: Table 9.7, Table 9.8

Office of Justice Programs: Figure 7.6, Table 7.5

Office of Juvenile Justice and Delinquency Prevention: Table 7.1, Table 7.2, Table 7.3, Figure 7.2, Figure 7.3, Figure 7.4, Table 7.6, Table 7.7, Table 7.8, Figure 7.7

Urban Institute: Table 9.2

U.S. Bureau of Justice Statistics: Table 1.1, Table 2.1, Table 2.2, Table 2.3, Figure 2.4, Figure 2.5, Figure 2.6, Table 3.1, Table 3.2, Table 3.3, Table 3.5, Table 3.6, Table 3.7, Table 3.8, Table 3.9, Table 3.10, Table 3.11, Table 3.14, Table 3.15, Table 3.16, Table 4.1, Table 4.2, Table 4.3, Figure 4.1, Table 4.4, Table 4.5, Table 4.6, Table 4.7, Figure 4.2, Table 4.8, Table 4.9, Table 4.10, Table 4.11, Figure 4.3, Table 5.1, Table 5.2, Table 5.3, Figure 5.1, Figure 5.2, Table 5.4, Table 5.6, Table 5.7, Table 5.8, Table 5.9, Table 5.10, Table 5.11, Table 5.12, Table 5.13, Figure 6.1, Table 6.1, Table 6.2, Table 6.3, Table 6.4, Figure 6.2, Table 6.5, Table 6.6, Table 6.7, Table 6.8, Table 6.9, Table 6.10, Table 6.11, Figure 6.3, Figure 6.4, Figure 7.5, Table 7.11, Figure 8.1, Table 8.1, Table 8.2, Figure 8.2, Figure 8.3, Table 8.3, Table 8.4, Table 8.5, Figure 8.4, Table 8.6, Table 8.7, Table 8.8, Figure 8.5, Table 8.9, Table 8.10, Figure 8.6, Figure 8.7, Table 8.11, Table 9.1, Table 9.2, Table 9.5, Table 9.6, Figure 10.1, Table 10.1, Table 10.3, Table 10.4, Table 10.5, Figure 10.3, Table 10.6, Figure 10.4, Figure 10.5, Figure 10.6, Table 10.7, Table 10.8

U.S. Census Bureau: Figure 2.2, Figure 2.3, Figure 6.1, Figure 7.1, Figure 8.6, Figure 10.1, Figure 10.2

U.S. Department of Justice: Table 3.13

U.S. Sentencing Commission: Table 9.3, Table 9.4

CHAPTER 1
HISTORY OF CORRECTIONS—
REVENGE OR REHABILITATION?

A terrible stinking dark and dismal place situated underground into which no daylight can come. It was paved with stone; the prisoners had no beds and lay on the pavement whereby they endured great misery and hardship.

— Inmate at Newgate Jail (1724)

Public views of punishment for crimes have changed over the centuries. History has its clement and its stormy seasons, and during times of war, famine, and disorder, gains made in peace and plenty are sometimes lost. Yet generally over time most societies have moved from the extraction of personal or family justice—vengeful acts such as blood feuds or the practice of "an eye for an eye"—toward formal systems based on written codes and orderly process. Jails and prisons have changed from being holding places where prisoners awaited deportation, maiming, whippings, beatings, or execution. Confinement itself has become the punishment. In the United States today, as articulated by the U.S. Supreme Court, punishment has at least four justifications: deterrence, societal retribution, rehabilitation, and incapacitation—the last category intended to protect society by permanently incarcerating those who cannot be reformed.

ANCIENT TIMES

Many ancient cultures allowed the victim or a member of the victim's family to deliver justice. The offender often fled to his or her family for protection. As a result, blood feuds developed in which the victim's family sought revenge against the offender's family. Sometimes the offender's family responded by striking back. Retaliation could continue until the families tired of killing or stealing from each other or until one or both families were destroyed or financially ruined.

As societies organized into tribes and villages, local communities increasingly began to assume the responsibility for punishing crimes against the community and its members. Punishments could be brutal—the condemned boiled in oil or fed to wild beasts. The development of writing led to the creation of lists of crimes and their respective punishments. The Code of Hammurabi in Babylon (circa 1750 B.C.E.) is generally considered the first such set of laws. The laws of Moses, as recorded in the Bible, also cited offenses against the community and their corresponding punishments. Nonetheless, personal revenge continued to be practiced. For example, the Bible reports 10 cities in which an accused murderer would be safe from the victim's family. The Justinian Code of Emperor Justinian of the Byzantine or Eastern Roman Empire (529–565) organized many of the early codes.

As empires developed, the owners of large tracts of land, and later the rulers, wanted a more orderly legal system than blood feuds and thus established courts. Such courts often sentenced the offender to slavery in the victim's family for several years as restitution for the offense. Other punishments included laboring on public works projects, banishment, or even death.

MEDIEVAL TIMES

As in ancient times, medieval Europe had very harsh punishments. Torture and death were commonly administered. From the depths of the "Dark Ages" came cruel instruments that tortured as they killed. For example, the rack stretched its victims until their bodies were torn apart. The Iron Maiden—a box thickly set with sharp spikes inside and on the inner side of its door—pierced its victims from front and back as it closed. People came to watch public executions to see the convicts burn, be hanged, or be beheaded.

Confinement

Those arrested were usually confined (imprisoned) until they confessed to the crime and their physical punishment occurred. The medieval church sometimes used long-term incarceration to replace executions. Some wealthy landowners built private prisons to enhance their own power, imprisoning those who dared dispute their pursuit of power or oppose their whims. With the enactment of King Henry II's set of ordinances, called the Assize of Clarendon (England, 1166), many crimes were classified as offenses against the "king's peace" and were punished by the state and not by the church, the lord, or the victim's extended family. At this time the first prisons designed solely for incarceration were constructed.

Prisons

The only comfort prisoners had in the cold, damp, filthy, rat- and roach-infested prisons of medieval Europe was what they could—or rather were required to—buy. The prison-keeper charged for blankets, mattresses, food, and even the manacles (chains). The prisoner had to pay for the privilege of being both booked (charged) and released. Wealthy prisoners could pay for plush quarters but most suffered in terrible conditions, often dying from malnutrition, disease, or victimization by other prisoners.

THE RISE OF NATIONS

In Europe in the 1500s, while most jails still housed people waiting for trial or punishment, workhouses and debtors' prisons developed as sources of cheap labor or places to house insane or minor offenders. Those found guilty of serious crimes could be transported instead of executed. England transported many prisoners to colonial Georgia in the United States and later to colonial Australia; France sent many to South America. Although transportation was a less severe punishment than the death penalty, many prisoners did not survive the harsh conditions either on board the transport ships or life in the early colonies to which they were sent.

COLONIAL AND EARLY POST-REVOLUTIONARY PERIODS

Just as in Europe, physical punishment was common in colonial America. Americans used stocks, pillories, branding, flogging, and maiming—such as cutting off an ear or slitting nostrils—to punish offenders. The death penalty was used frequently. In 1636 the Massachusetts Bay Colony listed 13 crimes that warranted execution, including murder, practicing witchcraft, and worshipping idols. In early New York State, 20 percent of offenses, including pickpocketing, horse stealing, and robbery, were capital crimes (warranting the death penalty).

Jails were used to hold prisoners awaiting trial or sentencing or as debtors' prisons, but were not the punishment itself. Puritans believed that humans were naturally depraved, which made it easier for the colonies and the first states to enforce harsh punishments. In addition, since

Puritans believed that humans had no control over their fate (predestination), many early Americans felt there was no need for rehabilitation.

Pennsylvania

The Quakers, led by William Penn, made colonial Pennsylvania an exception to the harsh practices often found in the other colonies. The early criminal code of colonial Pennsylvania abolished executions for all crimes except homicide, replaced physical punishments with imprisonment and hard labor, and did not charge the prisoners for their food and housing.

Ideas of the Enlightenment

The philosophy of the Enlightenment (the Age of Reason) emphasized the importance of the individual. After the French Revolution of 1789, which was based on the ideas of the Enlightenment, western European countries abolished torture as a form of punishment and emphasized that the punishment should fit the individual's crime(s). Rather than inflicting pain as the main element of correction, the idea of changing the individual became the goal. The French Revolution, however, also introduced the guillotine, a sophisticated beheading machine that was similar to instruments used in Britain.

In England John Howard (1726–1790) wrote *The State of the Prisons in England and Wales* (1777), in which he described the horrible treatment of prisoners. Howard thought that prisoners should not be harassed by keepers who extorted from them, nor should they have to suffer malnutrition and disease. He advocated segregating prisoners by age, sex, and type of crime; paying the staff; hiring medical officials and chaplains; and supplying prisoners with adequate food and clothing.

Howard called the facilities "penitentiaries" (from the word "penitent," meaning to be ashamed or sorry for committing a sin or offense) because he based his ideas on the Quaker philosophy of people repenting, reflecting on their sins, and changing their ways. Public concern led the British Parliament to pass the Penitentiary Act of 1779; it called for the first secure and sanitary penitentiary. The law eliminated the charging of fees. Prisoners would live in solitary confinement at night and work together silently during the day. Nonetheless, although Parliament passed the law, it did not actually go into effect until the opening of Pentonville Penitentiary in North London in 1842.

THE REFORM MOVEMENT

The ideas of individual freedom and the concept that people could change society for the better by using reason permeated American society in the 1800s. Reformers worked for the abolition of slavery, women's rights, and the prohibition of liquor, as well as changes in corrections.

Pennsylvania System

In 1787 in Pennsylvania, a group campaigning for more humane treatment of prisoners established the Philadelphia Society for Alleviating the Miseries of Public Prisons. Led by Dr. Benjamin Rush, this organization, which included many Quakers, campaigned for the imprisonment of criminals rather than physical and capital punishment. The Quakers thought solitary confinement could reform criminals. In such cells, the offenders could think over their wrongful ways, repent, and reform. In 1790 Pennsylvania established the Walnut Street Jail in Philadelphia for "hardened and atrocious offenders."

The association continued pressuring the legislature for more prisons. Eventually, in 1829, the state built the Western Penitentiary outside Pittsburgh and the Eastern Penitentiary near Philadelphia. The cells (12 by 8 by 10 feet in dimension) with individual exercise yards isolated inmates from everyone so they could work, read their Bibles, and contemplate in order to be rehabilitated. The only voice the inmates heard was that of the chaplain on Sunday.

The reformers thought solitary confinement not only allowed the offenders to repent but also served as a punishing experience since humans are social animals. In addition, the system would be economical since, under these conditions, prisoners would not take long to see the error of their ways and fewer guards would be needed. Many prisoners found the total isolation very difficult to endure. The jails, however, quickly became overcrowded warehouses for prisoners.

Auburn System

The Auburn System (New York, 1819) used the Quaker idea of solitary confinement at night but used a system of congregating inmates in a common workroom during the day. The prisoners could neither talk nor look at one another. Any violation of the rules was met with immediate and strict discipline. Each supervisor had the right to flog an inmate who violated the rules.

Reformers perceived the system as economical because a single guard could watch a group of prisoners at work. The work of the inmates would help pay for their upkeep; they would learn about the benefits of work and have time to meditate and repent. Both the Pennsylvania and Auburn systems dictated that offenders should be isolated and have a disciplined routine. European countries tended to adopt the Pennsylvania system while most American states chose the Auburn system. While these methods made it easier to run a prison, they did little to rehabilitate prisoners.

After the American Civil War (1861–65) huge industrial prisons were built to house thousands of prisoners in the Northeast, Midwest, and California. The western states used their old territorial jails while the South relied on leasing out prisoners for farm labor.

THE CINCINNATI DECLARATION

Because many prison administrators were corrupt, convicts were mistreated and used as cheap labor. However, a growing number of prison reformers were beginning to believe that the prison system should be more committed to reform. In 1870 the newly established National Prison Association (which later became the American Correctional Association) met in Cincinnati, Ohio, and issued a Declaration of Principles. The philosophy of the Auburn system (fixed sentences, silence, isolation, harsh punishment, lockstep work) was considered degrading and destructive to the human spirit. The values in the Declaration of Principles included the following:

- The penal system should be based on reformation, not suffering, and prisoners should be educated to be free, industrious citizens able to function in society, not orderly inmates controlled by the guards.

- Good conduct should be rewarded.

- Indeterminate sentencing (not a mandated exact sentence) should include the ability for prisoners to earn their freedom early through hard work and good behavior.

- Citizens should understand that society is responsible for the conditions that lead to crime.

- Prisoners should recognize that they can change their lives.

ELMIRA REFORMATORY

The superintendent of the Elmira Reformatory in New York, Zebulon Brockway (1827–1920), used some of these ideas when New York opened the reformatory in 1876 for male offenders 16 to 30 years old. Brockway believed that rehabilitation could be achieved through education.

Inmates who did well in both academic and moral subjects earned early release by accumulating points. Misbehavior and poor performance in the educational courses prolonged the individual's sentence. Brockway used this technique because the New York legislature had passed a law allowing indeterminate sentencing and the release of inmates on parole when they showed they had been reformed. Brockway recognized that it was difficult to distinguish between those inmates who had truly reformed and those who were pretending to be rehabilitated in order to be paroled.

PROGRESSIVE REFORMS

By 1900 this correctional philosophy had spread throughout the nation. Nonetheless, by World War I

(1914–18), the idea of using educational and rehabilitative approaches was being replaced by the use of strict discipline. The way the facilities were built, the lack of trained personnel, and the attitudes of the guards made Brockway's ideas difficult to implement. In addition, the introduction of a probation system kept the offenders easiest to rehabilitate out of the reformatories.

Despite this return to discipline, the reform movement survived. The progressives of the early 20th century believed that if prisons applied the ideas of behavioral science to the inmates, prisoners could be rehabilitated. The progressives worked to change the social environment from which criminals came and to design ways to rehabilitate individual inmates. By the 1920s reformers were strongly advocating indeterminate sentencing, parole, and treatment programs as a way to rehabilitate offenders. But this approach to corrections was not put into practice until decades later.

While many of the reforms had merit, most could not be properly implemented due to inadequate funding or the unwillingness of prison officials to act. As each reform apparently failed to solve the problem of crime, many people became disillusioned. By the beginning of the 21st century, while most people did not want to return to the exploitation and cruelty of prisons of the 19th and early 20th centuries, they did not want to hear inmates complain about their overcrowded conditions or their lack of services. After all, offenders were in prison to be punished for their actions.

PRISONS AS WORKPLACES

Despite the efforts of reformers, most citizens preferred prisons to pay their own way. Prison administrators constructed factories within the prison walls or hired inmates out for chain gangs. In rural areas, inmates worked on prison-owned farms. In the South, prisoners—predominantly black—were often leased out to local farmers. Prison superintendents justified the hard labor as teaching the offenders the value of work and self-discipline, but economics were the true motives behind the factories and farms. Some penologists (those who study prison management) believe that the harshness of the prisons made these inmates more vindictive against society.

With the rise of labor unions in the North, the 1930s saw an end to the large-scale prison industry. Unions complained about competing with the inmates' free labor, especially amid the rising unemployment of the Great Depression. By 1940 the states had limited what inmates could produce. By 1970 the number of prison farms had decreased substantially because they were expensive to operate and the prisons found it cheaper to purchase food. And agricultural work no longer prepared inmates for employment outside prison. Since the 1970s, however, support for prison factories as a way to train inmates for

outside jobs has grown. Penologists believe that working in prison factories helps keep prisoners from being bored and idle and teaches them skills. While they believe prisoners benefit from work, they also assert that prisoners should not suffer the exploitation that characterized the factories of the 1920s. Yet in 2003's sluggish economy, discussion sprung up in Congress about limiting the ability of federal prisoners to take work away from people outside prison walls.

REHABILITATION MODEL

The rehabilitation model of corrections began in the 1930s and reached its high point in the 1950s. Qualified staff were expected to diagnose the cause of an offender's criminal behavior, prescribe a treatment to change the individual, and determine when that individual had become rehabilitated. Group therapy, counseling, and behavior modification were all part of the approach. These techniques did not work with all inmates, most states did not budget enough money for their correctional institutions to achieve these goals, and there were too many prisoners for the prison staff to treat effectively.

COMMUNITY CORRECTIONS

Advocates of community corrections in the 1960s and 1970s thought that rehabilitation needed to be done within the community, not in the prisons. They favored probation, educational courses, and job training. Starting in the 1960s the judicial system began recognizing the constitutional rights of prisoners to live in tolerable conditions.

In 1965 President Lyndon B. Johnson's Commission on Law Enforcement and Administration of Justice, a panel of experts on crime and the justice system, recommended improvements to the correctional system and initiated the first standards for operating prison facilities. The president's task force asserted that the success of a correctional system depended upon having "a sufficient number of qualified staff."

It also recommended alternative community-based approaches, educational and vocational programs, and different treatments for special offender categories. As a result, the American Correctional Association's Commission of Accreditation established standards by which it assesses correctional facilities for voluntary accreditation.

JUSTICE MODEL

As crime increased in the late 1980s, the pendulum once again swung the other way. Pressure began mounting against rehabilitation, indeterminate sentencing, probation, parole, and treatment programs. Various people wanted criminals behind bars for a determinate amount of time, noting that offenders should be kept off the streets so that they can not commit more crimes. As a result, the

TABLE 1.1

Recidivism rates of state prisoners released in 1983 and 1994

Most serious offense for which released	Percent of prisoners released in		Percent rearrested within 3 years among prisoners released in:		Percent reconvicted within 3 years among prisoners released in:	
	1983	1994	1983	1994	1983	1994
All released prisoners	100%	100%	62.5%	67.5%	46.8%	46.9%
Violent	34.6	22.5	59.6	61.7	41.9	39.9
Property	48.3	33.5	68.1	73.8	53.0	53.4
Drug	9.5	32.6	50.4	66.7	35.3	47.0
Public-order	6.4	9.7	54.6	62.2	41.5	42.0
Other	1.1	1.7	76.8	64.7	62.9	42.1

Note: These data represent 272,111 prisoners released in 1994 from prisons in 15 states, and 108,580 prisoners released in 1983 from prisons in 11 states. All 11 states from 1983 are among the 15 states represented in 1994.

SOURCE: Ann L. Pastore and Kathleen Maguire, eds., "Table 6.46: Recidivism rates of State prisoners released in 1983 and 1994," in *Sourcebook of Criminal Justice Statistics 2001*, U.S. Bureau of Justice Statistics, Washington, DC, 2002

federal government and a growing number of states introduced mandatory sentencing and "three strikes you're out" life terms for habitual criminals. They also limited the use of probation, parole, and time off for good behavior.

The rising number of offenders on parole and in prisons and jails has taxed the system. Facilities have become overcrowded and states have had problems securing sufficiently large budgets to build new prisons and jails or to supply the needed treatment and educational programs.

Meanwhile, state and federal courts have put caps on how many prisoners each facility can hold and have told states that certain basic services are required. With determinate sentencing often eliminating parole, prisons have turned to a system called gain-time to prevent overcrowding and maintain control. Gain-time, or good time, allows prison officials to deduct a specified number of days from an offender's sentence for every month served without the inmate breaking any rules.

REHABILITATION OR PUNISHMENT—PUBLIC GOALS AND RECIDIVISM

About half of the public sees the goal of prisons as rehabilitation (48.4 percent). A minority (14.6 percent) see the goal as punishment. The remaining third (33.1 percent) hold the opinion that prison should prevent and deter crime. These data are the results of a 1996 survey conducted by the College of Criminal Justice (CCJ), Sam Houston State University, Texas. Since then, surveys have tended to concentrate on public opinion about capital punishment, and the CCJ survey has not been repeated.

Recidivism rates are an indirect indicator of the correctional system's performance in achieving the public goal of rehabilitation. The recidivism rate measures the relapse of a person into criminal behavior after incarceration. Table 1.1 presents state data on this subject for the years 1983 and 1994 as published in the 2001 *Sourcebook of Criminal Justice Statistics* (Bureau of Justice Statistics, Washington, D.C.). Statistics on recidivism tend to be old out of necessity: time must pass between a prisoner's release and his or her rearrest some time later.

This sample, based on 108,580 state prisoners released in 1983 and 272,111 prisoners released in 1994, shows that nearly two-thirds of prisoners (62.5 percent) released in 1983 were arrested again within three years. Among those released in 1994, more than two-thirds (67.5 percent) were rearrested. The rearrest rate thus increased during the period studied. The highest recidivism rate was for property offenses for those released in 1994—73.8 percent, up from 68.1 percent for those released in 1983. The lowest rate was for violent offenses, 61.7 percent in 1994, up from 59.6 percent in 1983. Drug rearrests experienced the largest overall growth, climbing from 50.4 percent in 1983 to 66.7 percent in 1994 for a change of 16.3 percent. In contrast, rearrests for violence grew 2.1 percent during that same timeframe.

Recidivism rates for federal prisoners were lower. In a study published by the Bureau of Justice Statistics in 2000, *Offenders Returning to Federal Prison, 1986–97,* the recidivism rate was 15.7 percent within three years of release during that period. A total of 215,263 released prisoners were tracked. The highest recidivism rate was for prisoners sentenced originally for robbery, 32.4 percent.

JUVENILES

By the late 1700s children ages seven years or younger were presumed to be incapable of criminal intent, a concept that has carried over to the present time. In the 19th century a movement arose based on 16th-century European educational reform movements that changed the concept of a child from a "miniature adult" to an individual with less fully developed cognitive capacity. This resulted in children being separated from adult offenders in many major U.S. city prisons and jails.

By passing the Juvenile Court Act of 1899, the state of Illinois established the first juvenile court, located in Cook County. Using the British doctrine of "parens patriae" (state as parent), this act formalized the right of the state to intervene in the lives of juveniles in a way that was different from the manner in which the state dealt with adults. The focus was placed on the welfare of the delinquent child, who was seen as in need of the justice system's benevolent intervention.

By 1925 most states had passed similar legislation. Unlike the adult criminal justice system, juvenile courts dealt with young delinquents by considering both legal and non-legal factors, such as home environment and schooling. However, by the 1960s the juvenile court's success in rehabilitating young offenders was being called into question, largely due to the growing population of juveniles institutionalized indefinitely while being "reformed."

In 1974 Congress passed the Juvenile Justice and Delinquency Prevention Act. It required not only the segregation of juveniles from adults but also the separation of juvenile delinquents (those charged with a crime) from juvenile status offenders (truants and so-called "incorrigibles"). This led to the development and expansion of community-based programs in an effort to discourage institutionalization. A decade later the public's perception was that serious juvenile crime was on the rise again and that the system devised to protect juveniles had become too lenient. This perception led to a trend in the 1990s to exclude certain serious offenses from juvenile court jurisdiction. Juveniles charged with certain crimes could legally be tried in adult court, in some states at the sole discretion of the prosecuting agency.

According to "Juvenile Justice: A Century of Change" (1999 National Report Series, Office of Juvenile Justice and Delinquency Prevention), by 1997 most states had adopted new, stricter laws for dealing with juvenile offenders in one or more of the following areas:

- Transfer provisions—making it easier to transfer juvenile offenders to the adult criminal justice system.

- Sentencing authority—giving criminal and juvenile courts expanded sentencing options.

- Confidentiality—modifying or removing traditional juvenile court confidentiality by making records and proceedings more open.

- Victims' rights—increasing the role of victims of juvenile crime in the juvenile justice system.

- Correctional programming—allowing for the development of new detention programs for certain adult offenders and for juveniles transferred to the adult justice system.

In addition, many states have added language to their juvenile codes aimed at holding juveniles accountable for criminal behavior and imposing punishment consistent with the seriousness of the crime.

CHAPTER 2
EXPENDITURES

According to the Bureau of Justice Statistics (BJS), the total amount spent on corrections at federal, state, and local levels rose from $6.9 billion in 1980 to $49 billion in 1999, a seven-fold increase. (See Table 2.1.) During the same time period, total expenditures for police protection more than quadrupled—from $15.2 to $65.4 billion. Total judicial and legal costs rose by roughly the same rate—from $7.8 billion in 1982 to $32.2 billion in 1999.

In 1999 states bore the largest share of these costs, accounting for 62.8 percent of direct expenditures on corrections. The federal government's share was 6.7 percent. (See Table 2.2.) Local governments accounted for 30.5 percent of total expenditures on corrections as well as for the largest share of spending on police protection (69.7 percent) and judicial and legal costs (43.2 percent).

Calculated on a per capita basis, in 1980 total spending on corrections cost each U.S. resident $30.37. By 1999 that figure rose to $174.17 per person, a 473-percent increase. (See Table 2.3.) By comparison, the per capita cost of police protection rose by 248 percent, from $66.73 in 1980 to $232.30. Judicial and legal costs per person rose 241 percent from $33.54 in 1982 to $114.38 in 1999.

INCARCERATION RATES RISING

The reason for the escalating costs of corrections is simple enough: More people are being sent to prison; some criminals are also being held for longer periods because of mandatory sentencing rules; and some courts are requiring stiffer sentences. The official crime rate, reported by the FBI in its *Uniform Crime Reports*, has declined since 1991 from a rate of 5,898 crimes per 100,000 population to a rate of 4,124 in 2000. Yet the incarceration rate as reported by the Bureau of Justice Statistics has increased from 309.6 per 100,000 to 476.8. These two trends appear paradoxical. Part of the explanation is that the official crime rate does not track drug offenses—or related money laundering

offenses and illegal weapons violations—which have been growing at high rates. For this reason, the official crime rate and the incarceration rate do not always move in parallel. They do not reflect the same underlying facts.

According to the *Sourcebook of Criminal Justice Statistics 2001* (U.S. Department of Justice, Washington, D.C., 2002), the number of sentenced prisoners under jurisdiction of state and federal correctional authorities increased 23.9 percent from 1995 to 2001. In the Western United States, the percentage change between 1995 and 2001 was 27.7 percent, with Idaho (10.3 percent) and Oregon (9.8 percent) seeing the biggest average annual percent change in their prison populations. The Midwest saw a 24.7 percent change, with North Dakota (11.0 percent) and Missouri (7.0) experiencing the largest average annual percent change. Percentage rates in the South grew 20.8, with West Virginia (9.0 percent) and Mississippi (8.9 percent) gaining the most on an average annual basis. The Northeast had the least growth (5.6 percent), with Connecticut (4.1 percent) and Vermont (3.8 percent) seeing the highest average annual percent change. Some states witnessed a decline in prison population during that timeframe, including Alaska, Massachusetts, New York, North Carolina, and Washington, D.C.

FEDERAL CORRECTIONS

The U.S. budget for fiscal year (FY) 2004 proposed $5.92 billion in budget authority for corrections, an increase of nearly $50 million over the FY 2003 authority of $5.87 billion. These values, as well as those that follow, appear in *The Budget of the United States for Fiscal Year 2004* (Executive Office of the President, Washington, D.C.). The federal prison population grew at an annual rate of 7.8 percent between 1995 and 2001, but growth in expenditures is projected to slow. The $251 million increase between FY 2002 and FY 2003, for instance, was much bigger than the currently proposed increase in authority. Figure 2.1 shows

TABLE 2.1

Justice system direct and intergovernmental expenditures by type of activity and level of government, fiscal years 1980–99

(Dollar amounts in thousands)

Level of government and fiscal year	Total expenditures			
	Total justice system	Police protection	Judicial and legal	Corrections
All governments				
1980	NA	$15,163,029	NA	$6,900,751
1981	NA	16,822,094	NA	7,868,822
1982	$35,841,916	19,022,184	$7,770,785	9,048,947
1983	39,680,167	20,648,200	8,620,604	10,411,363
1984	43,942,690	22,685,766	9,463,180	11,793,744
1985	48,563,068	24,399,355	10,628,816	13,534,897
1986	53,499,805	26,254,993	11,485,446	15,759,366
1987	58,871,348	28,767,553	12,555,026	17,548,769
1988	65,230,542	30,960,824	13,970,563	20,299,155
1989	70,949,468	32,794,182	15,588,664	22,566,622
1990	79,433,959	35,923,479	17,356,826	26,153,654
1991	87,566,819	38,971,240	19,298,379	29,297,200
1992	93,776,852	41,326,531	20,988,888	31,461,433
1993	97,541,826	44,036,756	21,558,403	31,946,667
1994	103,470,564	46,004,536	22,601,706	34,864,322
1995	112,868,448	48,644,529	24,471,689	39,752,230
1996	120,194,175	53,007,425	26,157,907	41,028,843
1997	129,793,452	57,753,530	28,528,774	43,511,148
1998	135,899,453	60,828,213	29,901,380	45,169,860
1999	146,555,501	65,364,070	32,184,560	49,006,871
Federal				
1980	NA	1,941,000	NA	408,000
1981	NA	2,118,000	NA	436,000
1982	4,458,000	2,527,000	1,390,000	541,000
1983	4,844,000	2,815,000	1,523,000	606,000
1984	5,868,000	3,396,000	1,785,000	687,000
1985	6,416,000	3,495,000	2,129,000	792,000
1986	6,595,000	3,643,000	2,090,000	862,000
1987	7,496,000	4,231,000	2,271,000	994,000
1988	8,851,000	4,954,000	2,639,000	1,258,000
1989	9,674,000	5,307,000	2,949,000	1,418,000
1990	12,798,000	5,666,000	5,398,000	1,734,000
1991	15,231,000	6,725,000	6,384,000	2,122,000
1992	17,423,000	7,400,000	7,377,000	2,646,000
1993	18,591,000	8,069,000	7,832,000	2,690,000
1994	19,084,000	8,059,000	8,184,000	2,841,000
1995	22,651,000	9,298,000	9,184,000	4,169,000
1996	23,344,000	10,115,000	9,459,000	3,766,000
1997	27,065,000	12,518,000	10,651,000	3,896,000
1998	22,833,998	12,207,611	7,461,582	3,164,805
1999	27,392,000	14,796,726	8,515,167	4,080,107
State				
1980	$9,256,443	$2,194,349	$2,051,108	$4,547,667
1981	10,372,682	2,479,905	2,332,434	5,179,448
1982	11,601,780	2,833,370	2,748,364	6,020,046
1983	12,785,244	2,963,067	2,949,598	6,872,579
1984	14,212,842	3,173,297	3,271,076	7,768,469
1985	16,252,377	3,468,821	3,635,984	9,147,572
1986	18,555,723	3,749,413	4,004,720	10,801,590
1987	20,157,123	4,066,692	4,339,306	11,691,125
1988	22,836,919	4,531,184	4,885,843	13,419,892
1989	25,268,915	4,780,353	5,441,743	15,046,819
1990	28,345,066	5,163,475	5,970,895	17,210,696
1991	31,484,371	5,507,249	6,754,491	19,222,631
1992	33,755,092	5,592,791	7,722,882	20,439,419
1993	34,227,194	5,603,484	7,820,251	20,803,459
1994	37,161,391	6,000,330	8,026,326	23,134,735
1995	41,196,021	6,451,364	8,675,619	26,069,038
1996	39,903,049	6,499,224	8,109,714	25,294,111
1997	42,353,331	6,669,520	8,566,938	27,116,873
1998	49,453,806	7,996,298	10,858,191	30,599,317
1999	57,186,495	9,631,583	12,874,850	34,680,062

Level of government and fiscal year	Total expenditures			
	Total justice system	Police protection	Judicial and legal	Corrections
Local, total				
1980	NA	11,398,808	NA	2,277,257
1981	NA	12,678,955	NA	2,636,064
1982	20,967,562	14,172,313	3,784,285	3,010,964
1983	23,186,040	15,276,352	4,361,362	3,548,326
1984	25,154,172	16,515,727	4,627,473	4,010,972
1985	27,461,643	17,847,016	5,090,344	4,524,283
1986	30,178,432	19,355,599	5,690,544	5,132,289
1987	33,265,315	21,089,053	6,229,510	5,946,752
1988	36,097,549	22,370,517	6,826,419	6,900,613
1989	38,825,015	23,671,582	7,682,188	7,471,245
1990	43,558,671	26,097,219	8,675,732	8,785,720
1991	47,075,424	28,017,151	9,418,374	9,639,899
1992	50,115,498	29,658,955	10,052,330	10,404,213
1993	52,561,979	31,733,159	10,282,702	10,546,118
1994	55,517,277	33,364,901	11,022,716	11,129,660
1995	58,932,933	35,364,493	11,673,851	11,894,589
1996	62,811,126	38,227,201	12,355,193	12,228,732
1997	66,916,121	40,974,010	13,078,836	12,863,275
1998	70,831,438	43,311,939	13,559,129	13,960,370
1999	74,829,679	45,592,589	14,141,549	15,095,541
Counties				
1980	NA	2,669,497	NA	1,777,763
1981	NA	3,091,038	NA	2,066,269
1982	8,635,936	3,486,823	2,805,312	2,343,801
1983	9,791,530	3,754,693	3,238,571	2,798,266
1984	10,616,787	4,051,074	3,401,793	3,163,920
1985	11,609,827	4,400,716	3,736,030	3,473,081
1986	13,031,109	4,801,572	4,209,092	4,020,445
1987	14,530,198	5,254,562	4,611,863	4,663,773
1988	15,883,574	5,574,280	5,047,003	5,262,291
1989	17,503,442	6,099,265	5,692,464	5,711,713
1990	19,644,273	6,669,385	6,416,194	6,558,694
1991	21,913,042	7,386,260	7,074,386	7,452,396
1992	23,820,019	8,012,151	7,521,219	8,286,649
1993	24,624,542	8,520,472	7,697,938	8,406,132
1994	26,070,804	8,955,664	8,275,007	8,840,133
1995	27,917,010	9,499,807	8,804,229	9,612,974
1996	29,610,765	10,425,771	9,358,446	9,826,548
1997	31,576,448	11,328,607	9,928,998	10,318,843
1998	33,916,286	12,235,307	10,326,936	11,354,043
1999	35,118,293	12,457,018	10,540,476	12,120,799
Municipalities				
1980	NA	$8,791,989	NA	$527,060
1981	NA	9,678,462	NA	602,148
1982	$12,455,487	10,765,207	$981,963	708,317
1983	13,550,117	11,630,815	1,130,261	789,041
1984	14,696,313	12,565,350	1,235,073	895,890
1985	16,011,251	13,549,507	1,367,982	1,093,762
1986	17,346,101	14,685,842	1,495,968	1,164,291
1987	18,973,049	16,005,162	1,626,223	1,341,664
1988	20,449,324	16,964,757	1,788,158	1,696,409
1989	21,579,228	17,756,525	2,003,083	1,819,620
1990	24,244,122	19,674,855	2,274,164	2,295,103
1991	25,599,404	20,972,085	2,358,669	2,268,650
1992	26,770,919	22,034,381	2,546,171	2,190,367
1993	28,321,497	23,506,869	2,595,607	2,219,021
1994	29,908,762	24,766,007	2,765,164	2,377,591
1995	31,580,565	26,328,895	2,886,803	2,364,867
1996	33,200,361	27,801,430	2,996,747	2,402,184
1997	35,339,673	29,645,403	3,149,838	2,544,432
1998	37,585,662	31,627,623	3,249,087	2,708,952
1999	39,324,285	33,133,214	3,373,785	2,817,286

Note: Duplicative transactions between levels of government are excluded from the total for all governments, the state and the local total. Such intergovernmental expenditure consists of payments from one goverment to another and eventually will show up as a direct expenditure of a recipient government. The state government total for 1980 and 1981 includes a residual "other" category not displayed separately. Detail may not add to total because of rounding. Data for local governments are estimates subject to sampling variation. Beginning in 1998, expenditure data for the federal government are taken directly from the Budget of the United States Government.

SOURCE: Kathleen Maguire and Ann L. Pastore, eds.,"Table 1.2: Justice system direct and intergovernmental expenditures," in *Sourcebook of Criminal Justice Statistics 2001*, U.S. Bureau of Justice Statistics, Washington, DC, 2002

TABLE 2.2

Justice system direct and intergovernmental expenditures by level of government and type of activity, fiscal year 1999

Activity	Dollar amounts (in thousands)				Percent distribution		
	Total all governments	Federal government	State governments	Local governments[1]	Federal	State	Local[1]
Total justice system[2]	$146,555,501	$27,392,000	$57,186,495	$74,829,679	X	X	X
Direct expenditure	146,555,501	22,148,000	49,964,923	74,442,578	15.1%	34.1%	50.8%
Intergovernmental expenditure	X	5,244,000	7,221,572	387,101	X	X	X
Police	65,364,070	14,796,726	9,631,583	45,592,589	X	X	X
Direct expenditure[2]	65,364,070	11,964,000	7,809,838	45,590,232	18.3	11.9	69.7
Intergovernmental expenditure	X	2,832,726	1,821,745	2,357	X	X	X
Judicial and legal[2]	32,184,560	8,515,167	12,874,850	14,141,549	X	X	X
Direct expenditure	32,184,560	6,885,000	11,385,299	13,914,261	21.4	35.4	43.2
Intergovernmental expenditure	X	1,630,167	1,489,551	227,288	X	X	X
Corrections[2]	49,006,871	4,080,107	34,680,062	15,095,541	X	X	X
Direct expenditure	49,006,871	3,299,000	30,769,786	14,938,085	6.7	62.8	30.5
Intergovernmental expenditure	X	781,107	3,910,276	157,456	X	X	X

[1] Data for local governments are estimates subject to sampling variation.

[2] The total category for each criminal justice activity, and for the total justice system excludes duplicative intergovernmental expenditure amounts. This was done to avoid the artificial inflation that would result if an intergovernmental expenditure of a goverment were tabulated and then counted again when the recipient government(s) expended that amount. The intergovernmental expenditure categories are not totaled for this reason.

SOURCE: Kathleen Maguire and Ann L. Pastore, eds., "Table 1.3: Justice system direct and intergovernmental expenditures by level of government and type of activity, United States, fiscal year 1999," in *Sourcebook of Criminal Justice Statistics 2001*, U.S. Bureau of Justice Statistics, Washington, DC, 2002

how federal corrections expenditures, measured as actual spending (outlays), have increased since 1992. Outlays tend to be slightly below authorizations. Increases in recent years have been due to tougher sentencing guidelines leading to longer sentences, the abolition of parole, minimum mandatory sentences, and the war on drugs. Drug offenders account for about two-thirds of the federal inmate population. The Federal Bureau of Prisons, however, has made progress in reducing costs per inmate, as reported in assessments published by the Office of Management and Budget with the 2004 budget documents at http://www.whitehouse.gov/omb/budget/fy2004/.

STATE CORRECTIONS

Based on data from the U.S. Bureau of the Census (Census of Governments and Annual Survey of Governments), corrections have represented a small but often growing percentage of states' direct expenditures (excluding intergovernmental expenditures): 2.6 percent in FY 1991–92 and 3.0 percent in 1999–2000. (See Figure 2.2.) However, expenditures in FY 1999–2000 were down slightly from the two previous fiscal years' 3.1 percent. A decreasing proportion of the states' correctional dollars have been allocated to capital spending since FY 1995–96. (See Figure 2.3). Capital expenditures reached 11.4 percent of corrections budgets in FY 1994–95 but have been declining in proportion since then, reaching 7.6 percent of corrections expenditures in FY 1999–2000. This shift in direction, as shown in Figure 2.3, may have been brought about by the 1994 Crime Act passed by Congress

which, for the first time ever, offered federal funds to states to build prisons.

According to the Bureau of Justice Statistics, using its own surveys which result in slightly different data than those reported by the Census Bureau, in 1999 direct corrections expenditures by states were $30.77 billion. (See Table 2.2.) Total expenditures were 82 percent for prisons and 18 percent for other correctional activities, including juvenile facilities, parole and probation activities, and administrative functions not related directly to prisons. Looked at another way, the operation of prisons represented 74.8 percent of costs, capital outlays at prisons 7.2 percent, operations of other correctional activities were 17 percent, and capital outlays for these 0.9 percent. Trends for the period 1980 to 1999 are shown in Figure 2.4 in billions of dollars.

In this 19-year period, using the BJS data, direct correctional expenditures increased at an average rate of 11 percent a year. The highest rate of growth was for prison operations (averaging 11.6 percent a year) and the lowest for capital outlays (averaging 7.7 percent annually). The capital outlays category consists of construction (nearly 79 percent of the capital outlay total) and "other capital outlays" (21 percent); these are not broken out in Figure 2.4 but can be found at http://www.albany.edu/sourcebook/1995/pdf/t18.pdf. Construction grew at an average rate of 7 percent a year whereas the "other" category increased at an average rate of 11.6 percent annually—suggesting that spending on vehicles and computers grew at a higher rate than expenditures on prison beds and the structures

TABLE 2.3

Justice system per capita expenditures, fiscal years 1980–99

Fiscal year	July 1 population[1] (in thousands)	Total justice system[2]	Police protection	Judicial and legal	Corrections
1980	227,225	NA	$66.73	NA	$30.37
1981	229,466	NA	73.31	NA	34.29
1982	231,664	$154.72	82.11	$33.54	39.06
1983	233,792	169.72	88.32	36.87	44.53
1984	235,825	186.34	96.20	40.13	50.01
1985	237,924	204.11	102.55	44.67	56.89
1986	240,133	222.79	109.34	47.83	65.63
1987	242,289	242.98	118.73	51.82	72.43
1988	244,499	266.79	126.63	57.14	83.02
1989	246,819	287.46	132.87	63.16	91.43
1990	249,402	318.50	144.04	69.59	104.87
1991	252,131	347.31	154.57	76.54	116.20
1992	255,028	367.71	162.05	82.30	123.36
1993	257,783	378.39	170.83	83.63	123.93
1994	260,341	397.44	176.71	86.82	133.92
1995	262,755	429.56	185.13	93.14	151.29
1996	264,741	454.01	200.22	98.81	154.98
1997	267,252	485.66	216.10	106.75	162.81
1998	269,773	503.75	225.48	110.84	167.44
1999	281,375	520.85	232.30	114.38	174.17

[1] Population figures are for July 1 of each year from the U.S. Census Bureau, *Current Population Reports.* They are consistent with the 1980 and 1990 decennial enumerations. They do not include adjustments for census coverage errors. They may differ from population data taken from previous *Justice Expenditure and Employment Extracts Reports* because those tables were developed when only preliminary estimates were available.

[2] Detail may not add to total because of rounding.

SOURCE: Kathleen Maguire and Ann L. Pastore, eds.,"Table 1.6: Justice system per capita expenditures, by type of activity, United States, fiscal years 1980–99," in *Sourcebook of Criminal Justice Statistics 2001*, U.S. Bureau of Justice Statistics, Washington, DC, 2002

FIGURE 2.1

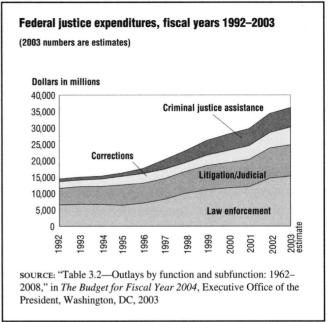

Federal justice expenditures, fiscal years 1992–2003

(2003 numbers are estimates)

SOURCE: "Table 3.2—Outlays by function and subfunction: 1962–2008," in *The Budget for Fiscal Year 2004*, Executive Office of the President, Washington, DC, 2003

that house them. Crowded prison conditions are indirectly reflected in patterns of expenditure. The "other correctional activities category" grew at an average rate of 10.4 percent a year.

These same data are shown as percentages of total correctional expenditures in Figure 2.5. The graphic shows that capital expenditures for prisons decreased as a percent of total expenditures in the 1980 to 1999 period. In 1980 they were 12.7 percent of the total, and in 1999 only 7.2 percent, a drop of 5.5 percent. The share of dollars spent on "other correctional activities" shrank nearly 2 percent, from 19.9 percent of the total in 1980 to 18 percent in 1999. The share of prison expenditures, operations and capital outlays combined, increased from 80.1 percent in 1980 to 82 percent in 1999.

Statistics providing further breakdowns of prison operating expenditures have not been updated by the Bureau of Justice Statistics for some time. The most recent information (1996) shows that more than two-thirds are allocated to pay employees' salaries and employee benefits; the rest are expended on prisoners' food and clothing, medical expenses, educational programs, and the cost of operating the prison (utilities and upkeep).

In its 1996 study, the BJS noted that the total outlay amounted to an annual operating expenditure of about $20,100 per state inmate. The five highest states in terms of annual costs per inmate were Minnesota ($37,800), Rhode Island ($35,700), Maine ($33,700), Alaska ($32,400), and Utah ($32,400). The five lowest states measured by cost per inmate were Alabama ($8,000), Oklahoma ($10,600), Mississippi ($11,200), Texas ($12,200), and Missouri ($12,800).

Inmate medical care accounted for the highest proportion of per-inmate dollars, at $6.54 per inmate, for a total of nearly $2.5 billion nationwide. Food service was $2.96 per inmate, followed by utilities (water, heating, lighting) at $1.81 per inmate, and transportation costs at 52 cents per inmate. According to the study, each year a higher number of inmate health dollars is spent on inmates who test positive for the human immunodeficiency virus (HIV). This number includes those who contract the virus while in prison and inmates who were HIV-positive at the time of incarceration, often due to prior drug use.

The Correctional HIV Consortium in San Francisco, California, reports that in 1998, the estimated annual cost of providing treatment for an HIV-positive state prison inmate was $80,396. A breakdown of these per-inmate costs includes: $38,500 for normal housing and related security; $22,800 for medications; $4,750 for hospital transportation and related security; $2,800 for radiology and other tests; and $2,160 for special dietary and nutritional needs. The Consortium, which hopes to conduct more studies soon, notes that the estimated annual cost

FIGURE 2.2

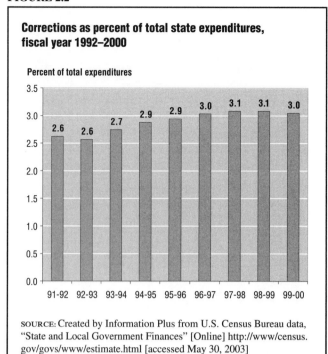

Corrections as percent of total state expenditures, fiscal year 1992–2000

SOURCE: Created by Information Plus from U.S. Census Bureau data, "State and Local Government Finances" [Online] http://www/census.gov/govs/www/estimate.html [accessed May 30, 2003]

FIGURE 2.3

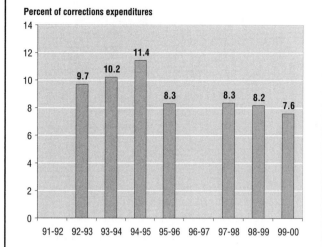

Capital expenditures as percent of state expenditures on corrections, fiscal year 1992–2000

Note: Capital expenditure data were not available in the same format in the Census of Governments years, 1991-92 and 1996-97.

SOURCE: Created by Information Plus from U.S. Census Bureau data, "State and Local Government Finances" [Online] http://www/census.gov/govs/www/estimate.html [accessed May 30, 2003]

FIGURE 2.4

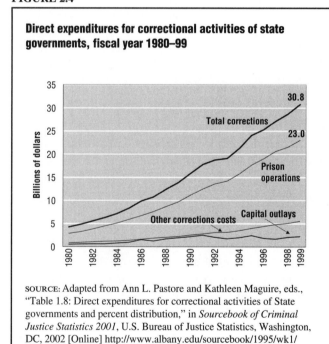

Direct expenditures for correctional activities of state governments, fiscal year 1980–99

SOURCE: Adapted from Ann L. Pastore and Kathleen Maguire, eds., "Table 1.8: Direct expenditures for correctional activities of State governments and percent distribution," in *Sourcebook of Criminal Justice Statistics 2001*, U.S. Bureau of Justice Statistics, Washington, DC, 2002 [Online] http://www.albany.edu/sourcebook/1995/wk1/t18.wk1 [accessed April 21, 2003]

each accounted for $1,200, and the costs of medical laboratory fees and education about HIV, tuberculosis, and hepatitis, were more than $800 per inmate.

According to the BJS, the number of HIV-positive inmates has experienced small increases and declines between 1995 (24,256 cases) and 2000 (25,088), hitting its highest level in 1999 (25,801). Among the states with the highest number of HIV-positive inmates in 2000 were New York (6,000), Florida (2,640), California (1,638), and Texas (2,492). Southern prisons house the most HIV-positive patients (10,767), while the Midwest houses the fewest (2,252).

LOCAL JAIL EXPENDITURES BY COUNTIES AND MUNICIPALITIES

As reported in *Sourcebook of Criminal Justice Statistics, 2001* (Bureau of Justice Statistics, Washington, D.C., 2002), the total costs for corrections at the local level rose from $2.3 billion in 1980 to $15.1 billion in 1999. (See Table 2.1.) This represents a nearly seven-fold increase. Expenditures for local corrections grew more rapidly than other local expenditures. Police expenditures increased four-fold while judicial and legal expenditures increased three times (from 1982). Total justice expenditures grew from 1982 at about the same rate as police expenditures. Spending on police is around 61 percent of total justice spending at the local level and total spending, therefore, tends to reflect the rate of growth of expenditures on police.

of providing treatment for an AIDS-diagnosed inmate is higher—$105,963. The increase in costs is mainly due to the need for more medications, which results in $46,440 per AIDS-diagnosed inmate.

In addition, in-patient hospital stays for HIV-positive state prison inmates averaged $1,400 annually in 1998, hazardous waste disposal and special case management

FIGURE 2.5

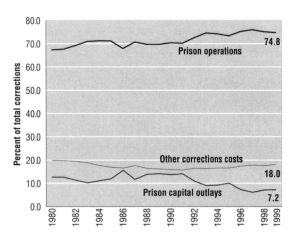

Expenditures for correctional activities of state governments, percent distribution, fiscal year 1980–99

Note: Other corrections costs include capital outlays not shown separately.

SOURCE: Adapted from Ann L. Pastore and Kathleen Maguire, eds., "Table 1.8: Direct expenditures for correctional activities of State governments and percent distribution," in *Sourcebook of Criminal Justice Statistics 2001*, U.S. Bureau of Justice Statistics, Washington, DC, 2002 [Online] http://www.albany.edu/sourcebook/1995/wk1/t18.wk1 [accessed April 21, 2003]

Between 1983 and 1999 local jails added 390,765 beds and 382,392 inmates. Beds grew at an annual rate of 5.9 percent, inmates at a rate of 6.4 percent a year, and, in this period, jail capacity utilization as a consequence went from 83 percent in 1983 to 93 percent in 1999 (*Census of Jails 1999*, U.S. Bureau of Justice Statistics, Washington, D.C., 2001). Based on data collected by the Criminal Justice Institute, Inc. (*The 2001 Corrections Yearbook: Jails*), the cost of a bed using new construction averaged $46,700 and the cost of a bed based on renovations and additions to existing facilities averaged $19,500 in 2001.

COSTS AND CONSEQUENCES

The costs of corrections for the United States have been rising in absolute terms, not simply as a reflection of a growing population. In the 1980–99 time period, the number of people held behind bars would have increased more than three-fold even if the U.S. population had stayed unchanged. In 1980 some 139 people were in state and federal prisons for every 100,000 U.S. residents. By 1999 that ratio had increased to 476 people. In 1980 correctional expenditures amounted to $30.37 for every man, woman, and child in the United States; by 1999 that cost had climbed to $174.17. (See Figure 2.6.) The incarceration rate increased an average of 6.7 percent per year; per capita expenditures increased by an average of 9.6 percent annually. Even if expenditures are expressed in constant year 2000 dollars (taking out the effects of inflation by applying the

FIGURE 2.6

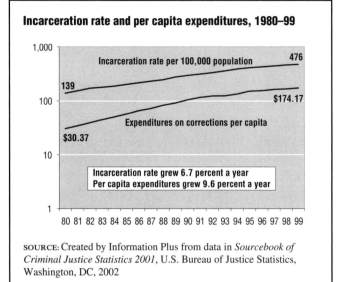

Incarceration rate and per capita expenditures, 1980–99

SOURCE: Created by Information Plus from data in *Sourcebook of Criminal Justice Statistics 2001*, U.S. Bureau of Justice Statistics, Washington, DC, 2002

Consumer Price Index deflator), annual per capita spending would have grown at 7.5 percent a year, from $43.40 in 1980 to $171.92 in 1999. During this period, the phenomenon of crime has increased in absolute terms, and more of the nation's resources have had to be expended on its consequences than in previous times.

Responses to rising costs have been variable and are documented in the remainder of this report. Cost containment strategies include some of the following:

Authorities have responded to budgetary pressures by crowding more people into available space and have thus caused increased crowding in correctional facilities. Crowding has been most serious in federal facilities, somewhat less so on average in state prison systems, and least in local jails, especially the smallest ones.

In its 1994 Crime Act, Congress provided funding to states for the construction of prisons. States bear a disproportionate financial burden for corrections. The Crime Act, however, requires that states qualify for funding by adopting truth-in-sentencing laws which, in effect, result in longer mandatory sentences.

Privately run prisons and jails have been created on the theory that the private sector can do the job at lower cost. Whether private prisons are more cost effective than public prisons is still being debated after more than a decade of this new approach, but the privately run prison populations have grown at a faster rate than the correctional population as a whole. Privately operated prison capacity increased from around 2,600 beds in 1986 to around 116,000 in 1998. At year-end in 2000, according to the Bureau of Justice Statistics (*Prisoners 2001*), 91,828 prisoners were in the 242 privately operated facilities—this was 5.8

percent of state and 12.3 percent of federal prison inmates. A private jail industry is also up and running.

A larger proportion of people convicted of felonies have been given probation in this period possibly in order to reduce prison populations. Intensive probation programs and electronic monitoring of convicted offenders have been introduced. This trend has, however, been countered by legislative efforts to eliminate parole so that those actually sentenced serve time are not released after serving only a portion of the sentence.

Most states have enacted some kind fee structure applicable to jail inmates under which inmates must pay fees. The most common type of requirement is that inmates pay for their own medical services.

CHAPTER 3
JAILS

Corrections institutions are organized in tiers by level of government and, at each level (federal, state, and local), specific types of institutions provide corrections functions based on the relative severity of the offenses committed. The most restrictive form of corrections is incarceration in a prison. Both the federal and the state governments operate their own prison systems; within the federal government, the military maintains its own prisons. Prison inmates serve time for serious offenses and are incarcerated for a year or longer.

In contrast, most people sentenced to jail serve less than a year for misdemeanors and offenses against the public order. Jails are operated at the local level—by cities and counties. The federal government operates some jails as well, and within the federal government, the Immigration and Naturalization Service has its own detention facilities. In some states, jails and prisons are operated under a single state authority, but the distinction—prisons for long terms and for serious offenses, jails for lesser terms and for less serious offenses—are still maintained.

Probation is the most common form of corrections without incarceration and is one form of what is known as "community corrections." In addition to holding offenders for short terms of confinement, jails also serve other purposes, including:

- To receive individuals pending arraignment and to hold them until their trials, conviction, or sentencing. Arraignment is the action of bringing an offender before a court to hear the charges.

- To readmit probation, parole, and bail-bond violators and absconders (those who run away or "skip bail").

- To detain juveniles temporarily pending their transfer to juvenile authorities.

- To hold mentally ill offenders pending their movement to appropriate health facilities.

TABLE 3.1

Number of persons held in state or federal prisons or in local jails, 1990–2001

Year	Total inmates in custody	Prisoners in custody		Inmates held in local jails	Incarceration rate[1]
		Federal	State		
1990	1,148,702	58,838	684,544	405,320	458
1995	1,585,586	89,538	989,004	507,044	601
1996	1,646,020	95,088	1,032,440	518,492	618
1997	1,743,643	101,755	1,074,809	567,079	648
1998	1,816,931	110,793	1,113,676	592,462	669
1999[2]	1,893,115	125,682	1,161,490	605,943	691
2000[3]	1,935,919	133,921	1,176,269	621,149	683
2001[3]					
June 30	1,964,301	140,741	1,187,763	631,240	690
December 31	--	143,337	1,181,128	--	
2002[3]					
June 30	2,019,234	148,783	1,200,203	665,475	702
Percent change, 6/30/01 - 6/30/02	2.8%	5.7%	1.0%	5.4%	
Annual average increase, 12/31/95 - 6/30/02	3.8%	8.1%	3.0%	4.3%	

Note: Jail counts are for midyear (June 30). Counts for 1994-2002 exclude persons who were supervised outside of a jail facility. State and federal prisoner counts for 1990-2000 are for December 31.

– Not available.

[1] Persons in custody per 100,000 residents in each reference year.

[2] In 1999, 15 states expanded their reporting criteria to include inmates held in privately operate correctional facilities. For comparisons with previous years, the state count of 1,137,544 and the total count 1,869,169 should be used.

[3] Total counts include Federal inmates in non-secure privately operated facilities (5,977 in 2000, 6,192 in 2001, and 6,762 in 2002.

SOURCE: Adapted from Paige M. Harrison and Jennifer C. Karberg, "Table 1: Number of persons held in State or Federal prisons or in local jails, 1990-2002," in *Prison and Jail Inmates at Midyear 2002*, U.S. Bureau of Justice Statistics, Washington, DC, April 2003

- To hold individuals for the military, for protective custody, for contempt, and for the courts as witnesses.

- To hold convicted inmates just before their release to the community upon completion of their sentences.

TABLE 3.2

TABLE 3.3

Number held in jail and incarceration rate, 1990 and 1995–2002

Year	Number held in jail	Incarceration rate[1]
2002	665,475	231
2001[2]	631,240	222
2000[2]	621,149	220
1999	605,943	222
1998	592,462	219
1997	567,079	212
1996	518,492	196
1995	507,044	193
1990	405,320	163

[1] Number of jail inmates per 100,000 U.S. residents on July 1 of each year.
[2] Rates for 2000 and 2001 are based on estimates from the 2000 Census and updated for July 1 of each year; rates for 1990–99 are based on estimates from the 1990 Census.

SOURCE: Adapted from Paige M. Harrison and Jennifer C. Karberg, "Number of jail inmates up 5.4% in 12 months ending June 28, 2002," in *Prison and Jail Inmates at Midyear 2002*, U.S. Bureau of Justice Statistics, Washington, DC, April 2003

- To transfer inmates to federal, state, or other authorities.

- To operate as bases for community-based programs in which offenders are monitored electronically or are subjected to other types of intensive supervision.

NUMBER OF JAIL INMATES

People in jail represent the smallest percentage on individuals in custody. On June 30, 2002, the nation's jails held 665,475 inmates, 33 percent of those behind bars. The jail population was up 5.4 percent from the year before as reported in *Prison and Jail Inmates at Midyear 2002* (Bureau of Justice Statistics, Washington, D.C., April 2003). (See Table 3.1.) The increase was above the average annual growth of 4.3 percent experienced between December 31, 1995 and June 30, 2002.

The jail inmate population rose from 163 per 100,000 U.S. residents in 1990 to 231 per 100,000 in 2002. (See Table 3.2.) The average daily jail population for 2002 was 652,082, up from 625,966 in 2001 and 408,075 in 1990, corresponding to an average rate of increase of 4 percent a year from 1990 to 2002. (See Table 3.3.)

Significant changes have occurred in the profile of this population in the 12-year period shown. Men represented the overwhelming majority of the jail population throughout the period, but females have become proportionately more numerous. In 1990 women represented 9.2 percent of the local jail population; in 2002 they were 11.8 percent, and the female population grew at an average annual rate of 6.2 percent compared with the male local jail population's 3.9 percent average annual growth rate. But juveniles have seen the most dramatic increase. Their proportion more than doubled from 0.6 percent in 1990 to 1.1

Average daily population and the number of men, women, and juveniles in local jails, midyear 1990, 1995, and 2000–02

	1990	1995	2000	2001	2002
Average daily population[1]	408,075	509,828	618,319	625,966	652,082
Number of inmates, June 30[2]	405,320	507,044	621,149	631,240	665,475
Adults	403,019	499,300	613,534	623,628	658,228
Male	365,821	448,000	543,120	551,007	581,411
Female	37,198	51,300	70,414	72,621	76,817
Juveniles[3]	2,301	7,800	7,615	7,613	7,248
Held as adults[4]	–	5,900	6,126	6,757	6,112
Held as juveniles	2,301	1,800	1,489	856	1,136

Note: Data are for June 30 in 1995 and 2000 and for June 29 in 1990 and 2001 and June 18 for 2002. Detailed data for 1995 were estimated and rounded to the nearest 100.
– Not available.
[1] The average daily population is the sum of the number of inmates in a jail each day for a year, divided by the total number of days in the year.
[2] Inmate counts for 1990 include an unknown number of persons who were under jail supervision but not confined.
[3] Juveniles are persons defined by state statute as being under a certain age, usually 18, and subject initially to juvenile court authority even if tried as adults in criminal court.
[4] In 1994 the definition was changed to include all persons under age 18. Includes juveniles who were tried or awaiting trial as adults.

SOURCE: Adapted from Paige M. Harrison and Jennifer C. Karberg, "Table 9. Average daily population and the number of men, women, and juveniles in local jails, midyear 1995 and 2000–2002," in *Prison and Jail Inmates at Midyear 2002*, U.S. Bureau of Justice Statistics, Washington, DC, April 2003

percent of the jail population in 2002. In 1990 all juveniles were held as juveniles; by 2002, 84.3 percent were held as adults—reflecting changes in public's attitude toward crime and legislation reflecting this "get tough" mood.

REASONS FOR THE GROWING INMATE POPULATION

Arrest Statistics

The FBI collects data on arrests and publishes the numbers in its *Crime in the United States* series. During the period 1990–2001, total estimated arrests first rose from 14.2 million in 1990 to 15.3 million in 1997, the peak year in this timeframe. Thereafter, arrests declined every year to reach 13.7 million in 2001. For the period as a whole, arrests decreased at the rate of 0.3 percent a year—versus a growth in jail population of 4 percent a year in the same period. The overall arrest rate, therefore, does not explain the increase in jail population. Individuals are jailed for periods of less than a year, and therefore a peak in arrests in 1997 does not influence the jail population in 2001.

Table 3.4 shows arrests by categories for 2001. The largest single category is "drug abuse violations." The even larger classification, "all other offenses" is an aggregation of offenses against specific state and local statutes that are not used elsewhere in the tabulation. Arrests for drug abuse violations were 1.09 million in 1990 and 1.59 million in

TABLE 3.4

Estimated arrests by type of crime, 2001

Type of crime	Number arrested	Type of crime	Number arrested
Total[1,2]	13,699,254	Embezzlement	20,157
		Stolen property; buying, receiving, possessing	121,972
Murder and nonnegligent manslaughter	13,653	Vandalism	270,645
Forcible rape	27,270	Weapons; carrying, possessing, etc.	165,896
Robbery	108,400	Prostitution and commercialized vice	80,854
Aggravated assault	477,809	Sex offenses (except forcible rape and prostitution)	91,828
Burglary	291,444	Drug abuse violations	1,586,902
Larceny-theft	1,160,821	Gambling	11,112
Motor vehicle theft	147,451	Offenses against the family and children	143,683
Arson	18,749	Driving under the influence	1,434,852
		Liquor laws	610,591
Violent crime[3]	627,132	Drunkenness	618,668
Property crime[4]	1,618,465	Disorderly conduct	621,394
Crime Index total[5]	2,245,597	Vagrancy	27,935
		All other offenses	3,618,164
Other assaults	1,315,807	Suspicion	3,955
Forgery and counterfeiting	113,741	Curfew and loitering law violations	142,889
Fraud	323,308	Runaways	133,259

[1] Does not include suspicion.

[2] Because of rounding, the figures may not add to total.

[3] Violent crimes are offenses of murder, forcible rape, robbery, and aggravated assault.

[4] Property crimes are offenses of burglary, larceny-theft, motor vehicle theft, and arson.

[5] Includes arson.

SOURCE: "Table 29. Estimated Arrests United States, 2001," in *Crime in the United States, 2001*, U.S. Department of Justice, Federal Bureau of Investigation, Washington, DC, 2002

2001, increasing at an annual rate of 3.4 percent. Other categories showing increases are simple assault (shown as "other assaults,") growing at a rate of 2.4 percent a year and "offenses against the family and children," which includes domestic violence, growing at a rate of 4.8 percent yearly. More rigorous prosecution of drug violations may, in part, explain why the rate of growth in jail populations is higher than the growth rate of total arrests.

Jail Inmates Held for State/Federal Authorities

Midway through 2001, local jails were operating 10 percent below capacity whereas state prisons were at between 100 and 115 percent of capacity and federal facilities exceeded their capacity by 31 percent (*Prison and Jail Inmates at Midyear 2001*, Bureau of Justice Statistics, Washington, D.C., 2002). Local jails had more room than prisons and federal penitentiaries. It is customary in corrections to house prisoners in jails until the prison can receive them and for jails to hold prisoners for state or federal authorities under contract. In 2001, for instance, the State of Massachusetts was housing 6,200 prisoners (of a total of 16,900) in local jails. The Criminal Justice Institute, Inc. estimated (1999) that jails on average held 38 inmates awaiting transfer to state facilities and that 80 inmates were housed under state and/or federal contracts. In a number of states/districts (Alaska, Connecticut, Delaware, District of Columbia, Hawaii, Rhode Islands, and Vermont), prisons and jails are integrated. Increase in prison populations is, therefore, reflected in jail populations.

Sentencing Status and Procedural Delays

According to the Bureau of Justice Statistics (BJS), as of June 29, 2001 an estimated 58.5 percent of adult jail inmates in the United States were awaiting some type of court action on their charge—up from 56 percent the year before. This increase is in line with data shown in the Bureau's series titled *Felony Sentences in State Courts*. In the period between 1992 and 1998, the median number of days required to dispose of all cases increased from 138 days to 149. Cases disposed of by jury trial increased from 231 days in 1992 to 300 days in 1998. Crowded dockets cause delays because people are held in jails longer awaiting disposition of their cases.

LARGEST JAIL JURISDICTIONS

In 2001 the country's 50 largest jail jurisdictions held about one-third (32.6 percent) of all jail inmates, accounting for a total jail population of 205,875. This was down from 206,914 jail inmates in 2000 and 208,204 in 1999.

Twenty-two states had jails that made the top 50 based on average daily population. Some states had more than one "top 50" jails, including California (10), Florida (7), Texas (7), Georgia (3), Ohio (3), Pennsylvania (3), and Tennessee (2). Los Angeles County and New York City together accounted for 5.4 percent of the national total, or 34,200 inmates.

Twenty-three of the 50 largest jurisdictions had a drop in jail population. Those with the largest decreases

TABLE 3.5

Rated capacity of local jails and percent of capacity occupied, 1990 and 1995–2002

Year	Rated capacity[1]	Amount of capacity added[2]	Percent of capacity occupied[3]
2002	713,899	14,590	93%
2001	699,309	21,522	90
2000	677,787	25,466	92
1999	652,321	39,541	93
1998	612,780	26,216	97
1997	586,564	23,593	97
1996	562,971	17,208	92
1995	545,763	41,439	93
1990	389,171		104
Average annual increase 1995–2002	3.9%	24,019	

Note: Capacity data for 1990, 1995-98 and 2000-02 are survey estimates subject to sampling error.
[1] Rated capacity is the number of beds or inmates assigned by a rating official to facilities within each jurisdiction.
[2] The number of beds added during the 12 months before June 30 of each year.
[3] The number of inmates divided by the rated capacity times 100.

SOURCE: Paige M. Harrison and Jennifer C. Karberg, "Table 11: Rated capacity of local jails and percent of capacity occupied, 1990 and 1995–2002," in *Prison and Jail Inmates at Midyear 2002*, U.S. Bureau of Justice Statistics, Washington, DC, 2003

TABLE 3.7

Gender, race, Hispanic origin, and conviction status of local jail inmates, midyear 1995 and 2000–02

Characteristics	Percent of jail inmates			
	1995	2000	2001	2002
Total	100.0%	100.0%	100.0%	100.0%
Gender				
Male	89.8%	88.6%	88.4%	88.4%
Female	10.2	11.4	11.6	11.6
Race/Hispanic origin				
White, non-Hispanic	40.1%	41.9%	43.0%	43.8%
Black, non-Hispanic	43.5	41.3	40.6	39.8
Hispanic	14.7	15.1	14.7	14.7
Other[1]	1.7	1.6	1.6	1.6
Conviction status (adults only)				
Convicted	44.0%	44.0%	41.5%	40.0%
Male	39.7	39.0	36.6	35.4
Female	4.3	5.0	4.9	4.6
Unconvicted	56.0	56.0	58.5	59.9
Male	50.0	50.0	51.9	53.0
Female	6.0	6.0	6.6	6.9

Note: Detail may not add to total because of rounding.
[1] Includes American Indians, Alaska Natives, Asians, and Pacific Islanders.

SOURCE: Paige M. Harrison and Jennifer C. Karberg, "Table 10: Gender, race, Hispanic origin, and conviction status of local jail inmates, midyear 1995 and 2000-2002," in *Prison and Jail Inmates at Midyear 2002*, U.S. Bureau of Justice Statistics, Washington, DC, 2003

TABLE 3.6

Jail occupancy as a percent of capacity, 2000–02

Size of jurisdiction[1]	Percent of capacity occupied		
	2000	2001	2002
Total	92%	90%	93%
Fewer than 50 inmates	66	67	68
50-99	80	87	89
100-249	94	92	93
250-499	96	90	95
500-999	94	94	98
1,000 or more	94	92	95

[1] Based on the average daily population in the year ending June 30.

SOURCE: Adapted from Paige M. Harrison and Jennifer C. Karberg, "At midyear 2002, 93% of jail capacity occupied," in *Prison and Jail Inmates at Midyear 2002*, U.S. Bureau of Justice Statistics, Washington, DC, 2003

were Oklahoma County, OK (down 22.4 percent), Harris County, TX (21.1 percent), Tarrant County, TX (16.6 percent), Shelby County, TN (13 percent), and San Diego County, CA (down 10.2 percent).

Reeves County, TX had the largest increase among the leading 50. Its jail population rose 75.7 percent due in large part to an expansion of its capacity by 87.1 percent. Others experiencing growth were Essex County, NJ (up 21.2 percent), King County, WA (17 percent), and York County, PA (up 16 percent).

RATED CAPACITY

State or local rating officials define "rated capacity" as the maximum number of beds or inmates that may be housed in a jail. In 2002 U.S. jails added 14,590 beds to total jail capacity, bringing it to 713,899. (See Table 3.5.) This was the smallest increase in the 1995–2002 period. Capacity utilization had dropped to 90 percent in 2001 but increased to 93 percent in 2002, the same level experienced in 1999. Jail administrators were adding beds but the number of inmates entering the system was increasing more quickly. Nonetheless, jail administrators were doing a better job than those who ran state and federal prisons. In 2001 state prisons were operating 1 percent above capacity and federal prisons 31 percent above capacity.

At midyear 2002 jail systems with 500 to 999 beds reported the highest occupancy rate, 98 percent. (See Table 3.6.) The occupancy rate was 95 percent in jail systems with an average daily population of 1,000 or more inmates, higher than in 2001, when the rate was 92 percent. Jurisdictions with fewer than 50 inmates had a 68 percent capacity experience, up slightly from a rate of 67 percent the year before.

TABLE 3.8

TABLE 3.9

Racial characteristics of jail inmates, 2002

	Estimated count	Incarceration rate[1]
Total	665,475	231
Gender		
Male	588,106	417
Female	77,369	53
Race/Hispanic origin		
White[2]	291,800	147
Black[2]	264,900	740
Hispanic[3]	98,000	256
Other[3]	10,800	72

Note: Inmate counts were estimated and rounded to the nearest 100. Resident population figures were estimated for July 1, 2002, based on the 2000 Census..

[1] Number of inmates per 100,000 residents in each group.

[2] Non-Hispanic only.

[3] Includes American Indians, Alaska Natives, Native Hawaiians, and other Pacific Islanders.

SOURCE: Paige M. Harrison and Jennifer C. Karberg, "Table 10: Gender, race, Hispanic origin, and conviction status of local jail inmates, midyear 1995 and 2000-2002," in *Prison and Jail Inmates at Midyear 2002*, U.S. Bureau of Justice Statistics, Washington, DC, 2003

JAIL INMATE CHARACTERISTICS

Gender and Race

In midyear 2002, incarceration rates in jail were 113 women per 100,000 female residents in the United States. During that time, the rate for men was 1,309 men per 100,000 adult male residents. In 1995 females represented 10.2 percent of jail inmates, and in 2002, 11.6 percent, the same percentage as in 2001. (See Table 3.7.)

Most local jail inmates in 2002 were minorities, but the percentage of whites increased while other groups decreased or stayed the same in proportion. At midyear 2002, non-Hispanic whites made up 43.8 percent of the jail population, up from 43.0 percent at midyear 2001. Non-Hispanic blacks were 39.8 percent of jail inmates, down from 40.6 percent in 2001 and 43.5 percent in 1995. Hispanics were 14.7 percent, unchanged from 2001, and other races (Asians/Pacific Islanders, Native Americans, and Alaska Natives) were 1.6 percent, also unchanged from the previous year.

Relative to their proportion in the U.S. population, blacks were 5 times more likely than whites to be held in local jails, 2.9 times more likely than Hispanics, and 10 times more likely than persons of other races. Men were 8 times more likely to be jailed than women. (See Table 3.8.)

Juveniles in Jail

According to the Bureau of Justice Statistics, there was a 339 percent rise in the number of juveniles confined in adult jails between 1983 and 2000—from a total of 1,736

Juveniles in adult jails, 1983–2000

Year	Total adult inmates	All males	All females	Juveniles
1983	221,815	206,163	15,652	1,736
1984	233,018	216,275	16,743	1,482
1985	254,986	235,909	19,077	1,629
1986	272,736	251,235	21,501	1,708
1987	294,092	270,172	23,920	1,781
1988	341,893	311,594	30,299	1,676
1989	393,248	356,050	37,198	2,250
1990	403,019	365,821	37,198	2,301
1991	424,129	384,628	39,501	2,350
1992	441,780	401,106	40,674	2,804
1993	455,600	411,500	44,100	4,300
1994	479,800	431,300	48,500	6,700
1995	499,300	448,000	51,300	7,800
1996	510,400	454,700	55,700	8,100
1997	557,974	498,678	59,296	9,105
1998	584,372	520,581	63,791	8,090
1999	596,485	528,998	67,487	9,458
2000	613,534	543,120	70,414	7,615
% Change:				
1983–1990	82	77	138	33
1990–2000	52	48	89	231
1983–2000	177	163	350	339

SOURCE: Adapted from James Austin, Kelly Dedel Johnson, Maria Gregoriou, "Table 2: Juveniles in Adult Jails, 1983–1998," in *Juveniles in Adult Prisons and Jails: A National Assessment*, U.S. Department of Justice, U.S. Bureau of Justice Assistance, Washington, DC, 2000 and "Jail populations by age and gender, 1990-2000," *Demographic Trends in Jail Populations*, U.S. Bureau of Justice Statistics [Online] http://www.ojp.usdoj.gov/bjs/glance/tables/jailagtab.htm [accessed March 5, 2003]

juveniles in 1983 to 7,615 juveniles in 2000. (See Table 3.9.) By comparison, during the same period, the rate of all female jail inmates rose by 350 percent and all male inmates rose by 163 percent. Increases were higher in the 1983 to 1993 period in all categories except juveniles. Juveniles in adult jails grew most in the 1990 to 2000 period.

Approximately 8 of 10 of the more than 7,600 juveniles held in adult prison had been convicted or were being held for trial as adults. Most states require that persons under 18 be subject to juvenile court jurisdiction, but exceptions are made based on the severity of the offense or the offender's criminal history.

Adult Conviction Status

Convicted inmates include those awaiting sentencing, serving a sentence, or returned to jail for a violation of probation or parole. As shown at the bottom of Table 3.7, fewer than half (41.5 percent) of all adults under supervision by jail authorities had been convicted of their current charges in 2001. This figure is down from 44.0 percent in 2000, and still lower than 48.5 percent conviction rate in 1990. Corresponding figures for women were 4.9 percent in 2001, down from 5 percent in 2000 but up from the 4.5 percent conviction rate in 1990. The largest proportion of

TABLE 3.10

TABLE 3.11

Offenses committed by women on probation or in jail/prison, 1990–96

Most serious offense[1]	Percent of women offenders			
	Probation	Local jails	State prisons	Federal prisons
Violent offenses	9%	12%	28%	7%
Homicide	1	1	11	1
Property offenses	44%	34%	27%	12%
Larceny	11	15	9	1
Fraud	26	12	10	10
Drug offenses	19%	30%	34%	72%
Public-order offenses	27%	24%	11%	8%
Driving while intoxicated	18	7	2	0
Number of women offenders	721,400	27,900	75,200	9,200

[1] Based on the offenders' most serious offense. Overall offense categories are shown with selected detail categories containing larger percentages of women offenders.

SOURCE: Lawrence A. Greenfeld and Tracy L. Snell, "Offenses of women on probation or in jail or prison," in *Women Offenders*, U.S. Bureau of Justice Statistics, Washington, DC, December 1999

Persons under jail supervision, by confinement status and type of program, midyear 1995, 2000–2002

Confinement status and type of program	Number of persons under jail supervision			
	1995	2000	2001	2002
Total	541,913	687,033	702,044	737,912
Held in jail	507,044	621,149	631,240	665,475
Supervised outside jail facility[1]	34,869	65,884	70,804	72,437
Electronic monitoring	6,788	10,782	10,017	9,706
Home detention[2]	1,376	332	539	1,037
Day reporting	1,283	3,969	3,522	5,010
Community service	10,253	13,592	17,561	13,918
Weekender programs	1,909	14,523	14,381	17,955
Other pretrial supervision	3,229	6,279	6,632	8,702
Other work programs[3]	9,144	8,011	5,204	5,190
Treatment programs[4]	–	5,714	5,219	1,256
Other/unspecified	887	2,682	7,729	9,663

– Not available.

[1] Excludes persons supervised by a probation or parole agency.

[2] Includes only those without electronic monitoring.

[3] Includes persons in work release programs, work gangs, and other work alternative programs.

[4] Includes persons under drug, alcohol, mental health, and other medical treatment.

SOURCE: Paige M. Harrison and Jennifer C. Karberg, "Table 8: Persons under jail supervision, by confinement status and type of program, midyear 1995, 2000–2002," in *Prison and Jail Inmates at Midyear 2002*, U.S. Bureau of Justice Statistics, Washington, DC, 2003

female jail inmates held in U.S. jails were either convicted of or facing property offenses (34 percent), followed by drug offenses (30 percent), public-order offenses such as driving while intoxicated (24 percent), and violent crime offenses (12 percent). (See Table 3.10.) Of unconvicted adult inmates at year-end 2001, 51.9 percent were males and 6.6 percent females. (See Table 3.7.)

Confinement Status

In 1995, for the first time, the Annual Survey of Jails (Bureau of Justice Statistics, Washington, D.C.) obtained the count of the number of offenders under community supervision. Respondents were asked if their jail jurisdictions operated any community-based programs and how many persons participated in them.

From midyears 1995 to 2002 the number of persons supervised outside a jail facility rose from 34,869 to 72,437. (See Table 3.11.) The largest number of persons supervised outside a jail facility (17,955) were sentenced to weekender programs (they had to spend their weekends in jail). Next were persons sentenced to community service (13,918). The next largest category was individuals on electronic monitoring (9,706), people who wear electronic bracelets from which their location can be determined.

PAYING FOR SERVICES

Inmate fees

The last comprehensive survey of statutory state authority permitting jails to charge fees for some kinds of services was conducted by the National Institute of Corrections (NIC), U.S. Department of Justice, in 1997

and published as *Fees Paid by Jail Inmates: Findings from the Nation's Largest Jails*. Data from that study indicate that most states authorized some kind of fee for services to inmates. In 34 states, fees for medical services were authorized; in 17, fees could be collected for specific programs; in 16, per diem fees could be levied. (See Table 3.12.) An explanation of such fees follows:

- Medical services—collecting copayments or other fees for medical care

- Per diem fees—requiring jail inmates to reimburse the county for all or a portion of their daily incarceration costs, including housing, food, and basic programs

- Other nonprogram functions—charging for services such as bonding, telephone use, haircuts, release escort, and drug testing

- Participation in programs—imposing a fee or collecting a portion of any compensation earned by inmates in programs, such as work release, weekend incarceration, and electronic monitoring; or charging for participation in rehabilitation programs such as education or substance abuse treatment

Jurisdiction Fees

The NIC's 1997 survey was an update of earlier work tracking what has become a major trend in the management of jails, a trend still going strong in 2003 as

TABLE 3.12

Statutes on charging fees to jail inmates as of 1997

	Statutes provide authority to charge fees for:					No statutory authority indicated
	General cost of incarceration	Medical services	Per diem	Specific programs	Other specific functions	
Alabama[1,2]						
Alaska	NA					
Arizonza		x				
Arkansas						x
California		x	x	x	x	
Colorado				x		
Connecticut	x					
Delaware						
D.C.						x
Florida		x	x	x		
Georgia		x				
Hawaii		x		x		
Idaho		x	x			
Illinois[1]		x				
Indiana[1]		x				
Iowa		x	x			
Kansas						
Kentucky				x		
Louisiana	NA			x		
Maine		x				
Maryland		x				
Massachusetts						x
Michigan		x	x			
Minnesota		x				
Mississippi		x				
Missouri		x		x		
Montana		x	x			
Nebraska		x		x		
Nevada		x	x			
New Hampshire		x	x	x		
New Jersey		x		x		
New Mexico		x				x
New York						x[3]
North Carolina		x	x			
North Dakota						
Ohio		x	x		x	
Oklahoma[1]		x	x			
Oregon		x		x		
Pennsylvania						x
Rhode Island		x	x	x	x	
South Carolina		x				
South Dakota		x	x	x	x	
Tennessee		x		x		
Texas		x	x	x		
Utah						x
Vermont						x
Virginia		x		x		
Washington	x					
West Virginia[1]		x				
Wisconsin		x	x	x		
Wyoming		x	x		x	
U.S. Code						x

Note: NA stands for no data available.

[1] Statutory data for these states was supplemented by information from the National Conference of State Legislatures ("Selected Laws on Offender Fees," January 1997).

[2] Legislation is specific to individual counties: intent varies.

[3] Jail standards in New York permit the charging of a per diem fee for work release participation; statutes permit payment of medical charges by third-party insurance.

SOURCE: "Table 1: Statutes on Charging Fees to Jail Inmates," in *Fees Paid by Jail Inmates: Findings from the Nation's Largest Jails*, U.S. Department of Justice, National Institute of Corrections, Logmont, CO, 1997

evidenced by even a cursory review of journalistic reports of new proposals on the Internet. However, the trend has not been surveyed authoritatively in recent years.

Jails are also attempting to finance a portion of their operations by charging other jurisdictions for housing inmates, as noted earlier. In the *Census of Jails, 1999* (Bureau of Justice Statistics, Washington, D.C., August 2001), the Department of Justice reported that around 71 percent of all jail systems have established charges for keeping inmates for other jurisdictions. Fees charged averaged $48 a day for federal prisoners, $36 for state prisoners, and $38 for jail inmates held for other local jails. (See Table 3.13.)

THE 1999 CENSUS OF JAILS

The BJS conducted its census of jails in 1999 and published the results in 2001. The Bureau usually reports on jails only as part of an annual survey of prisons and jails combined. The 1999 census provides a slightly dated but a more comprehensive look at jail staffing, facilities, and privately run jails. An overview of facilities and staffing is provided in Table 3.14.

Facilities and Staffing

The number of jails across the country has remained relatively steady since 1983, rising from 3,338 in that year to 3,365 in 1999. There are 3,043 counties in the United States. The number of jails is roughly one per county plus additional jails in large urban areas. But while the total facilities increased by just 27 jails between 1983 and 1999, their capacity to house offenders has increased significantly. In 1983 rated capacity of the nation's jails was 261,556 or about 78 beds per jail on average. In 1999 capacity had increased to 652,321, 194 beds per jail on average. Jails, therefore, have grown in size if not significantly in number. The utilization of available jail capacity increased from 85 percent occupancy in 1983 to 101 percent crowding in 1988. Capacity growth then began, reflected in decreasing jail utilization: 97 percent of capacity was being used in 1993, 93 percent in 1999. As reported earlier, capacity utilization stood at 93 percent in 2002, but it had been as low as 90 percent in 2001.

The nation's publicly operated local jails employed 207,600 people in 1999, up from 64,560 in 1983, a 222-percent increase, more than matching the 171-percent increase in jail inmates, which stood in 1999 at 605,943 inmates, up from 223,551. In 1999 there was a staff member present for every 2.9 prisoners and a correctional officer for every 4.3 prisoners. Staff and guards had more inmates to administer in 1983 when there were 3.5 inmates per member of staff and 5.0 per correctional officer.

Two-thirds of jail staff members were male in 1999; 66 percent were white, 24 percent were black, 8 percent Hispanic, and 2 percent of other races. Inmates in 1999 were 89 percent male and, by race, they were 41 percent white, 42 percent black, 15 percent Hispanic, and 2 per-

TABLE 3.13

Average daily fees charged by jails to house an inmate for other correctional authorities, 1999

Region and jurisdiction	Average daily fees charged by jail jurisdictions to house an inmate for —		
	Federal authority	State authority	Other local authority
U.S. total	$48	$36	$38
Federal	/	/	/
State	$48	$36	$38
Northeast	**$66**	**$53**	**$63**
Maine	75	72	69
Massachusetts	69	81	65
New Hampshire	57	40	45
New Jersey	67	58	/
New York	78	52	78
Pennsylvania	54	47	48
Midwest	**$49**	**$43**	**$43**
Illinois	45	40	39
Indiana	38	35	36
Iowa	53	52	52
Kansas	38	39	34
Michigan	41	35	34
Minnesota	57	56	54
Missouri	43	29	31
Nebraska	48	43	43
North Dakota	42	39	35
Ohio	64	61	56
South Dakota	44	46	42
Wisconsin	55	53	44
South	**$39**	**$25**	**$25**
Alabama	26	4	11
Arkansas	32	25	26
Dist. of Col.	70	/	/
Florida	49	47	36
Georgia	34	22	27
Kentucky	33	25	28
Louisiana	35	22	8
Maryland	51	49	42
Mississippi	29	21	20
North Carolina	43	26	27
Oklahoma	36	24	21
South Carolina	36	35	30
Tennessee	39	31	21
Texas	40	39	35
Virginia	51	17	24
West Virginia	43	33	36
West	**$54**	**$48**	**$48**
Alaska	105	100	79
Arizona	54	42	47
California	58	53	53
Colorado	49	46	44
Idaho	42	39	43
Montana	45	47	42
Nevada	59	50	38
New Mexico	75	73	71
Oregon	69	64	63
Utah	45	41	35
Washington	54	47	50
Wyoming	45	41	43

Note: / stands for not reported.

SOURCE: "Appendix table 11: Average daily fees charged by jails to house an inmate for other correctional authorities, June 30, 1999," in *Census of Jails, 1999*, U.S. Department of Justice, Washington, DC, 2000

TABLE 3.14

Highlights of jails, 1983, 1988, 1993, and 1999

	Census of jails at midyear –			
	1983	1988	1993	1999
Number of jail inmates	223,551	343,569	459,804	605,943
Rated capacity of jails	261,556	339,949	475,224	652,321
Percent of capacity occupied	85%	101%	97%	93%
Number of jails	3,338	3,316	3,304	3,365
Number of jail employees	64,560	99,631	165,500	207,600
Number of inmates per employee (total staff)	3.5	3.4	2.8	2.9
Number of inmates per correctional officer	5.0	4.7	3.9	4.3

SOURCE: James J. Stephan, "Highlights," in *Census of Jails 1999*, U.S. Bureau of Justice Statistics, Washington, DC, August 2001

16,656 offenders. Of these, 13,814 were inmates in the private jails and 2,842 were supervised but not confined. (See Table 3.15.) On average, private jails were bigger than those operated by public agencies. Excluding offenders supervised, the average population of the 47 private jails in 1999 was 294 inmates. Inmates by gender were predominantly male, as in the public jails, 89 percent. The racial composition was somewhat different: whites were 31.7 percent, blacks 38.0 percent, Hispanics 16.0 percent, and other races 14.2 percent of the population. Among private jail staff, women accounted for nearly half (46.3 percent of total staff, 40.8 percent of correctional officers). Private jails staffs supervised 3.3 inmates per person, a somewhat higher workload than in publicly-run jails (2.9 inmates per staff). Private correctional officers supervised 5.3 inmates each, one more than publicly employed guards (4.3).

Federal Jails

While the emergence of private jails is often mentioned in the press, less known is the fact that the federal government operates jails of its own—in addition to the much better known federal penitentiaries—and federal jails have also grown in number. The government increased such facilities from 7 in 1993 to 11 in 1999. In 1999 they held nearly as many inmates as private jails—11,209, up from 5,899 in 1993, a near doubling of the federal jail population. (See Table 3.16.) Federal jail inmates were overwhelmingly male (93 percent); the majority, 63 percent, were white, 32 percent were black, and 5 percent were of all other races. Federal jail staff was 74.5 percent male. The total employee-to-inmate ratio in 1999 was 3.6, and each correctional officer supervised 6.7 inmates. Federal jails were crowded; they operated 39 percent above rated capacity—but the 1999 results were better than in 1993 when federal jails were 55 percent above capacity.

cent of other races. Hispanics may be of any race. In the data presented here, blacks and whites are non-Hispanics.

Privately Operated Jails

In 1993 there were 17 privately operating jails. Six years later, the number had increased to 47 and supervised

TABLE 3.15

TABLE 3.16

Characteristics of privately operated jails, 1999

Facilities	47	Race/Hispanic origin		
		White	4,324	
Gender of inmates housed		Black	5,187	
Men only	15	Hispanic	2,188	
Women only	2	Other classifications[1]	1,942	
Both men and women	30			
		Average daily population[2]	13,618	
Size of facility				
Fewer than 50 inmates	13	Staff		
59-99	5	Total staff	4,178	
100-249	6	Male	2,242	
250-499	12	Female	1,936	
500-999	9	Inmates per employee	3.3	
1,000-1,499	2			
		Correctional officers only	2,617	
Inmates		Male	1,548	
		Female	1,069	
Total under supervision	16,656	Inmates per correctional officer	5.3	
Inmates	13,814			
Non-confined persons	2,842			
Confined on June 30, 1999				
Males	12,239			
Females	1,575			

Note: Detail may not add to total.
[1] Includes American Indians, Alaska Natives, Asians and Pacific Islanders.
[2] Based on the average daily population for the 12 months ending June 30, 1999.

SOURCE: James J. Stephan, "Table 9. Characteristics of privately operated jails, June 20, 1999," in *Census of Jails 1999*, U.S. Bureau of Justice Statistics, Washington, DC, August 2001

Characteristics of federal jails, 1993 and 1999

Characteristic	1993	1999
Number of facilities	7	11
Number of inmates	5,899	11,209
Male	5,490	10,455
Female	409	754
White	4,271	7,080
Black	1,462	3,559
Other[1]	166	570
Status of inmates		
Convicted	47%	26%
Unconvicted	53%	74%
Rated capacity	3,810	8,040
Percent of capacity occupied	155%	139%
Number of employees	2,009	3,110
Male	1,499	2,318
Female	510	792
Administrators	89	253
Correctional officers	1,080	1,685
Clerical and maintenance	263	93
Educational	26	30
Other[2]	551	1,049
Number of inmates per employee		
All employees	2.9	3.6
Correctional officers	5.5	6.7

Note: The 11 federal jails in 1999 were in Los Angeles, CA; San Diego, CA; Miami, FL; Chicago, IL; Oakdale, LA; Brooklyn, NY; New York, NY; Otisville, NY; Oklahoma City, OK; Guaynabo, PR; and Seattle, WA.
[1] Includes American Indians, Alaska Natives, Asians, and Pacific Islanders.
[2] Includes professional and technical workers such as health service employees, case managers, and transportation specialists.

SOURCE: Adapted from James J. Stephan, "11 Federal jails held 11,209 inmates on June 30, 1999," in *Census of Jails 1999*, U.S. Bureau of Justice Statistics, Washington, DC, August 2001

JAIL INDUSTRIES

The National Institute of Justice defines a jail industry as one that uses inmate labor to create a product or provide a service that has value to a public or private client and for which the inmates receive compensation, whether it be pay, privileges, or other benefits. This definition describes a variety of activities. If a convict cuts the grass in front of the jail and thereby earns permission to watch television an extra hour, the elements of labor, service provision, value, and compensation are all present. At the other end of the spectrum are those jail inmates who work for private sector industry and earn real dollars.

Jail officials hoped these programs would develop inmate work habits and skills, generate revenues or reduce costs for the county, reduce inmate idleness, and meet needs in the community. The 1984 Justice Assistance Act (PL 98-473) removed some of the long-standing restrictions on interstate commerce of prisoner-made goods, thereby opening new opportunities for prison labor to work for the private sector. Both state prisons and county jails have entered into private-sector work programs.

In most programs, inmates receive no or low wages. In some instances, a portion of the money they earn is used to pay child support, victim restitution, or other obligations. Their work often serves the public sector and they

are usually credited with "good time." Thus, the offenders pay for their crimes with public service labor, and their early release makes scarce bed space available for other offenders.

Jail Industries at Work

In an effort to help inmates learn new skills and establish solid work habits, the Santa Clara County Department of Correction in California offers a jail industry program. Inmates manufacture a range of products, from computer and office desks, to bookshelves, benches and toys. The items are sold to government and non-profit organizations throughout the United States.

In Clark County, Washington, among the services provided by inmates is a computer recycling program. The service is geared to train inmates in electronics; reduce the number of discarded computers that become hazardous waste in landfills; and provide rebuilt computers to non-profit organizations, which distribute the rebuilt machines to low-income families. Programs in other regions include habitat restoration and enhancement as well as litter cleanup.

One factor that limits the development of jail industries is that individuals sentenced to jail serve relatively short periods of time compared with those in prison (who serve one year or longer). Continuity of employment in jail industries is difficult to maintain. Work undertaken must call for skills widely distributed in the population; projects must be of short duration; and organization of the workplace and of the workflow must accommodate relatively rapid turn-over. These considerations limit the usefulness of jail industries, as compared with prison industries, as training places for offenders intending to acquire new skills to be used as part of their rehabilitation after release.

CHAPTER 4
PRISONS

In *Prisoners in 2001*, the Bureau of Justice Statistics reported that the prison population increased between 2000 and 2001 although at a lower rate than between 1999 and 2000. Individuals in custody grew by 14,275 between 2000 and 2001 and those under federal/state jurisdiction by 14,770. The latter category includes people sentenced to prison but residing in jails or in hospitals and also people on work release, furlough, or bail. People under custody grew by 1.1 percent between 2000 and 2001. The rate of increase has declined both for those in custody and those under prison jurisdiction since 1997. Since 1995 the prison population has grown by 37,057 inmates per year on average. (See Table 4.1.)

The incarceration rate of prisoners with sentences of more than one year was 476 persons per 100,000 U.S. residents in 1999. The rate in 2001 had declined by 1.1 percent to 470. This decline came about because the state incarceration rate declined by 2.8 percent, from 434 to 422 per 100,000 residents, but the federal component increased 14.3 percent, from 42 to 48 prisoners per 100,000 residents. (See Table 4.2.)

RATE OF INCARCERATION

The inmate population in the United States is measured by the rate of incarceration—that is, the number of people sent by the courts to prisons and jails per 100,000 people in the general population. As reported by The Sentencing Project, an advocacy group promoting alternatives to incarceration, in "U.S. Prison Populations—Trends and Implications" (Washington, D.C., May 2003), the United States had the highest incarceration rate in the world in 2002 with 702 individuals confined in prisons or jails per 100,000 population, higher than Russia (628), other successor states of the Soviet Socialist Republic (ranging from 489 for Turkmenistan to 554 for Belarus), and South Africa (400). Other states with high rates are small island nations. The Cayman Islands is second in

TABLE 4.1

Change in the state and federal prison populations, 1995–2001

Years	Annual increase in the number of prisoners		Percent change, under state/federal jurisdiction
	In state/federal custody	Under state/federal jurisdiction	
1995	88,395	71,172	6.7
1996	49,222	57,494	5.1
1997	48,800	58,785	5.0
1998	47,905	58,420	4.7
1999	36,957	43,796	3.4
2000	25,182	18,191	1.3
2001	14,275	14,770	1.1
Average annual increase, 1995–2001	37,057	41,919	3.8%

Note: In years in which states changed their reporting methods, counts based on comparable methods were used to calculate the annual increase and percent change.

SOURCE: Allen J. Beck and Paige M. Harrison,"Table 2: Change in the State and Federal prison populations, 1995-2001," in *Prisoners in 2001*, U.S. Bureau of Justice Statistics, Washington, DC, 2002

the world with 664 per 100,000; Bermuda makes the top ten with 457.

The incarceration rate for federal and state prisoners in the United States, excluding those in jail, has risen from a low of 79 in 1925 to 470 in 2001. (See Table 4.3.) The most recent data, from *Prison and Jail Inmates at Midyear 2002* (U.S. Bureau of Justice Statistics, Washington, D.C., April 2003) shows the rate increasing further to 474 in 2002. Beginning in 1925, the rate of incarceration of U.S. prisoners rose steadily for 15 years to a peak of 137 in 1939. The rate declined somewhat and more or less leveled out to between 100 and 120 for the next 35 years. Then, in 1973, the rate began to rise steadily. (See Figure 4.1.) From 1974 to 2001, the rate increased more than four-fold. The rate for males jumped from about 200 inmates per 100,000 people in the mid-1970s to around 900 per 100,000 in 2000.

TABLE 4.2

Prisoners under the jurisdiction of state or federal correctional authorities, by region and jurisdiction, yearend 2000 and 2001

	Advance 2001	2000	Percent change, 2000-01	Incarceration rate, 2001 [1]
U.S. total	1,344,512	1,329,367	1.1 %	470
Federal	136,509	125,044	9.2	48
State	1,208,003	1,204,323	0.3	422

[1] The number of prisoners with sentences of more than 1 year per 100,000 U.S. residents.

SOURCE: Adapted from Allen J. Beck and Paige M. Harrison,"Table 4: Prisoners under the jurisdiction of State or Federal correctional authorities, by region and jurisdiction, yearend 2000 and 2001," in *Prisoners in 2001*, U.S. Bureau of Justice Statistics, Washington, DC, 2002

Female incarceration rates began to rise in the mid-1980s, yet males still represented the overwhelming majority (93.7 percent) of all prisoners in 2001.

The highest rate of incarceration reported in 2001, the last year for which all data are in, was in Louisiana (800 prisoners per 100,000 residents). Second and third place were occupied by Mississippi (715) and Texas (711). Maine led the states with the lowest incarceration rate, 127 per 100,000, followed by Minnesota (132) and North Dakota (161). North Dakota, however, also had the highest overall growth in prison population in the 1995–2001 period, 11 percent a year, followed by Idaho (10.3 percent) and Oregon (9.8 percent a year). States with the most rapidly declining prison populations for the same period were Massachusetts, declining at an average rate of 1.8 percent annually, followed by Alaska (1 percent) and New York (0.2 percent). (See Table 4.4.)

PRISONS AND THEIR CAPACITIES

The Bureau of Justice Statistics conducts a census of prisons at five year intervals. The most recent census was held in 2000 but has not yet been published except for a few preliminary totals. As reported in *Census of State and Federal Correctional Facilities, 1995* (Bureau of Justice Statistics, Washington, D.C., August 1997), 1,375 state prisons housed 941,642 inmates and 125 federal facilities housed 81,930—for a total count of 1,500 prisons and slightly more than 1.13 million prisoners. State prisons were up from 1,207 in 1990 (up 13.9 percent) and federal facilities had increased from a total of 80 in 1990 (up by 56 percent). At the state level, the biggest growth was in facilities labeled maximum, high, or close security (up 29.6 percent); at the federal level, the increase was in the minimum/low category (up 184.3 percent) while maximum security facilities had declined by 18.2 percent between 1990 and 1995 and medium security facilities were down by 32.4 percent. To the 1,500 state and federal prisons must be added privately operated prisons. Professor Charles W. Thomas, retired, cited in the *Sourcebook of Criminal Statistics 2001*, estimates, based on his own survey, that 142 such prisons operated in 1997. If private prisons are added, the 1995 count of facilities was 1,642.

The report, *Mental Health Treatment in State Prisons, 2000* (Bureau of Justice Statistics, Washington, D.C., July 2001), reports numbers from the still unpublished 2000 prison census indicating that, in that year, 1,320 state prisons, 264 privately operated facilities, and 84 federal facilities were in operation, indicating that the "physical plant" housing prison inmates stood at 1,668, not much higher than five years before. The total prison population was 1.38 million, 22 percent higher than in 1995.

Crowding in Prisons

From 1995 to 2000, the number of state and federal prisons decreased, but capacity in the state-run or state-supervised prison system increased. Old prisons were replaced with new ones; more prisoners were housed in privately operated prisons; and additions to capacity at existing sites added new beds. In 1995 states operated their prisons 14 percent above capacity; in 2000 they were operating at capacity. Federal capacity, already strained in 1995, decreased further. In the federal sector, prisons operated 26 percent above capacity in 1995 and 31 percent over capacity in 2000. Data for 2001 indicate a slight increase in state capacity and no change in federal capacity. (See Table 4.5.) These are averages. The state reporting the least crowding in 2001 was Rhode Island; the state was using only 86 percent of its highest capacity. New Jersey reported operating at 37 percent above the capacity of its prison system, the highest among states. Capacity measures exclude prisoners housed in private facilities or in local jails under contract.

What does crowding mean? The American Correctional Association guidelines call for a standard cell area of 60 square feet for inmates spending no more than 10 hours per day in their cells. In many prisons, inmates are double-bunked in cells designed for one or sleep on mattresses in unheated prison gyms or on the floors of dayrooms, halls, or basements. Some are housed in tents; others share the same bunks at different times of the day. Crowding makes it more difficult to segregate violent from nonviolent prisoners and contributes to the spread of communicable diseases, such as tuberculosis. Overcrowded conditions can also cause tension, which can lead to fights and injuries.

State and Federal Prisoners Held Elsewhere

IN PRIVATELY RUN PRISONS. At the end of 2001 a total of 91,828 prisoners under the jurisdiction of federal and state correctional authorities were housed in private facilities. (See Table 4.6.) This accounted for 5.8 percent of all

TABLE 4.3

Number and rate (per 100,000 resident population in each group) of sentenced prisoners under jurisdiction of state and federal correctional authorities on December 31, by sex, 1925–2001

Year	Total	Rate	Male Number	Male Rate	Female Number	Female Rate	Year	Total	Rate	Male Number	Male Rate	Female Number	Female Rate
1925	91,669	79	88,231	149	3,438	6	1964	214,336	111	206,632	219	7,704	8
1926	97,991	83	94,287	157	3,704	6	1965	210,895	108	203,327	213	7,568	8
1927	109,983	91	104,983	173	4,363	7	1966	199,654	102	192,703	201	6,951	7
1928	116,390	96	111,836	182	4,554	8	1967	194,896	98	188,661	195	6,235	6
1929	120,496	98	115,876	187	4,620	8	1968	187,914	94	182,102	187	5,812	6
							1969	196,007	97	189,413	192	6,594	6
1930	129,453	104	124,785	200	4,668	8							
1931	137,082	110	132,638	211	4,444	7	1970	196,429	96	190,794	191	5,635	5
1932	137,997	110	133,573	211	4,424	7	1971	198,061	95	191,732	189	6,329	6
1933	136,810	109	132,520	209	4,290	7	1972	196,092	93	189,823	185	6,269	6
1934	138,316	109	133,769	209	4,547	7	1973	204,211	96	197,523	191	6,004	6
1935	144,180	113	139,278	217	4,902	8	1974	218,466	102	211,077	202	7,389	7
1936	145,038	113	139,990	217	5,048	8	1975	240,593	111	231,918	220	8,675	8
1937	152,741	118	147,375	227	5,366	8	1976	262,833	120	252,794	238	10,039	9
1938	160,285	123	154,826	236	5,459	8	1977[1]	278,141	126	267,097	249	11,044	10
1939	179,818	137	173,143	263	6,675	10	1977[2]	285,456	129	274,244	255	11,212	10
							1978	294,396	132	282,813	261	11,583	10
1940	173,706	131	167,345	252	6,361	10	1979	301,470	133	289,465	264	12,005	10
1941	165,439	124	159,228	239	6,211	9							
1942	150,384	112	144,167	217	6,217	9	1980	315,974	139	303,643	275	12,331	11
1943	137,220	103	131,054	202	6,166	9	1981	353,673	154	339,375	304	14,298	12
1944	132,456	100	126,350	200	6,106	9	1982	395,516	171	379,075	337	16,441	14
1945	133,649	98	127,609	193	6,040	9	1983	419,346	179	401,870	354	17,476	15
1946	140,079	99	134,075	191	6,004	8	1984	443,398	188	424,193	370	19,205	16
1947	151,304	105	144,961	202	6,343	9	1985	480,568	202	459,223	397	21,345	17
1948	155,977	106	149,739	205	6,238	8	1986	522,084	217	497,540	426	24,544	20
1949	163,749	109	157,663	211	6,086	8	1987	560,812	231	533,990	453	26,822	22
							1988	603,732	247	573,587	482	30,145	24
1950	166,123	109	160,309	211	5,814	8	1989	680,907	276	643,643	535	37,264	29
1951	165,680	107	159,610	208	6,070	8							
1952	168,233	107	161,994	208	6,239	8	1990	739,980	297	699,416	575	40,564	32
1953	173,579	108	166,909	211	6,670	8	1991	789,610	313	745,808	606	43,802	34
1954	182,901	112	175,907	218	6,994	8	1992	846,277	332	799,776	642	46,501	36
1955	185,780	112	178,655	217	7,125	8	1993	932,074	359	878,037	698	54,037	41
1956	189,565	112	182,190	218	7,375	9	1994	1,016,691	389	956,566	753	60,125	45
1957	195,414	113	188,113	221	7,301	8	1995	1,085,022	411	1,021,059	796	63,963	48
1958	205,643	117	198,208	229	7,435	8	1996	1,137,722	427	1,068,123	819	69,599	51
1959	208,105	117	200,469	228	7,636	8	1997	1,194,581	444	1,120,787	853	73,794	54
							1998	1,245,402	461	1,167,802	885	77,600	57
1960	212,953	117	205,265	230	7,688	8	1999	1,304,074	463[3]	1,221,611	913	82,463	59
1961	220,149	119	212,268	234	7,881	8							
1962	218,830	117	210,823	229	8,007	8	2000	1,331,278	469[3]	1,246,234	915	85,044	59
1963	217,283	114	209,538	225	7,745	8	2001[4]	1,344,512	470	1,259,481	896	85,031	58

Note: These data represent prisoners sentenced to more than 1 year. Both custody and jurisdiction figures are shown for 1977 to facilitate year-to-year comparison.

[1] Custody counts.

[2] Jurisdiction counts.

[3] Rates have been revised and are now based on population estimates from the 2000 decennial census.

[4] Preliminary; subject to revision.

SOURCE: Kathleen Maguire and Ann L. Pastore, eds., "Table 6.23: Number and rate (per 100,000 resident population in each group) of sentenced prisoners under jurisdiction of State and Federal correctional authorities on December 31," in *Sourcebook of Criminal Justice Statistics 2001*, U.S. Bureau of Justice Statistics, Washington, DC, 2002

state inmates and 12.3 percent of federal prisoners. The states with the highest percentage of prisoners under private management were New Mexico (43.8 percent), Montana (32.7 percent), and Alaska (31.7 percent). The District of Columbia also had a high percentage, 35.9. Eighteen states had no prisoners in privately operated facilities.

Privately managed prisoners have increased in number, from 71,208 in 1999 to 87,369 in 2000 to 91,828 in 2001. The increase between 1999 and 2000 was 22.7 percent;

growth from 2000 to 2001 was 5 percent, possibly signaling a tightening of private prison capacities.

IN LOCAL JAILS. Table 4.6 also shows that 70,681 prisoners were housed in local jails in 2001, 1.9 percent of all federal prisoners and 5.4 percent of state prisoners. Louisiana, with 44.9 percent of its prisoners in jails rather than in prisons, led this category, followed by Kentucky (30.5 percent) and Tennessee (26.3 percent).

The number of prisoners held in jails appears to fluctuate with capacity in state systems. Between 1999 and 2000,

FIGURE 4.1

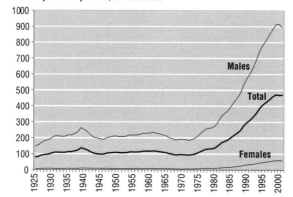

Number of sentenced prisoners per 100,000 residents, 1925–2000

Number of prisoners per 100,000 residents

Note: Prison population data are compiled by a yearend census of prisoners in state and federal institutions. Data for 1925 through 1939 include sentenced prisoners in state and federal prisons and reformatories whether committed for felonies or misdemeanors. Data for 1940 through 1970 include all adult felons serving sentences in state and federal insti-tutions. Since 1971, the census has included all adults or youthful offenders sentenced to a state or federal correctional institution with maximum sentences of over 1 year.

SOURCE: Kathleen Maguire and Ann L. Pastore, eds., "Table 6.23: Number and rate (per 100,000 resident population in each group) of sentenced prisoners under jurisdiction of State and Federal correctional authorities on December 31," in *Sourcebook of Criminal Justice Statistics 2001*, U.S. Bureau of Justice Statistics, Washington, DC, 2002

the number held in jails decreased by 495 prisoners but went up from 2000 to 2001 by 7,541, possibly reflecting tightening capacity in the state systems, as shown in Table 4.5.

RISING PRISON POPULATIONS

More People Coming to Court

Data on felony convictions at the state level tend to be reported later than data on prisoners, but trends can be discerned after a lag in time. In the decade 1988 to 1998, felony convictions in state courts increased from 667,366 to 927,717, an average annual growth rate of 3.3 percent. (See Table 4.7.) During the same period, prisoners held in state and federal facilities increased from 603,732 to 1,245,402 (as shown in Table 4.3). This represents an average annual increase of 7.5 percent. Felony convictions cause prison populations to increase because each prisoner serves more than a year in prison. Of those arrested, 44 percent received a felony sentence in 1988, 1992, and 1998. The rate dropped to 38 percent in 1996. As shown in Figure 4.2, conviction rates for all major crimes have increased between 1988 and 1998 except for burglary, but, as shown in the tabulation that accompanies the graphic, rates of conviction fluctuate over time; more detail for 1998 felony convictions is shown in Table 4.8.

Rising prison populations appear to be due to the fact that more people are "coming to court" and are convicted at the same rates as in earlier years. During the 1988 to 1998 period shown by available data, the population of adults 18 years old and older increased 1.1 percent a year as reported by the Bureau of the Census. Conviction rates of offenders grew at a rate three times higher annually. What other factors are at work?

Drug Offenses Are Up

The rise in drug offenders confined to federal prison has contributed dramatically to the overcrowding of those prisons. According to the U.S. Bureau of Prisons, of 20,686 total sentenced federal prisoners in 1970, some 3,384 were drug offenders—16.3 percent. By 1980, such offenders had climbed to 24.9 percent of the federal prison population. By 2001 the number of sentenced drug offenders in federal prisons had risen to 67,037, or 55.5 percent of all federal prisoners. (See Table 4.9.) Using data in this table, one can calculate that in the 1988 to 1998 period, during which state and federal prison populations increased 7.5 percent a year, imprisoned drug offenders increased at an average rate of 14 percent a year. Federal prisoners, however, are a small fraction of total prisoners.

As reported in *Correctional Populations in the United States, 1997* and *Prisoners 2001*, both published by the Bureau of Justice Statistics, drug offenders were 6.5 percent of the state correctional population in 1980 and 20.9 percent in 2000. In the 1988–98 period, drug offenders at the state level also increased rapidly—11.6 percent a year.

Is More Time Served?

Prison populations are influenced both by the length of a sentence a court imposes and by the percentage of the sentence the felon actually serves. Between 1988 and 1998, for all offenses, the average sentence imposed went from 76 months in 1988 to 57 months in 1998. However, at the same time, the percentage of time actually served increased from 32 percent of the sentence in 1988 to 47 percent in 1998. The net effect of these averages is to increase the time actually served between 1988 and 1998: 32 percent of 76 months produces an actual average sentence of 24 months; and 47 percent of 57 months produces 27 months. (See Table 4.10.)

A closer look at the details shown in Table 4.10 reveals that, on average, sentences are longer for every category except drug offenses if time served and imposed sentence are combined. This is shown in the last panel of the table. Thus the estimated actual time served in prison for robbery increased from 38 to 54 months between 1988 and 1998, but the time served for drug offenses went from 20 to 19 months in this same period. The data are the product of multiplying average sentences imposed by the percent of average time served for each category.

TABLE 4.4

The 10 highest and lowest jurisdictions for selected characteristics of the prison population, yearend 2001

Prison population	Number of inmates	Incarceration rates, 2001	Rate per 100,000 state residents[1]	1-year growth, 2000–01	Percent change	Growth since 1995	Average percent change[2]
10 highest:							
Texas	162,070	Louisiana	800	West Virginia	9.3%	North Dakota	11.0%
California	159,444	Mississippi	715	Alaska	8.9	Idaho	10.3
Federal	156,933	Texas	711	Idaho	8.5	Oregon	9.8
Florida	72,406	Oklahoma	658	Oregon	8.3	West Virginia	9.0
New York	67,534	Alabama	584	Federal	8.0	Montana	8.9
Michigan	48,849	Georgia	542	Hawaii	7.9	Mississippi	8.9
Georgia	45,937	South Carolina	529	South Dakota	7.5	Federal	8.5
Ohio	45,281	Missouri	509	Montana	7.2	Colorado	7.9
Illinois	44,348	Delaware	504	Tennessee	6.8	Tennessee	7.7
Pennsylvania	38,062	Arizona	492	New Mexico	6.1	Utah	7.3
10 lowest:							
North Dakota	1,111	Maine	127	New Jersey	-5.5%	Massachusetts	-1.8%
Wyoming	1,684	Minnesota	132	Utah	-5.2	Alaska	-1.0
Maine	1,704	North Dakota	161	New York	-3.8	New York	-0.2
Vermont	1,741	Rhode Island	181	Texas	-2.8	Ohio	0.2
New Hampshire	2,392	New Hampshire	188	California	-2.2	New Jersey	0.7
South Dakota	2,812	Vermont	213	Illinois	-2.1	Rhode Island	0.8
Rhode Island	3,241	Nebraska	225	Oklahoma	-1.7	Maryland	1.9
Montana	3,328	Utah	230	Rhode Island	-1.4	Florida	2.1
Nebraska	3,937	West Virginia	231	Ohio	-1.2	South Carolina	2.2
West Virginia	4,215	Massachusetts	243	Massachusetts	-1.1	Virginia	2.3

[1] The number of prisoners with a sentence of more than 1 year per 100,000 residents in the state population. The Federal Bureau of Prisons and the District of Columbia are excluded.
[2] The average annual percentage change from 1995 to 2001 in sentenced prisoners.

SOURCE: Allen J. Beck and Paige M. Harrison, "Table 6: The 10 highest and lowest jurisdictions for selected characteristics of the prison population, yearend 2001," in *Prisoners in 2001*, U.S. Bureau of Justice Statistics, Washington, DC, 2002

TABLE 4.5

Trends in prison population, 1990–2001

December 31	Number of inmates		Sentenced prisoners per 100,000 resident population		Population housed as a percent of highest capacity	
	Federal	State	Federal	State	Federal	State
1990	65,526	708,379	20	272	–	115%
1995	100,250	1,025,624	32	379	126%	114
1999	135,246	1,228,455	42	434	132	101
2000	145,416	1,236,476	45	432	131	100
2001	156,993	1,249,038	48	422	131	101

– Not available.

SOURCE: Allen J. Beck and Paige M. Harrison, "Highlights," in *Prisoners in 2001*, U.S. Bureau of Justice Statistics, Washington, DC, July 2002

The net effect of sentencing and time served, therefore, is to increase the prison population because violent and property crimes represent the largest proportions of all felonies—while drug offenses are growing more rapidly.

Truth-in-Sentencing Laws

Beginning in the mid-1980s, the federal government and many states passed truth-in-sentencing laws as part of a wide-spread "get tough of crime" movement. The idea behind these laws was to ensure that all or a substantial portion of each sentence imposed would actually be served. States operating under federal guidelines require that 85 percent of sentences are served; parole is abolished. Forty-two states, the District of Columbia, and the federal government itself operate under truth-in-sentencing statues. Their effect has been longer retention of prisoners and thus a growth in prison populations.

Parole Violators

In 1990, 29.1 percent of all admissions to state prison systems were parole violators. That proportion had increased to 35 percent of all admissions by 2000—203,569 prisoners out of 582,232. Parole violators were increasing at an average annual rate of 4.3 percent, nearly twice as fast as all admissions to state systems. (See Table 4.11.) Although statistics on why parolees are recommitted to prison are not routinely collected by the Bureau of Justice Statistics, a survey conducted in 1997 and reported in *Trends in State Parole, 1990–2000* (Bureau of Justice Statistics, Washington, D.C., October 2001) indicated that 69.9 percent of imprisoned parolees had committed a new offense. Some 16 percent of parolees were rearrested for drug violations. In a legislative environment in which the use of parole is being curtailed by state courts, the rising incidence of rearrest of those who are paroled is yet another cause of a rising prison population.

TABLE 4.6

State and federal prisoners held in private facilities, local jails, or other states' facilities, by jurisdiction, yearend 2001

	Private facilities		Local jails		In other state or federal facilities	
	Number	Percent of all inmates[a]	Number	Percent of all inmates[a]	Number	Percent of all inmates[a]
U.S. total	91,828	6.5 %	70,681	5.0 %	6,111	0.4 %
Federal[b]	19,251	12.3	2,921	1.9	1,194	0.8
State	72,577	5.8	67,760	5.4	4,917	0.4
Northeast	3,131	1.8 %	2,593	1.5 %	1,262	0.7 %
Connecticut	0	0	--	--	497	2.6
Maine	11	0.6	3	0.2	50	2.9
Massachusetts	0	0	420	4.0	91	0.9
New Hampshire	0	0	12	0.5	71	3.0
New Jersey[c]	2,620	9.3	2,019	7.2	71	0.3
New York	0	0	139	0.2	0	0
Pennsylvania	500	1.3	0		45	0.1
Rhode Island[c]	0	0	--	--	46	1.4
Vermont[c]	0	0	--	--	391	22.5
Midwest	6,920	2.9 %	2,192	0.9 %	875	0.4 %
Illinois	0	0	0		31	0
Indiana	915	4.4	1,320	6.3	0	0
Iowa	0	0	0		0	0
Kansas	98	1.1	0		89	1.0
Michigan	449	0.9	237	0.5	0	0
Minnesota	0	0	184	2.8	144	2.2
Missouri	0	0	0		247	0.9
Nebraska	0	0	0		26	0.7
North Dakota	44	4	21	1.9	21	1.9
Ohio	1,924	4.2	0		35	0.1
South Dakota	35	1.2	16	0.6	39	1.4
Wisconsin	3,455	16.0	414	1.9	243	1.1
South	45,690	8.1 %	57,782	10.3 %	1,143	0.2 %
Alabama	0	0	601	2.2	491	1.8
Arkansas	0	0	951	7.8	38	0.3
Delaware	0	0	--	--	28	0.4
Dist. of Columbia	986	35.9	--	--	4	0.1
Florida	3,995	5.5	0		0	0
Georgia	4,561	9.9	4,682	10.2	0	0
Kentucky	1,028	6.7	4,706	30.5	18	0.1
Louisiana	2,928	8.2	16,050	44.9	0	0
Maryland	128	0.5	140	0.6	45	0.2
Mississippi	3,634	16.9	3,736	17.4	0	0
North Carolina	191	0.6	0		0	0
Oklahoma	6,658	29.2	903	4.0	70	0.3
South Carolina	6	0	446	2.0	290	1.3
Tennessee	3,678	15.5	6,230	26.3	0	0
Texas	16,331	10.1	15,158	9.4	0	0
Virginia	1,566	5.0	3,440	10.9	86	0.3
West Virginia	0	0	739	17.5	73	1.7

PRIVATIZATION OF PRISONS

Rising prison populations and the need to expand the prison system in the states has led to calls for privatization in this sphere as in others (telecommunications, electric power). The basic assumption behind this movement is that the private sector is inherently more efficient and flexible than public bureaucracies because it is less constrained by regulations and is stimulated to be more cost-effective by competition. In this view, a privatized or even a partially privatized corrections system would cost the taxpayer less money. Corrections functions, however, are ultimately vested in governmental hands, and private prisons must operate under established rules and regulations. The complexity of corrections activities is such that comparisons between private and public facilities are very difficult to make, and the cost savings achieved by private corrections are in dispute because the evidence is inconclusive.

Speaking before the National Conference of State Legislatures in July 2000 in Chicago, J. Michael Quinlan of the Corrections Corporation of America, the leading private prison company, cited statistics from the *1999 Corrections Yearbook* (Criminal Justice Institute, Inc., Middletown, CT, 1999) stating that, in 1998, public prisons cost $56.51 per day to operate per prisoner whereas private prison costs were $43.00 per diem. Survey results, however, are not universally accepted in the field of

TABLE 4.6

State and federal prisoners held in private facilities, local jails, or other states' facilities, by jurisdiction, yearend 2001 [CONTINUED]

	Private facilities		Local jails		In other state or federal facilities	
	Number	Percent of all inmates[a]	Number	Percent of all inmates[a]	Number	Percent of all inmates[a]
West	16,836	6.2 %	5,193	1.9 %	1,637	0.6 %
Alaska	1,441	31.7	--	--	1	0
Arizona	1,429	5.2	349	1.3	101	0.4
California	4,452	2.8	2,727	1.7	628	0.4
Colorado	2,390	13.7	129	0.7	0	0
Hawaii	1,251	22.9	--	--	29	0.5
Idaho	1,348	22.4	249	4.1	91	1.5
Montana	1,087	32.7	496	14.9	37	1.1
Nevada	478	4.7	188	1.8	205	2.0
New Mexico	2,484	43.8	0		18	0.3
Oregon	0	0	8	0.1	209	1.8
Utah	0	0	1,020	19.1	146	2.7
Washington[c]	0	0	0		81	0.5
Wyoming	476	28.3	27	1.6	91	5.4

-- Not applicable. Prison and jails form an integrated system

... Not reported.

[a] Based on the total number of inmates under State or Federal jurisdiction.

[b] Includes 6,515 Federal inmates held in privately operated community correctional centers.

[c] Inmates held in other State facilities include interstate compact cases.

SOURCE: Allen J. Beck and Paige M. Harrison, "Table 9: State and Federal prisoners held in private facilities, local jails, or other States' facilities, by jurisdiction, yearend 2001," in *Prisoners in 2001*, U.S. Bureau of Justice Statistics, Washington, DC, July 2002

TABLE 4.7

Number of felony convictions in state courts, 1988–98

Year	Number of convictions
1988	667,366
1990	829,344
1992	893,630
1994	782,217
1996	997,970
1998	927,717

SOURCE: Jodi M. Brown, Patrick A. Langan, and David J. Levin, "Number of felony convictions in state courts, 1988–96," in *Felony Sentences in State Courts, 1996*, and *Felony Sentences in State Courts, 1998*, U.S. Bureau of Justice Statistics, Washington, DC, 1998 and 2001

corrections because too many variables make generalizations impossible. While somewhat dated, a 1996 study by the General Accounting Office, the analytical arm of the U.S. Congress, undertook the study of five state-sponsored investigations comparing private and public prisons. ("Private and Public Prisons—Studies Comparing Operational Costs and/or Quality of Service," GAO/GGD-96-158, Washington, D.C., 1996). The following paragraph from the summary provides insight into the difficulties of comparing private and public facilities:

> Three of the studies we reviewed (California, Tennessee, and Washington) made comparisons of costs between reasonably matched private and public facilities that were operating within each state that was studied. Of the four private/public comparisons reported in these three studies, two showed no significant differences in operational

---

FIGURE 4.2

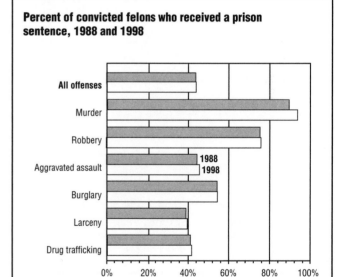

Percent of convicted felons who received a prison sentence, 1988 and 1998

Percent of convicted felons who received a prison sentence

	1988	1992	1996	1998
All offenses	**44%**	**44%**	**38%**	**44%**
Murder	91	93	92	94
Robbery	75	74	73	76
Aggravated assault	45	44	42	46
Burglary	54	52	45	54
Larceny	39	38	31	40
Drug trafficking	41	48	39	42

SOURCE: Adapted from Jodi M. Brown, Patrick A. Langan, and David J. Levin, "Percent of convicted felons who received a prison sentence," in *Felony Sentences in State Courts, 1998*, U.S. Bureau of Justice Statistics, Washington, DC, 1999

TABLE 4.8

Estimated number of felony convictions in state courts, 1998

Most serious conviction offense	Felony convictions in state courts	
	Number	**Percent**
All offenses	927,717	100.0%
Violent offenses	164,584	17.8
Murder[1]	9,158	1.0
Murder	6,944	0.7
Manslaughter	2,127	0.2
Sexual assault[2]	29,693	3.2
Rape	11,622	1.3
Other sexual assault	18,071	1.9
Robbery	38,784	4.2
Armed	11,977	1.3
Unarmed	10,358	1.1
Unspecified	16,450	1.8
Aggravated assault	71,060	7.7
Other violent[3]	15,889	1.7
Property offenses	283,002	30.5
Burglary	87,957	9.5
Residential	12,542	1.4
Nonresidential	20,419	2.2
Unspecified	54,996	4.9
Larceny[4]	107,621	11.6
Motor vehicle theft	14,368	1.5
Other theft	93,253	10.1
Fraud[5]	87,424	9.4
Fraud	43,975	4.7
Forgery	43,449	4.7
Drug offenses	314,626	33.9
Possession	119,443	12.9
Trafficking	195,183	21.0
Marijuana	22,975	2.5
Other	54,633	5.9
Unspecified	117,575	12.7
Weapons offenses	31,904	3.4
Other offenses[6]	133,601	14.4

Note: Detail may not sum to total because of rounding. This table is based on an estimated 927,717 cases.

[1] Includes manslaughter, defined as nonnegligent manslaughter only. A small number of cases were classified as nonnegligent manslaughter when it was unclear if the conviction offense was murder or nonnegligent manslaughter.

[2] Includes rape.

[3] Includes offenses such as negligent manslaughter and kidnaping.

[4] In a small number of cases, the type of larceny—vehicle theft versus other theft—was unknown. There were classified as "other theft."

[5] Includes embezzlement.

[6] Composed of nonviolent offenses such as receiving stolen property and vandalism.

SOURCE: Matthew R. Durose and Patrick A. Langham, "Table 1.1: Estimated number of felony convictions in State courts, 1998," in *State Court Sentencing of Convicted Felons, 1998,* U.S. Bureau of Justice Statistics, Washington, DC, 2001

TABLE 4.9

Drug offenders in the federal prison population, 1970–2001

Year	Total sentenced and unsentenced population	Total sentenced population	Total sentenced drug offenders	Percentage of sentenced prisoners who are drug offenders
1970	21,266	20,686	3,384	16.3%
1971	20,891	20,529	3,495	17.0%
1972	22,090	20,729	3,523	16.9%
1973	23,336	22,038	5,652	25.6%
1974	23,690	21,769	6,203	28.4%
1975	23,566	20,692	5,540	26.7%
1976	27,033	24,135	6,425	26.6%
1977	29,877	25,673	6,743	26.2%
1978	27,674	23,501	5,981	25.4%
1979	24,810	21,539	5,468	25.3%
1980	24,252	19,023	4,749	24.9%
1981	26,195	19,765	5,076	25.6%
1982	28,133	20,938	5,518	26.3%
1983	30,214	26,027	7,201	27.6%
1984	32,317	27,622	8,152	29.5%
1985	36,042	27,623	9,491	34.3%
1986	37,542	30,104	11,344	37.7%
1987	41,609	33,246	13,897	41.8%
1988	41,342	33,758	15,087	44.7%
1989	47,568	37,758	18,852	49.9%
1990	54,613	46,575	24,297	52.2%
1991	61,026	52,176	29,667	56.9%
1992	67,768	59,516	35,398	59.5%
1993	76,531	68,183	41,393	60.7%
1994	82,269	73,958	45,367	61.3%
1995	85,865	76,947	46,669	60.7%
1996	89,672	80,872	49,096	60.7%
1997	95,513	87,294	52,059	59.6%
1998	104,507	95,323	55,984	58.7%
1999	115,024	104,500	60,399	57.8%
2000	123,141	112,329	63,898	56.9%
2001	131,419	120,827	67,037	55.5%

Note: These data represent inmates housed in Federal Bureau of Prisons facilities; inmates housed in contract facilities are not included. Data for 1970–76 are for June 30; beginning in 1977, data are for September 30. Data for 2001 are as of December. Some data have been revised by the Federal Bureau of Prisons and may differ from previous editions.

SOURCE: Kathleen Maguire and Ann L. Pastore, eds., "Table 6.51: Federal prison population, and number and percent sentenced for drug offenses," in *Sourcebook of Criminal Justice Statistics 2001,* U.S. Bureau of Justice Statistics, Washington, DC, 2002

costs, one showed a 7-percent difference in favor of the private facility, and the other reported the private facility to be more costly than one public facility but less costly than another public facility. One additional study (Texas) reported a 14- to 15-percent savings from privatization; however, the analysis for the Texas study was problematic because the comparison was based on hypothetical public facilities, not existing ones. We could not conclude from these studies that privatization of correctional facilities will not save money. However, these studies do not offer substantial evidence that savings have occurred.

Despite these ambiguities, the political will to try out the concept of private prisons appears to be present in many states and at the federal level. The Bureau of Justice Statistics has been tracking private prisons and prison populations on a consistent basis only since 2000, but earlier numbers are available for 1990 and 1995. These data make it possible to get a statistical glimpse of developments from 1990 to 2001 or so. (See Figure 4.3.)

The graphic shows that the privately managed prison population has grown from 7,771 prisoners in 1990 to 91,828 in 2001—and from 1 percent to 6.9 percent of the correctional population under state and federal jurisdictions. Data for private prison capacity are available only for the 1997 to 2000 period. As shown in the graphic, the private prison population is beginning to come very close to private capacity. Private prisons are estimated to have

TABLE 4.10

Sentences imposed and time served, 1988, 1992, 1996, and 1998

Percent of imposed prison sentence actually served

	1988	1992	1996	1998
All offenses	32%	38%	45%	47%
Murder	33	44	50	52
Robbery	33	46	47	51
Aggravated assault	36	48	54	57
Burglary	30	35	42	45
Larceny	29	33	44	45
Drugs	30	34	42	41

Average imposed prison sentence length (in months)

	1988	1992	1996	1998
All offenses	76 mo	79 mo	62 mo	57 mo
Murder	239	251	257	263
Robbery	114	117	101	106
Aggravated assault	90	87	69	66
Burglary	74	76	60	52
Larceny	50	53	40	37
Drugs	66	72	55	47

Estimated actual time to be served in prison (in months)

	1988	1992	1996	1998
All offenses	24 mo	30 mo	28 mo	27 mo
Murder	79	110	128	136
Robbery	38	54	48	54
Aggravated assault	32	42	38	38
Burglary	22	27	25	24
Larceny	15	17	17	17
Drugs	20	24	23	19

SOURCE: Adapted from Matthew R. Durose and Patrick A. Langham, "Table 1.5. State court sentencing of convicted felons, 1998" and "Table 1.8. Mean sentence lengths for State felony sentences imposed, by the number and category of the conviction offense, 1998," in *State Court Sentencing of Convicted Felons, 1998,* U.S. Bureau of Justice Statistics, Washington, DC, 2001. Data for earliers years from David J. Levin, Patrick A. Langan, Jodi M. Brown, "Trends in the United States: 1988 to 1996" in *State Court Sentencing of Convicted Felons, 1996,* U.S. Bureau of Justice Statistics, Washington, DC, 2000

TABLE 4.11

Number of sentenced inmates admitted to state prisons, by type of admission, 1990–2000

Year	All admissions	New court commitments	Parole violators
1990	460,739	323,069	133,870
1991	466,286	317,237	142,100
1992	480,676	334,301	141,961
1993	475,100	318,069	146,366
1994	497,923	322,141	168,383
1995	521,970	337,492	175,726
1996	512,618	326,547	172,633
1997	538,375	334,525	186,659
1998	572,779	347,270	206,751
1999	573,013	345,648	198,639
2000	582,232	350,431	203,569
Percent change			
1990–1998	24.3%	7.5%	54.4%
1990–2000	26.3	8.5	52.1

Note: Sentenced inmates are those with a sentence of more than 1 year. Admissions exclude returned escapees and AWOLs and transfers from other jurisdictions. Admissions for Alaska were estimated for 1994. Parole violators for Idaho were estimated for 1998.

SOURCE: Allen J. Beck, Jennifer C. Karber, and Paige M. Harrison, "State Prison Admissions by Type," in *Prison and Jail Inmates at Midyear 2001,* U.S. Bureau of Justice Statistics, Washington, DC, 2002 (1998-2000 data). Earlier data from Allen J. Beck, *Prisoners in 1999,* U.S. Bureau of Justice Statistics, Washington, DC, 2000

increased from 67 in 1990 to 242 in 2001. Other Bureau of Justice Statistics sources put the 2001 count at 264.

The data in Figure 4.3 are plotted on a logarithmic scale on which growth trends may be compared directly by the slope of the curves. The trend shown indicates that private prison populations are growing much faster than the correctional population as a whole. Although cost comparisons between private and public prisons produce ambiguous results, private prisons are evidently gaining political support despite energetic opposition by opponents who wish to ensure that the corrective function remains entirely under public management.

While privatization appears to be driven by a need to find solutions to the high costs of housing prisoners, not least high capital expenditures required to build new prisons in an era of severe budgetary shortfalls at the state level, it is also evident from the public debate that the privatization issue transcends budgets and cost effectiveness and mirrors the opposing views of those who would rely upon the private sector and those who prefer that officials responsive to the voting public manage the public's business. Both sides acknowledge that the ultimate responsibility for corrections rests with the government and, therefore, government cannot completely privatize corrections, always retaining at minimum a supervisory responsibility, whereas the private sector cannot act as a purely private entity but must do so as the agent of government under statutes and regulations.

PRISON WORK PROGRAMS AND INDUSTRIES

Work in fields, laundries, and kitchens has always been a part of many inmates' lives; some even participate in work-release programs. According to the 1995 BJS census of correctional facilities, the last such census published, more than 94 percent of all prisons operated inmate work programs. About 63 percent of state inmates and 90 percent of federal inmates participated in some type of work program.

According to the Criminal Justice Institute (*The Corrections Yearbook—1998*), among the reporting jurisdictions (including the District of Columbia and the federal government) 76,080 inmates (6.7 percent) worked in prison industries which produced goods or services that could be sold. Almost 29,854 (4.8 percent) worked on prison farms and another 393,275 (44.5 percent) did other work assignments such as laundry, which helped run the prisons. Another 156,888 (16.3 percent) were receiving full-time academic or vocational training.

FIGURE 4.3

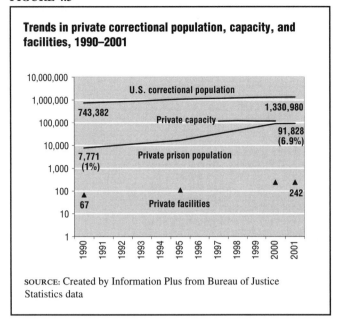

Trends in private correctional population, capacity, and facilities, 1990–2001

SOURCE: Created by Information Plus from Bureau of Justice Statistics data

State and local governments prevent prisoners from working at some jobs because they would be in competition with private enterprise or workers. In 1936 Congress barred convicts from working on federal contracts worth more than $10,000. In 1940 Congress made it illegal to transport convict-made goods in interstate commerce. As of May 2003 a debate was underway in Congress to permit private industry to bid on prison work in competition with federal prisons. Many states have laws prohibiting the sale of prisoner-made products within their state borders.

Some states allow prisoners to make goods for sale to governmental agencies only. In 1979 Congress allowed prisoners to work in other types of industries if they were paid the prevailing wage and local labor was not affected. Since 1990, 30 states have permitted the contracting out of prison labor to private companies.

According to the American Correctional Association, the number of inmates employed in prison industries varies from 1 percent in some states to 30 percent in others, with an average of 9 percent. Prisoners usually work at producing furniture, license plates, and textiles, and at printing and farming.

Wages

Some private industries pay minimum wage, but many prisons take most of prisoners' wages to pay for room and board, restitution, family support, and taxes. The Criminal Justice Institute (CJI) found that, in 1997, the average daily pay of inmates working for state prison industries ranged from a daily average low of $1.60 to an average high of $7.06. Inmates in Georgia received no wages while Nevada prisoners earned up to $48.75 per day. Private industry generally paid higher wages to the inmates—

an average of $24.27 to $38.23 per day. Florida paid inmates the lowest daily wages ($0.20) for private industry work, while Nebraska paid the highest ($67.50). According to the CJI, 48 jurisdictions reported annual prison industry gross sales of $1.5 billion for agency-operated industries.

Many prison administrators generally favor work programs. Some believe that work keeps prisoners productive and occupied, thus leading to a safer prison environment. Another cited benefit is that work programs help prisoners for re-entry into the noninstitutionalized world by helping them learn job skills and solid work habits that help them prepare for post-incarceration employment. Some prisons report that inmates who work in industry are less likely to cause problems in prison or be rearrested after release than convicts who do not participate in work programs.

Generally it is believed that the new skills developed through prison work programs, as well as educational opportunities, give prisoners an added edge in helping them readjust to normal life.

In addition, many inmates report that they like the opportunity to work. They assert that it gives them relief from boredom and some extra money. Yet, convicts are not allowed to protest about working conditions, nor are they permitted to talk to the media, to strike, or to change jobs.

UNICOR

UNICOR is the trade name for Federal Prison Industries, Inc., the government corporation that employs inmates in federal prisons. UNICOR should not be confused with state prison industry programs administered by the states. Under UNICOR, established in 1934, federal inmates get job training by producing goods and services for federal agencies. In 2001 items produced by inmates included industrial products (lockers, storage cabinets, shelving), clothing and textile products (draperies, canvas goods, military clothing), graphics and services (data entry, text editing, road signs), electronics (cable assemblies, connectors, power distribution systems), office furniture, and recycling activities.

UNICOR products and services must be purchased by federal agencies and are not for sale in interstate commerce or to nonfederal entities. UNICOR is not permitted to compete with private industry. If UNICOR cannot make the needed product or provide the required service, federal agencies may buy the product from the private sector through a waiver issued by UNICOR.

According to the agency's 2002 Annual Report, UNICOR employed 21,778 inmates in 111 factories at 71 locations. The agency had sales of $678.7 million, up from $583.5 million in 2001. UNICOR paid inmates between $0.23 and $1.15 per hour.

UNICOR is a self-supporting government corporation that may borrow funds from the U.S. Treasury and use the proceeds to purchase equipment, pay wages to inmates and staff (over 1,600 staffers who are not inmates are employed), and invest in expansion of facilities. No funds are appropriated for UNICOR operations.

CHAPTER 5
CHARACTERISTICS OF PRISON INMATES

Prisoners overwhelmingly represent societal "failures," young men (and a small percentage of women and older men) who have had unsuccessful experiences in their families, schools, military services, and labor force. They suffer disproportionately from child abuse, alcohol and drug abuse, poor self-concept, and deficient social skills. They tend to be hostile to others, and especially to authority.

— James B. Jacobs, "Inside Prisons" (Crime File Study Guide, National Institute of Justice, Washington, D.C., not dated)

RACE, ETHNICITY, AGE, AND GENDER

In 2001 some 1.26 million men and 85,000 women were serving sentences in state and federal prisons. (See Table 5.1.) Expressed in percentages, of total prisoners, 36.1 percent were non-Hispanic whites, 46.3 percent non-Hispanic blacks, 15.6 percent were Hispanics, and 2 percent were of other races (Asians, American Indians, Alaskan Natives, Native Hawaiians, and other Pacific Islanders). About 93.7 percent were men.

Among white prisoners, 7.5 percent were women, among blacks 5.9 percent, and among Hispanics 4.9 percent. But black women were the most numerous among all women in prison because the black prison population was the largest component.

The age group with the highest number of prisoners among men was 25–29. Women were most numerous in the 30–34 age group across all races. Among men, whites were more numerous in the 30–34 age group while blacks and Hispanics dominated the 25–29 group.

The largest number of prisoners were African Americans, both among men and women. Among men, blacks outnumbered whites in every age group except those age 45–54 and 55 and older. Among women, whites were more numerous than blacks in the 18–19, 20–24, 45–54, and 55 and older age categories. For every 100 white prisoners of both sexes, there were 128 black

TABLE 5.1

Number of sentenced prisoners under state or federal jurisdiction, by gender, race, Hispanic origin, and age, 2001

| | Number of sentenced prisoners | | | | | | | |
| | Males | | | | Females | | | |
Age	Total[1]	White[2]	Black[2]	Hispanic	Total[1]	White[2]	Black[2]	Hispanic
Total	1,259,481	449,200	585,800	199,700	85,031	36,200	36,400	10,200
18-19	35,600	8,900	17,400	7,000	1,300	700	500	100
20-24	214,600	60,000	106,500	40,600	8,500	3,700	3,200	1,500
25-29	241,800	71,000	122,500	42,100	15,200	5,600	6,600	2,000
30-34	238,600	85,100	110,700	39,100	21,100	8,700	9,400	2,400
35-39	214,500	81,900	102,000	28,900	18,600	8,000	8,400	2,000
40-44	145,900	58,400	64,300	21,200	10,100	4,200	4,700	1,000
45-54	124,800	59,500	48,400	16,100	8,000	3,900	3,000	1,000
55 or older	38,400	23,300	10,800	4,100	1,800	1,300	500	100

Note: Based on custody counts from National Prisoner Statistics (NPS-1A) and updated from jurisdiction counts by gender at yearend. Estimates by age derived from the *Survey of Inmates in State and Federal Correctional Facilities, 1997*. Estimates were rounded to the nearest 100.

[1] Includes American Indians, Alaska Natives, Asians, Native Hawaiians, and other Pacific Islanders.

[2] Excludes Hispanics.

SOURCE: Paige M. Harrison and Allen J. Beck, "Table 15: Number of sentenced prisoners under State or Federal jurisdiction, by gender, race, Hispanic origin, and age, 2001," in *Prisoners in 2001*, U.S. Bureau of Justice Statistics, Washington, DC, July 2002

prisoners. For every 100 Hispanic prisoners, there were 296 black prisoners.

Incarceration rates measured as prisoners per 100,000 residents of a gender/age group indicate that, overall, 462 white males 18 and older were in prison per 100,000 resident males of the same age group. For blacks this number was 3,535, for Hispanics 1,177. The rates for women were 36 for whites, 199 for blacks, and 61 for Hispanics. Whites and blacks in this context are non-Hispanic. (See Table 5.2.) These data, translated into percentages, indicate that 10 percent of black males age 25 to 29 were in prison in

TABLE 5.2

Number of sentenced prisoners under state or federal jurisdiction per 100,000 residents, by gender, race, Hispanic origin, and age, 2001

	Number of sentenced prisoners per 100,000 residents of each group							
	Males				Females			
Age	Total[1]	White[2]	Black[2]	Hispanic	Total[1]	White[2]	Black[2]	Hispanic
Total	896	462	3,535	1,177	58	36	199	61
18-19	838	321	2,858	1,092	31	25	83	23
20-24	2,199	941	7,901	2,627	91	61	225	105
25-29	2,624	1,173	10,028	2,946	164	94	483	150
30-34	2,401	1,267	8,791	2,681	211	130	682	176
35-39	1,906	1,029	7,536	2,030	165	102	561	147
40-44	1,286	699	4,932	1,786	88	51	320	88
45-54	685	422	2,652	1,032	42	27	136	61
55 or older	149	110	512	250	6	5	18	7

Note: Based on estimates of the U.S. resident population on July 1, 2000, and adjusted for the 1990 census undercount.

[1] Includes American Indians, Alaska Natives, Asians, Native Hawaiians, and other Pacific Islanders.

[2] Excludes Hispanics.

SOURCE: Paige M. Harrison and Allen J. Beck, "Table 16: Number of sentenced prisoners under State or Federal jurisdiction per 100,000 residents, by gender, race, Hispanic origin, and age, 2001," in *Prisoners in 2001*, U.S. Bureau of Justice Statistics, Washington, DC, July 2002

TABLE 5.3

Prisoners under the jurisdiction of state or federal correctional authorities, by gender, yearend 1995, 2000, and 2001

	Men	Women
All inmates		
Advance 2001	1,313,000	93,031
Final 2000	1,298,027	93,234
Final 1995	1,057,406	68,468
Percent change 2000–2001	1.2%	-0.2%
Average annual 1995–2001	3.7%	5.2%
Sentenced to more than a year		
Advance 2001	1,259,481	85,031
Final 2000	1,246,234	85,044
Percent change 1995–2001	1.1%	0.0%
Incarceration rate[1]		
2001	896	58
1995	789	47

[1] The number of prisoners with sentences of more than 1 year per 100,000 residents on December 31.

SOURCE: Paige M. Harrison and Allen J. Beck, "Table 7: Prisoners under the jurisdiction of State or Federal correctional authorities, by gender, yearend 1995, 2000, and 2001," in *Prisoners in 2001*, U.S. Bureau of Justice Statistics, Washington, DC, July 2002

2001 compared to 1.2 percent of white males in that age range and 2.9 percent of Hispanic males.

A somewhat expanded dataset, prisoners under the jurisdiction of state and federal correctional authorities (a grouping that includes people on probation and parole), shows correctional population trends for men and women since 1995. (See Table 5.3.) These data indicate that 1.31 million men and 93,031 women made up the correctional population in 2001. Men increased 1.2 percent from 2000 to 2001 with an annual average rate of 3.7 percent from 1995 to 2001. The female correctional population decreased by 0.2 percent from 2000 to 2001 but grew, overall, 5.2 percent on average each year from 1995 to 2001. Numbers for prisoners sentenced to more than one year show that the male correctional population in this category grew 1.1 percent in the 1995 to 2001 period whereas the female population remained essentially unchanged. The incarceration rate for men was 789 per 100,000 residents in 1995 and 896 in 2001. The corresponding rate for women was 47 in 1995 and 58 in 2001.

TYPES OF CRIMES

State Prisons

In the 1980 to 2000 time period, the number of people in the state correctional system increased by 309 percent, in the 1990 to 2000 period, by 77 percent. Most inmates are in state prisons rather than in federal facilities or local jails. Figure 5.1 shows a 20-year history of state incarcerations divided by type of crime committed. The largest

category is violent crime; the most rapidly growing category has been drug offenses. Drug offenses have had a 1,222 percent increase 1980 to 2000 as measured by state prison population. In the more recent 1990 to 2000 period, crimes against the public order have led the growth, increasing 905 percent. These crimes include illegal weapons possession, drunken driving, flight to escape prosecution, obstruction of justice, liquor law violations, and others.

The data graphed in Figure 5.1 are displayed as percentages of the total in Figure 5.2. The graphic shows that nearly half of all prison inmates are serving time for violent crimes (49 percent in 2000). A fifth of all prisoners are serving for drug offenses (21 percent) or property crimes (20 percent). The remaining 10 percent of prisoners have been convicted of offenses against the public order.

The distribution of offenses has changed somewhat over the 20-year period shown, dramatically in some instances. Thus in 1980 inmates incarcerated for drug offenses accounted for less than 7 percent of total prisoners; by 1990 they reached a peak of 22 percent, declining slightly thereafter. Violent crimes represented 59 percent of all incarcerations in 1980, dropped to a low in this period of 46 percent in 1990 but have been increasing in share of total offenses since, reaching 49 percent in 2000. The largest drop in share has been in property crime. The category dropped from 30 percent in 1980 to 26 percent in 1990 and finally to 20 percent of total inmates in 2000.

FIGURE 5.1

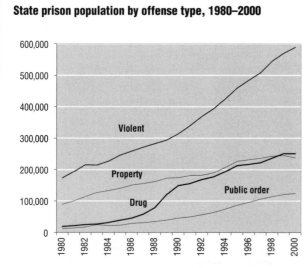

State prison population by offense type, 1980–2000

SOURCE: Adapted from Allen Beck and Paige Harrison, "Number of persons in custody of State correctional authorities by most serious offense, 1980–2000," in *Key Facts at a Glance,* U.S. Bureau of Justice Statistics, Washington, DC, July 25, 2002 [Online] http://www.ojp. usdoj.gov/bjs/glance/tables/corrtyptab.htm [accessed May 7, 2003]

FIGURE 5.2

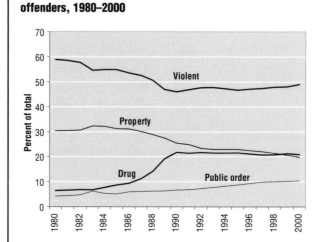

State prison population by offense type, by percent of total offenders, 1980–2000

SOURCE: Adapted from Allen Beck and Paige Harrison, "Number of persons in custody of State correctional authorities by most serious offense, 1980-2000," in *Key Facts at a Glance,* U.S. Bureau of Justice Statistics, Washington, DC, July 25, 2002 [Online] http://www.ojp. usdoj.gov/bjs/glance/tables/corrtyptab.htm [accessed May 7, 2003]

As measured by prisoners sentenced in state courts, the most frequently committed violent crime in 2000 was armed robbery. It was the leading violent crime among men—whose numbers dominate the prisoner population. Among women the leading violent crime was murder. Murder also outranked robbery among whites and Hispanics; among blacks, the leading crime was robbery. (See Table 5.4.) Burglary was the leading cause of a prison sentence in the property crime category. It was the leading category overall, among men, whites, blacks, and Hispanics. Among women, however, the top property crime was fraud.

Ranking types of crime by major category in 2000, the categories in descending order were violent crime, drug offenses, property crime, public order offenses, and miscellaneous offenses. This general pattern also held for males, blacks, and Hispanics. Among whites, property crime was second, drug offenses third. Among women, the top three offenses were drug violations, violent crime, and property offenses.

Federal Prisons

In 2001, there were nearly 8 people in state prison for every one in federal facilities. While in state prisons a fifth of all inmates were held for drug offenses, at the federal level more than half (55 percent) were imprisoned for drug violations as of January 2003. (See Table 5.5.) The next three categories in order of importance were weapons violations, explosives charges, and arson (10.6 percent of offenders), immigration violations (10.4 percent), and robbery (6.9).

According to the Federal Bureau of Prisons, federal inmates were predominantly male (93.2 percent) in 2003. The inmate population was 56.2 percent white, 40.6 percent black, and 1.6 percent each Asian and Native American.

EDUCATION OF PRISON AND JAIL INMATES

Early in 2003, the Bureau of Justice Statistics issued a special report, *Education and Correctional Populations,* on the educational attainment of prison and jail inmates. Data on prisoners are for the benchmark years of 1991 and 1997. The study utilized surveys of inmates in correctional facilities for those two years, surveys of local jail inmates conducted in 1989 and 1996, Current Population Survey data for 1997, and data from the 1992 Adult Literacy Survey sponsored by the National Center of Educational Statistics. Although the data are somewhat old, this study is the most recent to appear on the education of inmates.

Educational Attainment

A summary of the study's findings is presented in Table 5.6 where educational attainment of state and federal prison populations is compared to that of the general population in 1997. Also shown are data for 1991 and attainment of jail inmates for 1989 and 1996. Data for probationers is shown for 1995.

In 1997, 11.4 percent of state prisoners had "postsecondary/some college" education or were "college graduates or more." Federal prisoners in the same categories represented 23.9 percent of the federal prison

TABLE 5.4

Estimated number of sentenced prisoners under state jurisdiction, by offense, gender, race, and Hispanic origin, 2000

Offense	All	Male	Female	White	Black	Hispanic
Total	1,206,400	1,130,100	76,400	436,700	562,000	178,500
Violent offenses	589,100	565,100	24,000	212,400	273,400	87,100
Murder[a]	156,300	148,100	8,200	53,000	77,200	23,400
Manslaughter	17,300	15,400	1,800	6,600	6,800	2,900
Rape	30,800	30,400	300	15,400	12,100	2,300
Other sexual assault	83,100	82,200	900	50,500	20,700	10,400
Robbery	158,700	153,400	5,300	35,800	96,000	22,800
Assault	116,800	111,200	5,700	39,400	51,100	21,400
Other violent	26,100	24,400	1,700	11,800	9,600	3,900
Property offenses	238,500	219,300	19,200	108,600	96,800	28,400
Burglary	111,300	107,800	3,600	50,800	45,100	13,200
Larceny	45,700	39,900	5,800	17,900	21,100	5,300
Motor vehicle theft	18,800	18,100	700	7,700	7,100	3,700
Fraud	32,500	24,800	7,600	17,300	12,600	2,500
Other property	30,100	28,600	1,500	14,800	10,900	3,800
Drug offenses	251,100	226,400	24,700	58,200	145,300	43,300
Public-order offenses[b]	124,600	116,400	8,200	56,600	44,900	19,000
Other/unspecified[c]	3,200	2,900	300	700	1,600	700

Note: Data are for inmates with a sentence of more than 1 year under the jurisdiction of State correctional authorities. The number of inmates by offense were estimated using the *1997 Survey of Inmates in State Correctional Facilities* and rounded to the nearest 100.
[a] Includes nonnegligent manslaughter.
[b] Includes weapons, drunk driving, court offenses, commercialized vice, morals and decency charges, liquor violations, and other public-order offenses.
[c] Includes juvenile offenses and unspecified felonies.

SOURCE: Paige M. Harrison and Allen J. Beck, "Table 17: Estimated number of sentenced prisoners under State jurisdiction, by offense, gender, race, and Hispanic origin, 2000," in *Prisoners in 2001*, U.S. Bureau of Justice Statistics, Washington, DC, July 2002

TABLE 5.5

Federal prisoners by type of offense, 2003

	Number	Percent
Drug offenses	81,146	55.0
Weapons, explosives, arson	15,574	10.6
Immigration	15,358	10.4
Robbery	10,112	6.9
Property offenses	6,938	4.7
Extortion, fraud, bribery	6,956	4.5
Homicide, aggravated assault, and kidnapping	5,112	3.5
Sex offenses	1,557	1.1
Banking and insurance, counterfeit, embezzlement	1,054	0.8
Courts or corrections (e.g., obstruction of justice)	779	0.5
Continuing criminal enterprise	633	0.4
National security	85	0.1
Miscellaneous	2,711	1.8

SOURCE: "Type of offense," in *Federal Bureau of Prisons Quick Facts*, Federal Bureau of Prisons, Washington, DC, January 2003 [Online] http://www.bop.gov/fact0598.html#Offense [accessed April 15, 2003]

The groups of State prison inmates who had not completed high school or the GED included:

40% of males and 42% of females.

27% of whites, 44% of blacks, and 53% of Hispanics

52% of inmates 24 or younger and 35% of inmates 45 or older

61% of noncitizens and 38% of U.S. citizens

59% with a speech disability, 66% with a learning disability, and 37% without a reported disability

47% of drug offenders

12% of those with military service and 44% with no military service.

Women and Men

Among state prison inmates, 41.8 percent of women had an educational attainment of less than high school in 1997 compared with 39.6 percent for men ("8th grade or less" and "some high school"). Nearly 22 percent of women had a high school diploma, 20.4 percent of men. But if GED-certified prisoners are combined with high school graduates, men in these categories represented 49.3 percent of the prison population, women 43.9. Proportionately more women had an educational attainment exceeding the high school level: 14.3 percent had postsecondary education, some college, or were college graduates; 11.1 percent of males fell into these categories. (See Table 5.7.) A slightly smaller percentage of women participated in educational programs offered in state prisons than men, 50.1 percent versus the male participation rate of 52 percent.

Education by Race and Ethnicity

A breakdown of the state prison population by race and ethnicity shows that 27.2 percent of whites, 44.1 percent of blacks, and 53 percent of Hispanics had less than a high school education in 1997—all significantly higher than

population. In contrast, 48.4 percent of the general population had postsecondary education or a college degree or higher. In these two categories, both state and federal prisoners had a higher attainment in 1991 than in 1997.

Prisoners with less than a high school education were 39.7 percent of the state prison population and 26.5 percent of the federal prison population in 1997—compared to the general population with 18.4 percent in the less than high school categories.

In 1997, 33.2 percent of the general population had a high school diploma. By contrast, 20.5 percent of the state prison population and 27 percent of the federal prison population were high school graduates. More than a fifth of the prison populations had a General Education Development (GED) certificate—28.5 percent in state prisons, 22.7 percent in federal prisons. No comparable data for the general population were available. Concerning those in the state prisons (the majority) without a high school education, *Education and Correctional Population* presents the following summary:

TABLE 5.6

Educational attainment for state and federal prison inmates, 1991 and 1997, local jail inmates, 1989 and 1996, probationers, 1995, and the general population, 1997

| | Prison inmates | | | | Local jail inmates | | Proba- | General |
| | State | | Federal | | | | tioners | population |
Educational attainment	1991	1997	1991	1997	1989	1996		
8th grade or less	14.3 %	14.2 %	11.0 %	12.0 %	15.6 %	13.1 %	8.4 %	7.2 %
Some high school	26.9	25.5	12.3	14.5	38.2	33.4	22.2	11.2
GED*	24.6	28.5	22.6	22.7	9.2	14.1	11.0	...
High school diploma	21.8	20.5	25.9	27.0	24.0	25.9	34.8	33.2
Postsecondary/some college	10.1	9.0	18.8	15.8	10.3	10.3	18.8	26.4
College graduate or more	2.3	2.4	9.3	8.1	2.8	3.2	4.8	22.0
Number	706,173	1,055,495	53,677	88,705	393,111	503,599	2,029,866	192,352,084

Note: Probationers have been excluded from the general population. General population includes the noninstitutional population 18 or older.
Detail may not add to 100% due to rounding.
* General Educational Development certificate.
... Not available in the Current Population Survey.

SOURCE: Caroline Wolf Harlow, "Table 1: Educational attainment for State and Federal prison inmates, 1997 and 1991, local jail inmates, 1996 and 1989, probationers, 1995, and the general population, 1997," in *Education and Correctional Populations*, U.S. Bureau of Justice Statistics, Washington, DC, 2003

TABLE 5.7

Education, by gender for state prison inmates, 1997

| | Percent of state prison inmates | |
	Male	Female
Educational attainment		
8th grade or less	14.3%	13.6%
Some high school	25.3	28.2
GED	28.9	22.3
High school diploma	20.4	21.6
Postsecondary/some college	8.8	11.2
College graduate	2.3	3.1
Educational program participation		
Total	52.0%	50.1%
Basic	3.1	3.3
GED/high school	23.6	21.3
College	10.0	9.1
English as a second language	1.2	0.5
Vocational	32.4	29.5
Other	2.5	3.8
Number of prison inmates	989,419	66,076

Note: Detail may not add to total due to rounding or inmates' participation in more than one educational program.

SOURCE: Caroline Wolf Harlow, "Table 6: Education, by gender for State prison inmates, 1997," in *Education and Correctional Populations*, U.S. Bureau of Justice Statistics, Washington, DC, 2003

TABLE 5.8

Education, by race/Hispanic origin, for state prison inmates, 1997

| | Percent of state prison inmates | | |
	White	Black	Hispanic
Educational attainment			
8th grade or less	10.9%	11.7%	27.9%
Some high school	16.3	32.4	25.1
GED	35.2	24.8	24.7
High school diploma	22.8	21.0	14.9
Postsecondary/some college	11.4	8.4	5.5
College graduate or more	3.5	1.6	1.9
Educational program after admission			
Total	48.8%	53.8%	52.6%
Basic	2.1	3.3	4.8
GED/high school	18.7	26.1	25.4
College	12.4	9.0	7.1
English as a second language	0.1	0.1	6.4
Vocational	32.0	33.7	29.1
Other	3.0	2.5	1.8
Number of prison inmates	351,742	490,384	179,301

Note: Detail may not add to total due to rounding or inmates' participation in more than one educational program.

SOURCE: Caroline Wolf Harlow, "Table 7: Education, by race/Hispanic origin, for State prison inmates, 1997," in *Education and Correctional Populations*, U.S. Bureau of Justice Statistics, Washington, DC, 2003

the same group in the general population (18.4 percent). (See Table 5.6 and Table 5.8.) White prisoners with a high school diploma were 22.8 percent of the prison population, black prisoners in the same group were 21 percent, Hispanics 14.9. Prisoners with some postsecondary education or a college degree or higher attainment showed a similar pattern: whites were 14.9 percent of the population

with this attainment, blacks 10 percent, and Hispanics 7.4 percent. But among those participating in educational programs after admission to prison, blacks had the highest rate of participation, 53.8 percent, Hispanics second with 52.6 percent, and whites came last with 48.8 percent participation.

According to *Education and Correctional Populations* (Bureau of Justice Statistics, Washington, D.C., January

TABLE 5.9

Educational programs offered in state, federal, and private prisons, 1995 and 2000

Educational programs	State prisons 1995	State prisons 2000	Federal prisons 1995	Federal prisons 2000	Private prisons 1995	Private prisons 2000
With an education program	88.0%	91.2%	100.0%	100.0%	71.8%	87.6%
Basic adult education	76.0	80.4	92.0	97.4	40.0	61.6
Secondary education	80.3	83.6	100.0	98.7	51.8	70.7
College courses	31.4	26.7	68.8	80.5	18.2	27.3
Special education	33.4	39.6	34.8	59.7	27.3	21.9
Vocational training	54.5	55.7	73.2	93.5	25.5	44.2
Study release programs	9.3	7.7	5.4	6.5	32.7	28.9
Without an education program	12.0	8.8	0.0	0.0	28.2	12.4
Number of facilities	1,278	1,307	*	*	110	242

Note: Detail may not add to total because facilities may have more than one educational program.

* Changed definitions prevent meaningful comparisons of the numbers of federal facilities, 1995 and 2000

SOURCE: Adapted from Caroline Wolf Harlow, "Table 3: Educational programs offered in State, Federal, and private prisons, 2000 and 1995, and local jails, 1999," in *Education and Correctional Populations*, U.S. Bureau of Justice Statistics, Washington, DC, 2003

TABLE 5.10

Participation in educational programs since most recent incarceration or sentence, for state and federal prison inmates, 1991 and 1997

Educational programs	State 1991	State 1997	Federal 1991	Federal 1997
Total	56.6	51.9	67.0	56.4
Basic	5.3	3.1	10.4	1.9
GED/high school	27.3	23.4	27.3	23.0
College courses	13.9	9.9	18.9	12.9
English as a second language	...	1.2	...	5.7
Vocational	31.2	32.2	29.4	31.0
Other	2.6	2.6	8.4	5.6
Number of inmates	709,042	1,046,136	53,753	87,624

Note: Detail may not add to total due to rounding or inmates' participation in more than one educational program.
... Not available.

SOURCE: Adapted from Caroline Wolf Harlow, "Table 4: Participation in educational programs since most recent incarceration or sentence, for State and Federal prison inmates, 1997 and 1991, for local jail inmates, 1996, and for probationers, 1995," in *Education and Correctional Populations*, U.S. Bureau of Justice Statistics, Washington, DC, 2003

2003), young men in the 20 to 39 category dominate the prison population by sheer numbers. Young men in this age group, according to the report, were "markedly less educated than their counterparts in the general populations." The report presents the following summary: "Four times as many young males in the general population as in the prison population had attended some college classes or postsecondary courses—54% of whites in the general population and 11% in prison, 44% of blacks in the general population and 8% in prison, and 32% of Hispanics and 7% in prison."

Education Programs

Most prisons offer some kind of educational programs to inmates including basic adult education, secondary education, college courses, special education, vocational training, and study release programs. (See Table 5.9.) In 1995, 88 percent of state prisons offered educational opportunities; by 2000, 91.2 percent did. All federal facilities offer such courses of education. Private prisons participate in such programs at the lowest levels—71.8 percent did so in 1995, 87.6 percent did so by 2000. According to *Education and Correctional Populations*, 60.3 percent of local jails also offered educational programs in 1999. The most widely offered programs in 2000 were secondary education and basic adult education in that order. Study release programs were the least available in publicly run prisons; special education was the least available in privately run prisons.

Participation rates by prisoners have declined in state prisons from 56.6 percent in 1991 to 51.9 percent in 1997. A decline was also seen in federal facilities, from 67 percent in 1991 to 56.4 percent in 1997. (See Table 5.10.) No comparable data for private prisons were available. Although there has been a decrease as measured in percent of population, the actual numbers of prisoners participating has increased substantially—by 337,094 in state facilities and 33,871 in federal facilities. The lower participation rates are applied to a significantly increased prison population.

PAST ABUSE

The Bureau of Justice Statistics published a special report titled *Prior Abuse Reported by Inmates and Probationers* in 1999. The report was prepared from survey data collected from state and federal prisoners in 1997, inmates of local jails in 1996, and the 1995 Survey of Adults on Probation. The special report found that 18.7 percent of state prisoners, 9.5 percent of federal prisoners, 16.4 percent of jail inmates, and 15.7 percent of probationers had experienced abuse before being admitted to prison. (See Table 5.11.) The survey relied on the respondents' own definitions of physical and sexual abuse.

In general, most of the people who abused state and federal inmates before their incarceration were adults. Most victims knew their abuser(s). Men were most frequently abused by family members while women mainly suffered at the hands of husbands or boyfriends.

TABLE 5.11

Prior abuse of correctional populations by sex, 1997

| | Percent experiencing abuse before sentence | | | | |
| | | Ever | | Before 18 | |
	Total	Male	Female	Male	Female
Ever abused before admission					
State prison inmates	18.7 %	16.1%	57.2%	14.4 %	36.7 %
Federal prison inmates	9.5	7.2	39.9	5.8	23.0
Jail inmates	16.4	12.9	47.6	11.9	36.6
Probationers	15.7	9.3	40.4	8.8	28.2
Physically abused					
State prison inmates	15.4 %	13.4%	46.5%	11.9%	25.4 %
Federal prison inmates	7.9	6.0	32.3	5.0	14.7
Jail inmates	13.3	10.7	37.3	--	--
Probationers	12.8	7.4	33.5	--	--
Sexually abused					
State prison inmates	7.9 %	5.8%	39.0%	5.0 %	25.5 %
Federal prison inmates	3.7	2.2	22.8	1.9	14.5
Jail inmates	8.8	5.6	37.2	--	--
Probationers	8.4	4.1	25.2	--	--

Note: State and federal prison data were collected in 1997, data on jail inmates in 1996, and data on probationers in 1995.
-- Not available.

SOURCE: Adapted from Caroline Wolf Harlow, "Prior abuse of correctional populations, by sex," in *Prior Abuse Reported by Inmates and Probationers*, U.S. Bureau of Justice Statistics, Washington, DC, 1999

TABLE 5.13

Minor children in the resident population with an incarcerated parent, 1999

	Number of children	Percent of resident population
U.S. total*	1,498,800	2.1%
White	384,500	0.8%
Black	767,200	7.0
Hispanic	301,600	2.6

Note: Children were assumed to have the same race/ethnicity as the incarcerated parent.
* Includes children of other races.

SOURCE: Christopher J. Mumola, "1.5 million children in the U.S. had a parent in prison in 1999–up by more than 500,000 since 1991," in *Incarcerated Parents and Their Children*, U.S. Bureau of Justice Statistics, Washington, DC, August 2000

The report found that male respondents had experienced physical or sexual abuse before turning 18 at a rate of 5.8 percent for federal prisoners and 14.4 percent for state prisoners; 23 percent of females in federal prison cited abuse before age 18 compared to 36.7 percent of females in state prisons. The report states that "[a] review of 16 studies estimated that for the general adult population 5% to 8% of males and 12% to 17% of females were abused as children," suggesting that abuse in youth among prisoners, jail inmates, and probationers was higher than among members of the general population.

TABLE 5.12

Estimated number of state and federal prisoners with minor children, by gender, 1991 and 1999

| | State prisoners | | | Federal prisoners | | |
	Total	Male	Female	Total	Male	Female
Number of parents						
1991	413,100	386,500	26,600	39,400	36,500	2,900
1999	642,300	593,800	48,500	79,200	74,100	5,100
Number of minor children						
1991	852,300	794,500	57,800	84,200	78,300	5,900
1999	1,324,900	1,209,400	115,500	173,900	163,300	10,600

Note: Numbers are estimates based on responses to the 1991 and 1997 Surveys of Inmates in State and Federal Correctional Facilities, and custody counts from the National Prisoner Statistics program.

SOURCE: Christopher J. Mumola, "Table 2: Estimated number of State and Federal Prisoners with minor children, by gender, 1999," in *Incarcerated Parents and Their Children*, U.S. Bureau of Justice Statistics, Washington, DC, 2000

PRISONERS AND THEIR CHILDREN

In 1999 some 1.5 million children had a parent in prison. At the state level, 642,300 prisoners had 1.325 million minor children being taken care of by others. In federal prisons, 79,200 prisoners had left 173,900 children in others' care. Among state prisoners, males were parents to 92 percent of the minor children, female prisoners accounted for 8 percent of children left behind. (See Table 5.12.) In federal prisons, female prisoners were parents to 6 percent of minor children left behind, while male prisoners accounted for 94 percent.

Looking at state prisons only, prisoners' children increased by 55 percent since 1991. Prisoners with children had on average 2.1 children both in 1991 and 1999. Male parents in state prison increased 54 percent, the number of their children by 52 percent. The female parent prison population rose 82 percent, the children they had left doubled in number in this eight-year period.

Data for federal prisons show a somewhat different picture. Children with parents in federal prisons more than doubled—a 106.5 percent increase; federal prisoners with children increased 101 percent. Children with a male parent in prison increased 108.6 percent (from 78,300 to 163,300), those with a female parent by 79.7 percent (from 5,900 children in 1991 to 10,600 in 1999).

The 1.5 million children of prisoners were 2.1 percent of all children in the resident population of the United States. White children of prisoners were 0.8 percent of all white children, black children 7 percent of all black children, and Hispanic children with a parent in prison were 2.6 percent of all Hispanic children in the population. (See Table 5.13.)

The following statistics come from a study by the Bureau of Justice Statistics—*Special Report on Incarcerated Parents and Their Children*, issued August 2000 and written by Christopher J. Mumola. The report noted that:

- Half of the parents in state prison were never married.

- Fewer than half of the parents in state prison lived with their minor children before incarceration.

- One-third of mothers in prison had been living alone with their children in the months before arrest.

- Fathers cite the child's mother as the current caregiver; mothers cite child's grandparents or other relatives.

- About 40 percent of fathers and 60 percent of mothers in state prison had at least weekly contact with their children.

- A majority of parents in prison were violent offenders or drug traffickers.

GANG MEMBERSHIP

Prisons also house inmates who were part of gangs prior to their arrests. The BJS defines gangs as groups that commit illegal acts and have five or six of the following characteristics:

- Formal membership with a required initiation or rules for members

- A recognized leader or certain members whom others follow

- Common clothing or group colors, symbols, tattoos, or special language

- A group name

- Members from the same neighborhood, street, or school

- Turf or territory where the group is known and where group activities take place

In 1997 about 6 percent of prison inmates had belonged to groups that engaged in illegal activities and that had five or six gang characteristics. Another 6 percent had engaged in illegal activities with groups that had three or four gang characteristics. Among inmates who were gang members, half had belonged to the gang for 36 months or more and were active members at the time they were arrested for their current offenses. One third of prison inmates were still members of a gang while in prison.

CHAPTER 6
INMATE HEALTH

Through the mid-1990s, a number of studies, limited in scope, found a higher prevalence of certain infectious diseases, chronic diseases, and mental illness among prison and jail inmates. Further, each year the Nation's prisons and jails release more than 11.5 million inmates. The potential that ex-offenders may be contributing to the spread of infectious disease in the community became of increasing concern. In addition, as these ex-offenders' diseases get worse, society may have to pay substantially more to treat them than if these conditions had been treated at an earlier stage—or prevented altogether—while these individuals were still incarcerated.

— Edward A. Harrison, CCHP, President, National Commission on Correctional Health Care

DEATH RATES OF PRISONERS

Data on the health status of inmates in prisons and jails are not routinely collected by the Bureau of Justice Statistics (BJS). There are some exceptions. Surveys of prisoners conducted at intervals include questions about health. Since 1990 BJS has also collected data on the prevalence of Human Immunodeficiency Virus and Acquired Immune Deficiency Syndrome (HIV/AIDS) and has reported its findings on an annual basis. Estimates of prisoners' health conditions were developed by the National Commission on Correctional Health Care (NCCHC) and published in a report to Congress (*The Health Status of Soon-To-Be-Released Inmates*, Chicago, IL, 2002). These estimates, however, were not based on actual examinations of prison or jail inmates but were, instead, projections developed using studies of the general population with the results allocated to the prison population based on the economic, gender, and racial/ethnic composition of prisoners and inmates of jails.

An indirect measure of the health status of inmates is provided by mortality data that BJS makes available as part of its HIV/AIDS reporting. The age structure of prisoners is younger than that of the general population. The two

FIGURE 6.1

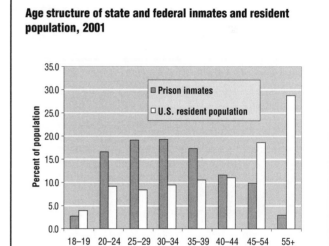

Age structure of state and federal inmates and resident population, 2001

SOURCE: Adapted from Paige M. Harrison and Allen J. Beck, "Table 15: Number of Sentenced Prisoners under State or Federal Jurisdiction, by gender, race, Hispanic origin, and age, 2001," in *Prisoners in 2001*, U.S. Bureau of Justice Statistics, Washington, DC, July 2002 and "Projections of the Total Resident Population by 5-year Age Groups, Race, and Hispanic Origin, with Special Age Categories: Middle Series, 2001 to 2005," in *Population Estimates*, U.S. Census Bureau, Washington, DC [Online] http://eire.census.gov/popest/estimates.php [accessed March 13, 2003]

largest age groups in state and federal prisons in 2001 were those age 25–29 and those age 30–34. In the general population, excluding those under 18 (to make the two populations comparable), the two largest groups were 45–54 and 55 and older. (See Figure 6.1.) In 2000 the relatively young state prison population had a death rate of 230 per 100,000 inmates. The 2000 death rate for the U.S. population as a whole was 873 per 100,000 as reported by the National Center for Health Statistics ("Deaths: Final Data for 2000," Centers for Disease Control and Prevention, September 16, 2002). But mortality data for a population with the age structure of state and federal prisoners would have been

TABLE 6.1

Number of inmate deaths in state prisons by cause, 1995–97

Cause of death	Number						Rate of death per 100,000 inmates					
	1995	1996	1997	1998	1999	2000	1995	1996	1997	1998	1999	2000
Total	3,133	3,095	2,872	2,805	2,933	2,865	311	308	255	239	240	230
Natural causes	1,569	1,715	1,859	1,905	2,179	2,139	156	170	165	162	178	172
AIDS	1,010	907	538	350	242	174	100	90	48	30	20	14
Suicide	160	154	159	176	169	185	16	15	14	15	14	15
Accident	48	43	37	41	44	24	5	4	3	3	4	2
Execution	56	45	74	68	98	84	6	4	7	6	8	7
By another person	86	65	75	55	56	56	9	6	7	5	5	4
Other/unspecified	204	166	130	210	145	203	20	16	12	18	12	16

Note: To calculate the rate of death, the number of inmates under state jurisdiction on June 30 of each year was used as an approximation of the average population exposed to the risk of death during the year. Detail may not add to total due to rounding.

SOURCE: Adapted from Laura M. Maruschak, "Table 4. Number of inmate deaths in State prisons, by cause, 1995–97," in *HIV in Prisons, 1997,* U.S. Bureau of Justice Statistics, Washington, DC, November 1999 (revised December 9, 1999); Laura M. Maruschak, "Table 4. Number of inmate deaths in State prisons, by cause, 1996–98," in *HIV in Prisons, 1998,* U.S. Bureau of Justice Statistics, Washington, DC, March 29, 2000; Laura M. Maruschak, "Table 4. Number of inmate deaths in State prisons, by cause, 1995 and 1999," in *HIV in Prisons and Jails 1999,* U.S. Bureau of Justice Statistics, Washington, DC, July 2001 and Laura M. Maruschak, "Table 5. Number of inmate deaths in State prisons, by cause, 1995 and 2000," in *HIV in Prisons, 2000,* U.S. Bureau of Justice Statistics, Washington, DC, October 2002 (revised February 24, 2003)

TABLE 6.2

Calculated and actual death rates of prison inmates, 2000

Age groups	Total prisoners	Percent of prisoners	Death rate per 100,000 in general population	Apportioned death rate (columns B x C)	Actual state prison population death rate
	A	B	C	D	E
18–19	33,300	2.7	68.2[a]	1.8	
20–24	199,600	16.2	96.0	15.6	
25–29	232,100	18.8	99.0	18.6	
30–34	234,000	19.0	116.3	22.1	
35–39	212,700	17.3	162.2	28.0	
40–44	149,400	12.1	237.3	28.8	
45–54	128,800	10.5	356.0	37.2	
55 and older	42,300	3.4	1003.9	34.5	
	1,232,200	100.0		186.6	230.0

Note: Actual prison population death rates are not available by age group.

[a] Death rate is for the 15-19 age group because the source did not provide sufficient detail to permit calculation of an 18-19 estimate.

SOURCE: Adapted from Allen J. Beck and Paige M. Harrison, "Table 14. Number of sentenced Prisoners under State or Federal Jurisdiction, by gender, race, Hispanic origin, and age, 2000," in *Prisoners in 2000,* U.S. Bureau of Justice Statistics, Washington, DC, August 2001 and Arialdi M. Ninino et al., "Table 3: Number of deaths and death rates by age, race, and sex: United States, 2000," in *Deaths: Final Data for 2000,* Centers for Disease Control and Prevention, Washington, DC, 2002 and Laura M. Maruschack, "Table 5. Number of inmate deaths in State prisons by cause, 1995 and 2000," in *HIV in Prisons, 2000,* U.S. Bureau of Justice Statistics, Washington, DC, October 2002 (revised February 24, 2003)

186.6 persons per 100,000 in 2000, lower than the 230 actually experienced. Data presented by the BJS account for this difference. (See Table 6.1 and Table 6.2.)

Table 6.1 shows deaths and death rates by cause of death. In 2000 the death rate from natural causes, excluding AIDS, was 172 per 100,000 inmates. If deaths from AIDS are added, the rate was 186, almost exactly what a population with the age structure of the prison population in 2000 would predictably experience. The actual higher value is produced by adding suicides (15), accidental deaths (2), executions (7), murders (4), and other causes (16) that were not known or not assigned to one of the other categories. Table 6.2 shows how age-specific death rates are apportioned to develop a calculated death rate for the prison population.

In the 1995–2000 period, the death rates generally dropped in the prisons as in the general population. The prison death rate declined from 311 per 100,000 inmates in 1995 to 230 in 2000. The national death rate dropped from 919 in 1995 to 873 in 2000—and to 855 in 2001 (preliminary release). The decreasing death rate in the general population—the inverse of which is an improving life expectancy—is due to improvements in methods of treating, controlling, and managing diseases and lower rates of accidental deaths. Within the prison population, the most dramatic change has been the sharply dropping death rate from AIDS. Deaths per 100,000 declined from 100 in 1995 to 14 in 2000, the rates dropping every year. If AIDS deaths are excluded from the total in prisons, the death rate would have increased rather than decreased, from 211 in 1995 to 216 in 2000.

MEDICAL CONDITIONS, SURVEYED AND MEASURED

The most recent survey of state and federal prisoners took place in 2000, but the Bureau of Justice Statistics has not yet published the results. Data from the 1997 survey provide a self-assessment of prisoners' state of health. To

TABLE 6.3

Medical problems among federal inmates and in the general public, 1997, 1998, 2000

Medical Problem	Percent of federal inmates		Percent of general public, 1998[2]
	Official records, midyear 2000[1]	1997 survey data	
Asthma	4.4%	0.9%	8.9%
Diabetes	3.6	1.5	6.2[3]
Heart	2.6	1.3	11.4
High blood pressure	7.8	1.7	19.0
HIV/AIDS	1.0	0.5	0.178[4]
Mental health	4.8	4.8	–

[1] Based on the clinical status on July 29, 2000, except for asthma, which was counted on September 20, 2000. Inmate totals were based on average daily population in each month.

[2] Unless otherwise noted, values are from J.R. Pleis and R. Coles, *Summary Health Statistics for U.S. Adults: National Health Interview Survey, 1998*, National Center for Health Statistics. Vital Health Statistics 10(209). 2002.

[3] Value is for 2000 from National Diabetes Information Clearinghouse, National Institutes of Health, obtained from http://www.niddk.nih.gov/health/diabetes/pubs/dmstats/dmstats.htm#7.

[4] Value is for 2001 from "Table 1: Persons reported to be living with HIV infection and with AIDS," in HIV/AIDS Surveillance Report, 2001; 13 (No. 2), Centers for Disease Control and Prevention, Atlanta, GA, accessible at http://www.cdc.gov/hiv/stats/hasr1302/table1.htm. Rate calculated using 2001 population projections, middle series, from the U.S. Census Bureau.

– Not reported.

SOURCE: Adapted from Laura M. Maruschak and Allen J. Beck, "Comparing estimates based on self-reported data to official records" in *Medical Problems of Inmates, 1997*, U.S. Bureau of Justice Statistics, Washington, DC, 2001

that the BJS has added data from official prison records for 2000. These data are shown for federal prisoners in Table 6.3 together with benchmark measures on the health status of the general public for selected conditions.

Federal prison records in 2000 showed that 4.4 percent of inmates suffered from asthma; 0.9 percent of inmates in the 1997 survey reported asthma as a medical problem; data for 1998 for the general public showed that 8.9 percent of the public suffered from asthma. Fewer prisoners report ailments than prison records show that they have. And, with the exception of the tracked conditions, HIV/AIDS, prisoners experience lower incidents of ailments than the general public. The data shown here are, of course, for different years and are therefore only indicative of patterns. Asthma illustrates well the differences between the prison population—predominantly young adults—and the general public. The prevalence of asthma is much higher in the general public which includes children and seniors; children are absent from prison and seniors are under-represented. Diabetes, heart disease, and high blood pressure (hypertension) are conditions that manifest later in life, hence the lower levels of such diseases in the prison population. The one sexually transmitted disease charted (HIV/AIDS) is substantially higher in prison than in the general public: 1 percent of federal inmates had been

TABLE 6.4

HIV-positive prison inmates, 1995–2000

		Percent of custody population		
		Total	State	Federal
1995	24,256	2.3%	2.4%	0.9%
1996	23,881	2.2	2.3	1.0
1997	23,886	2.1	2.2	1.0
1998	25,680	2.2	2.3	1.0
1999	25,801	2.1	2.3	0.9
2000	25,088	2.0	2.2	0.8

SOURCE: Adapted from Laura M. Maruschak, "HIV-positive and confirmed AIDS cases among inmates drop in 2000" and "Number of HIV-infected prison inmates at yearend 2000 down from 1999," in *HIV in Prisons, 2000*, U.S. Bureau of Justice Statistics, Washington, DC, October 2002 (revised February 24, 2003)

diagnosed with the condition compared with 0.18 percent of the general public as determined by the Centers for Disease Control and Prevention (CDC).

The prisoners, assessing themselves, significantly under-estimated their actual medical problems compared with measurements taken in prison infirmaries and hospitals. The exception was mental health problems. The most common form of diabetes, late-onset Type II, takes a long time to result in symptoms and requires blood-sugar testing for early detection. Only prisoners who experienced acute heart episodes were likely to know they had problems. Similarly, high blood pressure does not have symptoms.

These data are for the federal prison population which is a small part (11 percent) of the total prison population. With the exception of data on HIV/AIDS, the absence of data for the larger state prison population (data such as those shown in Table 6.3) illustrates indirectly some of the problems with health care in prisons. Congressional concern, based on a few limited studies, led Congress to have the National Commission on Correctional Health Care, a not-for-profit organization, produce estimates of the health status of prisoners in 1997. NCCHC published its report in 2002. Its findings were based mostly on projections rather than actual records. The commission, however, identified some of the problems involved in measuring prisoners' health and delivering services. The following four items are quoted from the NCCHC's Report to Congress, taken from page xiv. The issues highlight barriers to effective prevention, screening, and treatment:

Lack of leadership, such as failure to recognize the need for improved health care services, reluctance to consider that improving public health is a correctional responsibility, and unwillingness of public health agencies to advocate for improving correctional health care or to collaborate to promote improvement.

Logistical barriers, such as short periods of incarceration, security-conscious administration procedures for

FIGURE 6.2

Percent of the general population and prison population with confirmed AIDS, 1991–2000

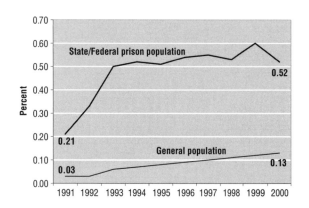

SOURCE: Adapted from Laura M. Maruschak, "Table 4: Percent of general population and prison population with confirmed AIDS," in *HIV in Prisons, 2000*, U.S. Bureau of Justice Statistics, Washington, DC, 2002 [Online] http://www.ojp.usdoj.gov/bjs/pub/sheets/hivp00.zip [accessed March 13, 2003] and Laura M. Maruschak, "Percent of general population and prison population with confirmed AIDS," in *HIV in Prisons, 1998*, U.S. Bureau of Justice Statistics, Washington, DC, 2000 [Online] http://www.ojp.usdoj.gov/bjs/pub/sheets/hivp98.zip [accessed March 13, 2003]

distributing medications, and difficulty coordinating discharge planning.

Limited resources that require difficult budgeting decisions to meet the high cost of many health care services and some medications, and that make it difficult to provide adequate space for medical services.

Correctional policies, such as failure to specify minimum levels of required care in contracts with private health care vendors, delays caused by the need to escort inmates to medical treatment, poor communication between public health agencies and prisons and jails, and lack of adequate clinical guidelines.

HIV/AIDS

An HIV-positive person is infected with the Human Immunodeficiency Virus. HIV interferes with and eventually destroys the body's immune system. Once the late stage of the disease is reached, the person has Acquired Immune Deficiency Syndrome. AIDS is incurable and leads to death. HIV/AIDS is transmitted in sexual contact, through breast-feeding of babies by an infected mother, and by blood. A common pathway is the use of unclean needles when injecting drugs. HIV can be treated but not cured. A very small percentage of those infected turn out to be so-called "non-progressors," indicating that their bodies are able to overcome the virus; they do not "progress" and acquire AIDS.

The prevalence of HIV infection was 2 percent among state and federal prisoners in 2000—2.2 percent among

TABLE 6.5

HIV-positive prison inmates by gender, 1995–2000

| | State prison inmates | | | |
| | Estimated number of HIV-positive inmates* | | Percent HIV/AIDS in custody population | |
Year	Males	Females	Males	Females
1995	21,144	2,230	2.3%	4.0%
1996	21,299	1,938	2.2	3.1
1997	20,608	2,258	2.1	3.5
1998	22,045	2,552	2.2	3.8
1999	22,175	2,402	2.2	3.5
2000	21,894	2,472	2.1	3.4
Annual average change, 1995-2000			0.7%	2.1%

*To provide year-to-year comparisons, estimates were made for states not reporting gender breakdown. For each state, estimates were made by applying the same percent breakdown by gender from the most recent year when data were provided.

SOURCE: Laura M. Maruschak, "Number of HIV-positive female inmates rose in 2000," in *HIV in Prisons, 2000*, U.S. Bureau of Justice Statistics, Washington, DC, October 2002 (revised February 24, 2003)

state prison inmates and 0.8 percent among federal prisoners. A total of 25,088 prisoners were HIV-positive, down 713 from 1999. (See Table 6.4.) Confirmed AIDS cases were 4 times higher in the prison population in 2000 than in the general public, 0.52 percent of prisoners and 0.13 percent of the general public. The differences between these two populations are narrowing. In 1991 the AIDS rate in prison was 7 times that of the general population. The biggest gap was reached in 1992 when the prison population had a rate 11-fold that of the general public. (See Figure 6.2.)

Higher Prevalence in Women

Women comprised about 6 percent of the prison population in 2000 but 10 percent of HIV-positive prisoners—2,472 females versus 21,894 males. Between 1995 and 2000, the average annual increase in the male infection rate was 0.7 percent, the increase in the female group was three times higher, 2.1 percent a year. (See Table 6.5.) These findings reflect trends also present in the prevalence of AIDS in the general population. In a study published in the *American Journal of Public Health*, John M. Karon of the CDC, with others, presented data for the prevalence of AIDS comparing 1990 to 1999 data ("HIV in the United States at the Turn of the Century: An Epidemic in Transition," vol. 91, no. 7, July 2001). The year-end prevalence of AIDS for men was 68.3 per 100,000 population in 1990, rising to 230.8 in 1999; the female rate was 8.2 in 1990 and rose to 55.1 in 1999. The male prevalence increased at 14.5 percent and the female at 23.6 percent on average each year in this nine-year period.

TABLE 6.6

Inmates ever tested for the human immunodeficiency virus (HIV) and results, by selected characteristics, 1997

| | Tested inmates who reported results | | | |
| | State prisons | | Federal prisons | |
Characteristic	Number	Percent HIV-positive	Number	Percent HIV-positive
All inmates	790,128	2.2	70,902	0.6
Race/Hispanic origin				
White non-Hispanic	257,919	1.4	21,128	0.3
Male	239,687	1.4	19,565	0.3
Female	18,232	2.3	1,563	0.3
Black non-Hispanic	384,870	2.8	28,178	0.8
Male	357,736	2.7	26,387	0.8
Female	27,135	3.9	1,791	1.3
Hispanic	123,725	2.5	18,466	0.7
Male	115,344	2.4	16,892	0.7
Female	8,382	4.2	1,573	0
Age				
17–24	154,181	0.5	5,528	0.1
25–34	310,161	2.3	26,262	0.5
35–44	232,835	3.1	22,228	0.4
45 or older	92,168	2.7	16,884	1.2

Note: Data are from the 1997 Surveys of Inmates in State and Federal Correctional Facilities.

SOURCE: Laura M. Maruschak, "Table 8: Inmates ever tested for the human immunodeficiency virus and results, by selected characteristics, 1997," in HIV in Prisons 1997, U.S. Bureau of Justice Statistics, Washington, DC, November 1999 (revised December 9, 1999)

Race and Ethnicity

Data on HIV/AIDS in prisons come from the *HIV in Prison* series that the Bureau of Justice Statistics has published since 1993. The most recent report that provides information broken down by race and ethnicity (and age) was the 1997 report published in 1999. Of 790,128 state prisoners tested for HIV, the highest percent testing positive were Hispanic women (4.2 percent), followed by non-Hispanic black women (3.9 percent) and non-Hispanic black men (2.7 percent). In federal prisons, where 70,902 people were tested, non-Hispanic black females had the highest results (1.3 percent), followed by black males (0.8 percent) and Hispanic men (0.7 percent). Fewer federal prisoners tested positive for HIV across all ethnic and racial categories (0.6 percent); 2.2 percent of all state prisoners tested positive. (See Table 6.6.)

The percentages, expressed as counts, indicate that 1,829 women tested positive in state prisons. Of these 22.9 percent were white, 57.8 percent were black, and 19.2 percent were Hispanic. A total of 15,783 males tested positive, distributed as follows: whites, 21.3 percent, blacks, 61.2 percent; and Hispanics 17.5 percent.

These results also reflect the situation in the general population. In an undated fact sheet, "HIV/AIDS Among African Americans," the Centers for Disease Control and

TABLE 6.7

Inmates receiving mental health treatment in state correctional facilities, by facility characteristic, 2000

| | Number of inmates receiving | | | | | |
| | 24-hour mental health care | | Therapy/ counseling | | Psychotropic medications | |
Facility characteristic	Number	%	Number	%	Number	%
Total						
Reported[1]	17,354	1.6	137,395	12.8	105,336	9.7
Estimated[2]	18,900		150,900		114,400	
Facility operation						
Public	16,429	1.8	118,933	12.8	92,414	9.8
Private	734	1.1	7,763	11.4	5,158	7.5
Authority to house						
Males only	13,161	1.5	102,235	11.7	75,664	8.5
Females only	834	1.4	15,262	26.5	12,536	21.5
Both	3,168	4.5	9,199	13.9	9,372	13.2
Type of facility						
Community-based	177	0.3	4,320	8.7	2,458	4.8
Confinement	16,986	1.8	122,376	12.9	95,114	9.8
Facility function[3]						
General confinement	11,485	1.3	109,009	12.8	82,929	9.6
Special function						
Reception/diagnostic center	1,029	2.5	6,362	14.7	5,392	11.7
Community corrections	107	0.3	2,588	7.4	1,662	4.6
Medical treatment	332	17.0	164	13.2	430	22.1
Mental health	3,335	47.5	3,373	46.7	3,277	45.3
Alcohol/drug treatment	0	0.0	1,323	7.7	761	4.5
Boot camp/youthful offenders	176	1.3	720	6.3	488	4.4
Other[4]	699	2.1	3,153	9.4	2,631	7.9

[1] Includes inmates receiving mental health treatment in Florida for whom only statewide totals were reported.
[2] National totals were estimated by multiplying the reported percentages by the total number of persons in state custody on June 30, 2000.
[3] Facilities could report more than one function. Primary function was the category with the largest number of inmates on June 30, 2000.
[4] Includes transfer facilities, juvenile confinement, protective custody, sex offender treatment, and death row.

SOURCE: Alan J. Beck and Laura M. Maruschak, "Table 3. Inmates receiving mental health treatment in State correctional facilities, by facility characteristic, June 30, 2000," in Mental Health Treatment in State Prisons, 2000, U.S. Bureau of Justice Statistics, Washington, DC, July 2001

Prevention reports that in 2001 African Americans represented 12 percent of the population but 50 percent of the new HIV cases reported in the United States. Whites accounted for 29 percent, Hispanics for 19, and other races for 2 percent of all new infections. Black women were most at risk. They represented 65 percent of new infections among women; black men were 43 percent of the newly infected among men.

Age

Older prisoners were more likely to test positive for HIV in 1997, the highest rate being for those age 35–44 and 45 and older in state prisons, 3.1 and 2.7 percent respectively. In federal prisons, the oldest group had the highest percentage testing positive, 1.2 percent of those

TABLE 6.8

Characteristics of state correctional facilities providing mental health services, 2000

Characteristic	Facilities that specialize in mental health/psychiatric confinement[1]			Other facilities	
	Total	Primary	Secondary	Confinement	Community-based
Number of facilities	155	12	143	961	442
Average daily population					
1,500 or more	44	2	42	169	3
750-1,499	54	1	53	310	3
250-749	37	5	32	278	32
100-249	13	3	10	157	114
Fewer than 100	7	1	6	47	290
Mean	1,400	690	1,460	928	130
Number of inmates held on June 30, 2000	217,420	8,124	209,296	902,976	58,411
Number of inmates receiving treatment[2]					
In 24-hour care	13,739	3,335	10,404	3,308	116
In therapy/counseling	38,992	3,373	35,619	83,828	3,876
Psychotropic medications	34,426	3,277	31,149	60,976	2,170
Percent of inmates					
In 24-hour care	6.8 %	47.5 %	5.3 %	0.4%	0.2 %
In therapy/counseling	19.2	46.7	18.2	11.2	8.1
Psychotropic medications	16.6	45.3	15.6	8.0	4.4
Rated capacity[3]	217,682	9,255	208,427	899,528	61,664
Percent of capacity occupied[4]	99.9 %	87.8 %	100.4 %	100.4 %	94.7%

[1] Facilities could report more than one function. Primary function was the category which applied to the largest number of inmates on June 30. Secondary function includes all other facilities that reported mental health/psychiatric confinement as a facility function.
[2] Excludes inmates in mental health treatment in Florida for whom only statewide totals were reported.
[3] Rated capacity is the maximum number of beds or inmates assigned by a rating official.
[4] Percent of capacity occupied is the ratio of number of inmates held to the rated capacity on June 30, 2000.

SOURCE: Alan J. Beck and Laura M. Maruschak, "Table 5. Characteristics of State correctional facilities providing mental health services, June 30, 2000," in *Mental Health Treatment in State Prisons, 2000*, U.S. Bureau of Justice Statistics, Washington, DC, July 2001

TABLE 6.9

Inmates and probationers identified as mentally ill, by gender, race/Hispanic origin, and age, 1998

Offender characteristic	Percent identified as mentally ill			
	State inmates	Federal inmates	Jail inmates	Probationers
Gender				
Male	15.8%	7.0%	15.6%	14.7%
Female	23.6	12.5	22.7	21.7
Race/Hispanic origin				
White*	22.6%	11.8%	21.7%	19.6%
Black*	13.5	5.6	13.7	10.4
Hispanic	11.0	4.1	11.1	9.0
Age				
24 or younger	14.4%	6.6%	13.3%	13.8%
25-34	14.8	5.9	15.7	13.8
35-44	18.4	7.5	19.3	19.8
45-54	19.7	10.3	22.7	21.1
55 or older	15.6	8.9	20.4	16.0

* Excludes Hispanics.

SOURCE: Paula M. Ditton, "Table 4. Inmates and probationers identified as mentally ill, by gender, race/Hispanic origin, and age," in *Mental Health and Treatment of Inmates and Probationers*, U.S. Bureau of Justice Statistics, Washington, DC, July 1999

45 and older, followed by the 25–35 group, 0.5 percent. (See Table 6.6.)

MENTAL ILLNESS IN PRISON

According to the National Institute of Mental Health (NIMH; "About Mental Illness and Mental Health," July 12, 2000, http://www.nimh.nih.gov/strategic/abmental.cfm):

> During a 1-year period, 22 to 23 percent of the U.S. adult population—or 44 million people—have diagnosable mental disorders, according to reliable, established criteria. In general, 19 percent of the adult U.S. population have a mental disorder alone (in 1 year); 3 percent have both mental and addictive disorders.

The U.S. prison population, at least as measured by looking at its largest component, the state prison population, experienced a prevalence of mental illness very much in line with that of the general population. Allen J. Beck and Laura M. Maruschak report, in *Mental Health Treatment in State Prisons, 2000* (BJS, Washington, D.C., 2001), that between 260,000 and 284,000 state prison inmates received some form of treatment for mental problems in 2000. In that year state prison facilities held 1.178 million inmates. The prevalence of mental illness, broadly defined, was thus 22 to 24 percent. Based on self-reporting of prisoners, extrapolated from 1997 levels to the 2000 population, the authors estimate that 191,000 prisoners described themselves as mentally ill—16 percent of the population. Those reporting themselves mentally ill may be those with the more acute conditions. Of those receiving treatment in prison, between 154,000 and 170,000 inmates were either under 24-hour mental health care or received therapy and counseling. The rest (105,000–114,400) received psychotropic medication. (See Table 6.7.)

Table 6.7 shows that treatment facilities were predominantly public in operation, most served only men, and they were largely in the prison environment rather than community-based. According to *Mental Health Treatment in State Prisons, 2000* (cited above), of 1,558 state-level correctional facilities, excluding jails and federal facilities, 1,394 provided mental health services in 2000. Of these 155 specialized in mental health and psychiatric confinement. (See Table 6.8.) Facilities specializing primarily in mental health confinement were the least crowded, running at 87.8 percent of capacity.

TABLE 6.10

Incarceration and the mentally ill, 1997

Offenses of mentally ill inmates compared to other inmates

	State prisoners	
Offense	Mentally ill inmates	Other inmates
Violent	52.9%	46.1%
Property	24.4	21.5
Drug	12.8	22.2
Public-order	9.9	9.8
Criminal history		
None	18.8%	21.2%
Priors	81.2	78.8

Rates of homelessness, abuse, and substance abuse among mentally ill inmates compared to other inmates

	State prisoners	
Before entering prison	Mentally ill inmates	Other inmates
Homeless in 12 months prior to arrest	20.1%	8.8%
Physical/sexual abuse		
Male	32.8%	13.1%
Female	78.4	50.9
Alcohol/drug use		
At time of offense	58.7%	51.2%
Drug use		
In month before offense	58.8%	56.1%

	Mentally ill Inmates	
Mental health treatment since admission	State prison	Jail
Any treatment	60.5%	40.9%
Medication	50.1	34.1
Counseling	44.1	16.2

SOURCE: Adapted from Paula M. Ditton, "Highlights" in *Mental Health and Treatment of Inmates and Probationers*, U.S. Bureau of Justice Statistics, Washington, DC, July 1999

Prisoner Characteristics

The most recent comprehensive survey of the prison population was issued in 1999 (*Mental Health and Treatment of Inmates and Probationers*, BJS, Washington, D.C., 1999). It was based on the 1997 Survey of Inmates in State and Federal Correctional Facilities, the 1996 Survey of Inmates in Local Jails, and the 1995 Survey of Adults on Probation. Although the data are now old, they bring into focus the differences between prison inmates with mental problems and those who do not have them.

More women were identified as mentally ill than men in 1998, 23.6 percent in state prisons and 12.5 percent in federal prisons in contrast with men of whom 15.8 percent (state) and 7 percent (federal) were mentally ill. Some 22.6 percent of whites in state prisons and 11.8 percent in federal facilities were mentally ill. Among black prisoners, the prevalence was lower, 13.5 percent (state) and 5.6 percent (federal). Hispanics had the lowest rates, 11 percent in state and 4.1 percent in federal facilities. Mental illness was slightly higher among those prisoners age 45–54 than other age groups. (See Table 6.9.)

Compared to other state prison inmates in 1998, more of those mentally ill were convicted of violent crimes, 52.9 versus 46.1 percent of other inmates. A higher proportion had committed property crimes (24.4 percent versus 21.5), but only 12.8 percent of mentally ill had been convicted of drug offenses versus 22.2 percent of other inmates. Some 81.2 percent of the mentally ill had a prior conviction compared with 78.8 percent of other inmates. The mentally ill were more than twice as likely to have been homeless in the 12 months before their arrest, and much more likely to have been sexually abused. (See Table 6.10.)

INJURIES IN PRISON

Data on injuries suffered by prisoners, whether in accidents or in fights, also date back to the 1997 survey of state and federal prisons. BJS has not published any new data since *Medical Problems of Inmates, 1997* (Washington, D.C., 2001), which includes data on injuries. The 1997 data are based on prisoner reporting. In that report, BJS shows the percent of prison inmates who reported injuries by time served in months. Both accidental injuries and injuries sustained in fights are reported.

It is difficult to compare injury rates, in this format, with injuries sustained by the general public. Data on the public are reported under various headings and for differing time frames. Industrial injuries are reported annually by the Bureau of Labor Statistics (see http://www.bls.gov/iif/oshwc/osh/os/ostb1109.txt) as a rate per 100 workers in private industry (5.7 percent of workers were injured in 2001). Criminal victimization data are collected at six months intervals and reported annually by the BJS; 2.4 percent of the public experienced violent crime in 2001, including simple assault (see http://www.ojp.usdoj.gov/bjs/glance/tables/viortrdtab.htm). Unintended injury data published most recently (see *Statistical Abstract of the United States: 2002*, U.S. Census Bureau, Washington, D.C., 2002, Table 171) indicates that 9.7 percent of the population suffered some kind of injury (excluding automotive) in 1999. Adding these figures produces a value that approximates the experience reported by prisoners. Roughly 18 percent of the public suffers some kind of injury every year. The BJS data indicate that, in 1997, 13.2 percent of state prisoners and 17 percent of federal prisoners, both with less than 12 months of time served, had suffered injuries. Of these, 2.9 percent of state and 0.8 percent of federal prisoners reported being injured in fights, while 10.2 percent of state and 15.6 percent of federal prisoners were injured in accidents in this group. Prisoners who had served 12 to 23 months had higher values: 19.8 percent of state prisoners and 22 percent of federal inmates reported an injury since admission. The longer prisoners serve, the higher the percentage of those injured. The survey format used by the BJS produces what amounts to a cumulative measure of injury over time. (See Table 6.11.)

TABLE 6.11

Injuries reported by state and federal inmates since admission, by time served, 1997

| | Percent of inmates who reported an injury since admission | | | | | |
| | Total | | Injured in an accident | | Injured in a fight | |
Time since admission	State	Federal	State	Federal	State	Federal
Less than 12 mo.	13.2%	17.0%	10.2%	15.6%	2.9%	0.8%
12-23 mo.	19.8	22.0	14.8	20.1	5.3	1.8
24-47 mo.	26.7	26.3	19.0	24.3	9.2	2.1
48-71 mo.	36.8	30.2	26.3	25.3	13.8	5.4
72 mo. or more	45.9	31.6	31.7	26.3	19.7	5.3

SOURCE: Laura M. Maruschak and Allen J. Beck, "Table 4. Injuries reported by State and Federal inmates since admission, by time served, 1997," in *Medical Problems of Inmates, 1997*, U.S. Bureau of Justice Statistics, Washington, DC, January 2001

FIGURE 6.3

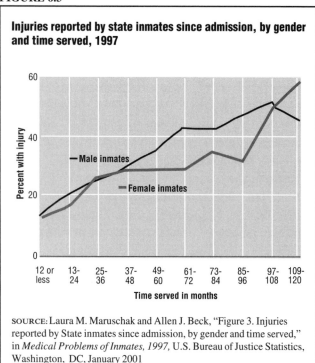

Injuries reported by state inmates since admission, by gender and time served, 1997

SOURCE: Laura M. Maruschak and Allen J. Beck, "Figure 3. Injuries reported by State inmates since admission, by gender and time served," in *Medical Problems of Inmates, 1997*, U.S. Bureau of Justice Statistics, Washington, DC, January 2001

FIGURE 6.4

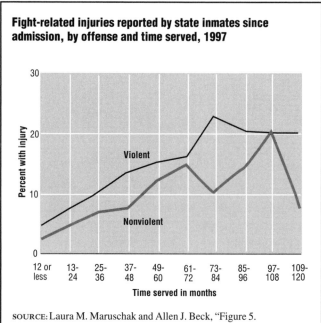

Fight-related injuries reported by state inmates since admission, by offense and time served, 1997

SOURCE: Laura M. Maruschak and Allen J. Beck, "Figure 5. Fight-related injuries reported by State inmates since admission, by offense and time served," in *Medical Problems of Inmates, 1997*, U.S. Bureau of Justice Statistics, Washington, DC, January 2001

Males experience more injuries than women, on average, until the women have served more than nine years in prison (108 months). Prisoners sentenced for violent crimes have a higher rate of injury from fights than those serving for nonviolent offenses. (See Figure 6.3 and Figure 6.4.)

REDUCING THE COST AND IMPROVING THE AVAILABILITY OF TREATMENT

Telecommunications links make it possible for physicians and other health care specialists to evaluate and treat patients who are hundreds or thousands of miles away. This technology, called telemedicine, offers the prospect of providing prisoners with cost-effective health care. For example, telemedicine makes it possible for physicians to examine prisoners without the inconvenience of traveling

to prison facilities, often located in remote or isolated areas. Likewise, the cost and security concerns of transporting prisoners to physicians are also eliminated.

In their article, "Can Telemedicine Reduce Spending and Improve Health Care?" (*National Institute of Justice Journal*, April 1999, U.S. Department of Justice, Washington, D.C.), authors Douglas McDonald, Andrea Hassol, and Kenneth Carlson reported on a demonstration program to evaluate a telemedicine system in prison. The pilot project was conducted jointly at four federal prisons:

- U.S. Penitentiary, Lewisburg, PA. Maximum security. Houses an average of 1,300 male prisoners

- U.S. Penitentiary, Allenwood, PA. Maximum security. Houses an average of 1,000 male prisoners

- Federal Correction Institution, Allenwood, PA. Low and medium security. Houses an average of 1,100 male prisoners

- Federal Medical Center, Lexington, KY. Medium and minimum security. Houses an average of 1,450 mostly male prisoners with chronic illnesses

The pilot program was conducted from September 1996 to December 1997. It did not replace routine medical care provided by prison staff. As reported, the goal of the telemedicine test program was to reduce three types of care:

- Consultations with specialty physicians who would normally visit the prison

- Prisoner trips to hospitals or off-site physicians

- Transfers of prisoners to federal medical centers for intensive or long-term treatment

At each prison a dedicated telemedicine room was equipped with interactive video-conferencing equipment, specialized medical cameras, an electronic stethoscope, and a computer workstation with appropriate software. For most examinations a medical staff member from the prison (usually a physician's assistant) presented the inmate patient to an off-site specialist linked via video-conferencing and equipped with remote controls that enabled the specialist to manipulate cameras located in the patient examination room.

During the 15 months of the demonstration project, physicians made approximately 100 telemedicine consultations each month, for a total of 1,321 consultations. About 58 percent of the telemedicine "visits" were for psychiatric consultations, followed by dermatology (13.3 percent), orthopedics (10.7 percent), dietary (6.4 percent), and podiatry (4.7 percent). The remaining 6.5 percent of telemedicine consultations were with specialist from other disciplines, including infectious diseases, cardiology, and neurology.

Four specialties were selected for purposes of comparing conventional medical care in prisons with telemedicine consultations—psychiatry, orthopedics, dermatology, and cardiology. Specialists in these four fields were among the most frequently consulted prior to the pilot project, and that frequently increased with the implementation of telemedicine.

During the pilot program, the cost of in-prison consultations decreased from approximately $108 per conventional consultation to $71 per telemedicine consultation, a savings of $37 per consultation. However, because there was not a one-for-one substitution of regular consultations and telemedicine consultations, the total number of consultations increased with the addition of telemedicine.

Some 35 trips for inmates to visit specialists outside of prison were eliminated through telemedicine for a total savings of about $27,500. Some trips were unavoidable when inmates required invasive tests, surgery, or intensive trauma care. The Bureau of Prisons estimated that it saved an additional $59,134 because, in certain cases, telemedicine eliminated the need for air transfers of inmates to federal medical centers. Most of the averted air transfers were for psychiatric patients who required intensive monitoring that was made possible through telemedicine consultations.

There were other nonfinancial benefits to the implementation of telemedicine consultations. Waiting time to see specialists decreased and new services became available, including more specialized HIV/AIDS care. Also, inmate patients reported feeling that the quality of care improved with telemedicine.

As a result of the success of this pilot program, the National Institute of Justice (NIJ) began studies using telemedicine in jails. It also funds a program to inform corrections staff of the benefits of telemedicine and to help prison administrators decide if telemedicine will succeed at their facilities. Some of the points to consider are space constraints and access to nearby medical centers. In addition, the program suggests ways to develop and launch prison telemedicine systems. Designing such systems is discussed in *Implementing Telemedicine in Correctional Facilities* (Peter L. Nacci, C. Allan Turner, Ronald J. Waldron, and Eddie Broyles, U.S. Department of Justice/U.S. Department of Defense, Washington, D.C., May 2002). One of the new systems implemented in 2003 involves the University of Texas Medical Branch (UTMB) and the Federal Medical Center in Lexington, Kentucky. Under the telemedicine agreement, medical specialists in Galveston treat inmates in Lexington nearly 1,000 miles away. Among the specialties offered are orthopedics and urology.

CHAPTER 7
JUVENILE CONFINEMENT

Since 1992, 45 states have passed or amended legislation making it easier to prosecute juveniles as adults. The result is that the number of youths under 18 confined in adult prisons has more than doubled in the past decade. This phenomenon is challenging the belief, enshrined in our justice system a century ago, that children and young adolescents should be adjudicated and confined in a separate system focused on their rehabilitation.

—Nancy E. Gist, Director, Bureau of Justice Assistance, 2003

WHO IS A JUVENILE?

In most states offenders age 18 or younger are considered juveniles and fall under the jurisdiction of juvenile courts rather than adult criminal courts. However, more states are trying more juveniles as adults as a result of changes in state law. These changes were triggered by an increase in youthful criminal behavior that began to manifest in the late 1980s but now appears, once more, to be diminishing. The laws, however, remain on the books.

As of April 2003, information maintained on the Internet by the Office of Juvenile Justice and Delinquency Prevention (OJJDP), an agency of the U.S. Department of Justice, and first published in 1999, indicates that most states retain juvenile court jurisdiction over offenders 17 years of age and younger. Those older are considered to be adults. In 10 states, those 16 and younger are juveniles. In Connecticut, New York, and North Carolina, juveniles are 15 and younger. (See Table 7.1. For full details, see http://www.ncjrs.org/html/ojjdp/0012_2/juv3.html.)

In some states, juvenile courts may retain jurisdiction over youthful offenders beyond the limits shown in Table 7.1 provided that this is in the interests of the juvenile and the public. Thus, in Alabama, Arkansas, Connecticut, and 30 other jurisdictions, juvenile courts may handle offenders until they turn 20. In Kansas the juvenile court's reach extends to those age 22; in California, Montana, Oregon, and Wisconsin, the age limit is 24. (See Table 7.2.) Such

TABLE 7.1

Oldest age for original juvenile court jurisdiction in delinquency matters, 1999

Age	State
15	Connecticut, New York, North Carolina
16	Georgia, Illinois, Louisiana, Massachusetts, Michigan, Missouri, New Hampshire, South Carolina, Texas, Wisconsin
17	Alabama, Alaska, Arizona, Arkansas, California, Colorado, Delaware, District of Columbia, Florida, Hawaii, Idaho, Indiana, Iowa, Kansas, Kentucky, Maine, Maryland, Minnesota, Mississippi, Montana, Nebraska, Nevada, New Jersey, New Mexico, North Dakota, Ohio, Oklahoma, Oregon, Pennsylvania, Rhode Island, South Dakota, Tennessee, Utah, Vermont, Virginia, Washington, West Virginia, Wyoming

SOURCE: Howard N. Snyder and Melissa Sickmund, "Oldest age for juvenile court jurisdiction in delinquency matters," in *Juvenile Offenders and Victims: 1999 National Report*, U.S. Department of Justice, Office of Justice Programs, Office of Juvenile Justice and Delinquency Prevention, Washington, DC, September 1999

extended jurisdiction may be legislatively limited to specific offenses or juveniles. The definition of a juvenile is, thus, not a cut-and-dried "18-and-younger." Many states have established exceptions to age criteria so that juveniles can be tried as adults or provide for procedures under which a prosecutor can decide how to dispose of the offender—be it under juvenile or adult jurisdiction.

CHANGING APPROACHES TO JUVENILE DELINQUENCY

Juvenile courts date to the late 19th century when Cook County, Illinois, established the first juvenile court under the Juvenile Court Act of 1899 passed by the state. The underlying concept was that if parents failed to provide children with proper care and supervision, the state had the right to intervene benevolently. Other states followed Illinois' initiative. Juvenile courts were in operation in most states by 1925. Juvenile courts favored a rehabilitative rather than a punitive approach and evolved much

TABLE 7.2

Oldest age over which the juvenile court may retain jurisdiction for disposition purposes in delinquency matters, 1999

Age	State
17	Arizona*, North Carolina
18	Alaska, Iowa, Kentucky , Nebraska, Oklahoma, Tennessee
19	Mississippi, North Dakota
20	Alabama, Arkansas, Connecticut, Delaware, District of Columbia, Florida, Georgia, Idaho, Illinois, Indiana, Louisiana, Maine, Maryland, Massachusetts, Michigan, Minnesota, Missouri, Nevada, New Hampshire, New Mexico, New York, Ohio, Pennsylvania, Rhode Island, South Carolina, South Dakota, Texas, Utah, Vermont, Virginia, Washington, West Virginia, Wyoming
22	Kansas
24	California, Montana, Oregon, Wisconsin
**	Colorado, Hawaii, New Jersey

* Arizona statute extends jurisdiction through age 20, but a 1979 State Supreme Court decision held that juvenile court jurisdiction terminates at age 18.
**Until the full term of the disposition order.
Note: Extended jurisdiction may be restricted to certain offenses or juveniles.

SOURCE: Howard N. Snyder and Melissa Sickmund, "Oldest age over which the juvenile court may retain jurisdiction for disposition purposes in delinquency matters," in *Juvenile Offenders and Victims: 1999 National Report*, U.S. Department of Justice, Office of Justice Programs, Office of Juvenile Justice and Delinquency Prevention, Washington, DC, September 1999

TABLE 7.3

Changes in juvenile justice laws, 1992–97

State	Changes in law or court rule*			State	Changes in law or court rule*		
Alabama	T		C	Montana	T	S	C
Alaska	T		C	Nebraska			
Arizona	T	S	C	Nevada	T		C
Arkansas	T	S	C	New Hampshire	T	S	C
California	T		C	New Jersey		S	C
Colorado	T	S	C	New Mexico	T	S	C
Connecticut	T	S	C	New York			
Delaware	T	S	C	North Carolina	T		C
District of Columbia	T	S		North Dakota	T		C
Florida	T	S	C	Ohio	T	S	C
Georgia	T	S	C	Oklahoma	T	S	C
Hawaii	T		C	Oregon	T	S	C
Idaho	T	S	C	Pennsylvania	T		C
Illinois	T	S	C	Rhode Island	T	S	C
Indiana	T	S	C	South Carolina	T		C
Iowa	T	S	C	South Dakota	T		
Kansas	T	S	C	Tennessee	T	S	C
Kentucky	T	S	C	Texas	T	S	C
Louisiana	T	S	C	Utah	T		C
Maine			C	Vermont			
Maryland	T		C	Virginia	T	S	C
Massachusetts	T	S	C	Washington	T		C
Michigan		S	C	West Virginia	T		C
Minnesota	T	S	C	Wisconsin	T	S	C
Mississippi	T		C	Wyoming	T		C
Missouri	T	S	C				

*T = Transfer provisions, S = Sentencing authority, C = Confidentiality

SOURCE: Howard N. Snyder and Melissa Sickmund, "From 1992 through 1997, legislatures in 47 States and the District of Columbia enacted laws that made their juvenile justice systems more punitive," in *Juvenile Offenders and Victims: 1999 National Report*, Office of Juvenile Justice and Delinquency Prevention, Washington, DC, 1999

less formal approaches than those in place in adult courts. They had exclusive jurisdiction over juveniles. Adult courts could try a juvenile only if the juvenile court waived its jurisdiction.

This approach began to change in the 1950s and 1960s because techniques of rehabilitation were not judged as uniformly effective. A growing number of juveniles were being institutionalized until they reached adulthood because "treatment" did not seem effective. Under the impetus of a number of U.S. Supreme Court decisions, juvenile courts became more formal to protect juveniles' rights in waiver situations or if they were to be confined. Congress passed the Juvenile Delinquency Prevention and Control Act in 1968. The act suggested that so-called "status offenders" (non-criminal offenders such as runaways) no longer be handled inside the court system. The Juvenile Justice and Delinquency Prevention Act of 1974 mandated that juvenile offenders be separated from adult offenders. The act was amended in 1980; part of the amendment required that juveniles be removed from adult jails. In the 1970s, the national policy became community-based management of juvenile delinquents.

Public perception changed again in the 1980s. Juvenile crime appeared to be growing and the systems in place were perceived as too lenient in dealing with delinquents. According to the Office of Juvenile Justice and Delinquency Prevention (*Juvenile Offenders and Victims: 1999 National Report*) public opinion was based on a "substantial misperception regarding increases in juvenile crime." Nonetheless, state legislatures responded in various ways:

> Some laws removed certain classes of offenders from the juvenile justice system and handled them as adult criminals in criminal court. Others required the juvenile justice system to be more like the criminal justice system and to treat certain classes of juvenile offenders as criminals but in juvenile court.

> As a result, offenders charged with certain offenses are *excluded* from juvenile court jurisdiction or face *mandatory* or *automatic waiver* to criminal court. In some States, concurrent jurisdiction provisions give prosecutors the discretion to file certain juvenile cases directly in criminal court…. In some States, some adjudicated juvenile offenders face *mandatory sentences.*

From 1992 to 1997, 47 states and the District of Columbia changed their laws. Forty-five states enacted provisions that made it easier to transfer juveniles to the jurisdiction of the criminal courts. In 31 jurisdictions, sentencing options were expanded. In 46 states, rules relating to confidentiality were modified or removed altogether, opening records and proceedings to public view. Nebraska, New York, and Vermont enacted no changes. (See Table

FIGURE 7.1

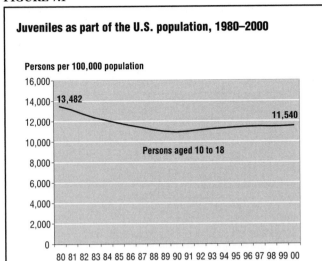

Juveniles as part of the U.S. population, 1980–2000

Persons per 100,000 population

Persons aged 10 to 18

Note: Persons shown are at least 10 and not yet 18 years of age. This group has decreased as a proportion of total population between 1980 and 2000, reaching its lowest point in this period in 1990, 10,928 per 100,000.

SOURCE: Adapted from "Civilian Population as of October 1," U.S. Bureau of the Census, Washington, DC [Online] http://eire.census.gov/popest/archives/national/nat_80s_detail.php [accessed December 12, 2002] and "Resident Population Estimates of the United States by Age and Sex," U.S. Bureau of the Census, Washington, DC [Online] http://eire.census.gov/popest/archives/national/nation2/intfile2-1.txt [accessed April 23, 2003]

FIGURE 7.2

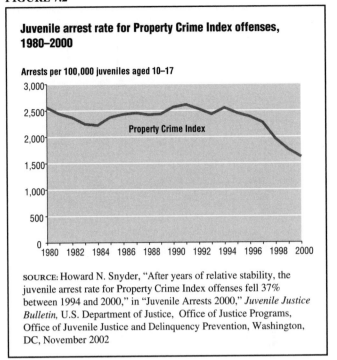

Juvenile arrest rate for Property Crime Index offenses, 1980–2000

Arrests per 100,000 juveniles aged 10–17

Property Crime Index

SOURCE: Howard N. Snyder, "After years of relative stability, the juvenile arrest rate for Property Crime Index offenses fell 37% between 1994 and 2000," in "Juvenile Arrests 2000," *Juvenile Justice Bulletin*, U.S. Department of Justice, Office of Justice Programs, Office of Juvenile Justice and Delinquency Prevention, Washington, DC, November 2002

7.3.) These legislative changes ushered in an era of incarcerating juvenile offenders at historically high rates.

TRENDS IN JUVENILE ARRESTS

During the period when the majority of states enacted tougher transfer, sentencing, and confidentiality statutes relating to juveniles, juveniles age 10 to under 18 declined as a proportion of total population from 13,482 per 100,000 in 1980 to 11,540 in 2000. (See Figure 7.1.) Juvenile arrest and incarceration trends are thus not simply a reflection of a growing population of people in their teens—pure demographics, in other words—but some mix in behavior and the legislative/law enforcement response to that behavior.

Juvenile arrests rates for the crimes included in the FBI's Property Crime Index and Violent Crime Index are charted as Figures 7.2 and 7.3 for the same period—during which the juvenile incarceration rate began to rise. Measured as arrests per 100,000 juveniles in the 10–17 age bracket, the data show both property and violent crime arrests decreasing at first from 1980 to around 1983. Property crime arrests then began increasing gradually while violent arrests rates began to climb more sharply by 1988. Arrest rates began to drop again in 1995 for both property and violent crimes, more steeply for violent crimes.

Arrest Rates by Gender

Data on juvenile arrest rates for three types of violent crime and for drug abuse (see Figure 7.4) show that the majority of juveniles arrested were males, but arrest rates for females grew proportionately more than for males. In 2000, 28 percent of juveniles arrested were female. Data for females are shown graphed both with males, indicating much lower female involvement, as well as separately to show the trend lines more clearly than is possible in combination with the much more numerous male arrests in each category.

Juvenile Offenders by Race

According to the OJJDP ("Juvenile Arrests 2000," *Juvenile Justice Bulletin*, Washington, D.C., November 2002), the majority of all juveniles arrested in 2000 were white, representing 55 percent of violent crime arrests and 69 percent of property crime arrests. Forty-two percent of violent crime arrests and 27 percent of arrests for property crimes involved blacks. Asians/Pacific Islanders comprised 2 percent of those arrested for both violent and property crimes; American Indians represented 1 percent of arrests in each category.

When arrest data are expressed as proportions of each racial population, blacks had higher rates of arrest in 2000 than whites and other races in all but three categories—driving under the influence, liquor law violations, and drunkenness. (See Table 7.4.) American Indians had the highest arrest rates for liquor law violations, whites for driving under the influence and drunkenness. Whites were arrested nearly twice as frequently as Asians/Pacific

FIGURE 7.3

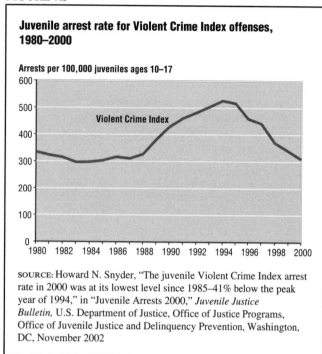

Juvenile arrest rate for Violent Crime Index offenses, 1980–2000

Arrests per 100,000 juveniles ages 10–17

SOURCE: Howard N. Snyder, "The juvenile Violent Crime Index arrest rate in 2000 was at its lowest level since 1985–41% below the peak year of 1994," in "Juvenile Arrests 2000," *Juvenile Justice Bulletin,* U.S. Department of Justice, Office of Justice Programs, Office of Juvenile Justice and Delinquency Prevention, Washington, DC, November 2002

FIGURE 7.4

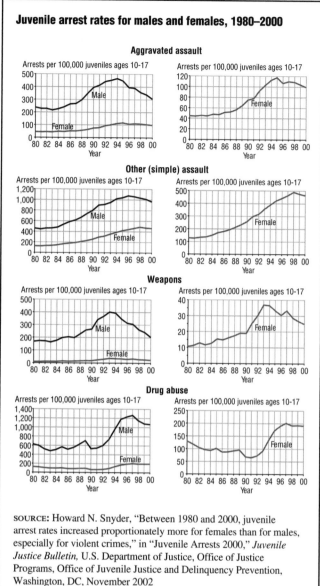

Juvenile arrest rates for males and females, 1980–2000

SOURCE: Howard N. Snyder, "Between 1980 and 2000, juvenile arrest rates increased proportionately more for females than for males, especially for violent crimes," in "Juvenile Arrests 2000," *Juvenile Justice Bulletin,* U.S. Department of Justice, Office of Justice Programs, Office of Juvenile Justice and Delinquency Prevention, Washington, DC, November 2002

Islanders for violent crimes, blacks nearly four times as frequently as whites. Whites were arrested nearly twice as often for property crimes than Asians/Pacific Islanders, blacks nearly twice as often as whites. Total arrest rates for whites increased from 1980 to 1990 and from 1990 to 2000. Black rates increased 1980 to 1990 but declined between 1990 and 2000. American Indian total arrest rates declined from 1980 to 1990 and then rose again in 2000. The total rates for Asians/Pacific Islanders declined uniformly from 1980 to 2000. These data do not identify arrest rates by Hispanic origin. Hispanics may be of any race. The largest racial grouping among Hispanics as reported by the 2000 Census was white (47.9 percent).

Disposition of Juveniles Arrested

A change in the disposition of juveniles arrested appeared in the 1970s. In 1972, 50.8 percent of those arrested were referred to juvenile courts; 45 percent were handled within police departments and released; only 1.3 percent were transferred by referral to criminal or adult courts. By 2000 cases handled internally (followed by release) had dropped to 20.3 percent. The majority of cases were referred to juvenile court (70.8 percent). The cases referred to adult jurisdictions had quintupled to 7 percent of all cases. (See Figure 7.5.)

Juvenile arrest trends have mirrored those of the adult population during the period examined. According to the FBI's Official Crime Index, published in the *Uniform Crime Reports* (Federal Bureau of Investigation, Washington, D.C., multiple years), the violent crime rate in the 1980 to 2000 period peaked in 1992 and declined

thereafter. The property crime rate reached its highest point (in the 1980–2000 period) in 1991 and has been decreasing since that time. As among juveniles, so among adults, the official crime rate for property crimes dropped more gradually than did violent crimes.

JUVENILES IN JAIL AND PRISON

In 2002, 10,303 juveniles were in jail or prison according to the Bureau of Justice Statistics (Paige M. Harrison and Jennifer C. Karberg, *Prison and Jail Inmates at Midyear, 2002,* U.S. Bureau of Justice Statistics, Washington D.C., 2003). Of these juveniles, 7,248 were in jail (6,112 held as adults) and 3,055 were in state prisons. Since 1985 (a year for which comparable statistics are available) juveniles in jail/prison have increased at the rate of 4.3 percent a year. During that same period, the number of juveniles in the 14–17 age group grew at around 0.3

TABLE 7.4

Juvenile arrest rates by offense and race, 1980, 1990, and 2000

(Arrest of persons age 10–17 per 100,000 persons age 10–17)

Offense	White			Black			American Indian			Asian and Pacific Islander		
	1980	1990	2000	1980	1990	2000	1980	1990	2000	1980	1990	2000
Total including suspicion	6,905.8	7,232.9	7,353.2	11,599.9	14,077.6	12,804.4	7,456.2	7,242.5	7,598.5	3,417.0	3,407.1	3,065.3
Violent Crime Index[1]	189.4	253.7	239.2	1,190.4	1,435.3	909.4	211.8	217.0	243.5	134.0	133.5	122.1
Property Crime Index[2]	2,251.6	2,341.0	1,568.5	4,885.9	4,412.6	3,087.8	2,759.1	2,566.7	1,857.3	1,693.8	1,248.8	834.4
Weapons carrying, possessing, etc.	78.2	112.3	109.1	176.2	354.5	249.1	74.0	54.6	79.7	47.3	61.3	46.6
Drug abuse violations	386.2	188.0	618.2	375.1	966.9	1,237.4	208.2	107.7	396.8	107.6	54.4	160.2
Driving under the influence	125.5	84.6	78.6	19.8	16.3	19.8	128.6	97.6	76.1	12.5	11.0	15.5
Liquor laws	589.5	666.9	610.6	80.2	162.2	151.6	608.9	1,033.5	1,136.9	78.2	102.8	90.4
Drunkenness	168.4	98.0	86.0	43.8	55.4	35.2	369.5	124.1	34.6	16.0	8.2	12.8
Disorderly conduct	405.1	376.0	471.3	767.1	931.8	1,160.7	414.9	276.3	385.5	51.3	88.3	109.9
Curfew and loitering law violations	236.9	304.0	500.3	294.3	439.1	856.0	356.2	283.0	468.8	85.2	187.8	250.8
Runaways	512.5	622.7	467.2	499.7	658.6	549.3	684.9	695.9	513.1	316.9	362.5	488.1

[1] Violent Crime Index includes murder and nonnegligent manslaughter, forcible rape, robbery, and aggravated assault.
[2] Property Crime Index includes burglary, larceny-theft, motor vehicle theft, and arson.

SOURCE: Adapted from "Juvenile Arrest Rates by Offense, Sex, and Race (1980-2000)," in *OJJDP Statistical Briefing Book,* U.S. Department of Justice, Office of Justice and Delinquency Prevention, National Center for Juvenile Justice, Washington, DC, March 15, 2002 [Online] http://ojjdp.ncjs.org/ojstatbb/asp/JAR.asp [accessed March 10, 2003]

FIGURE 7.5

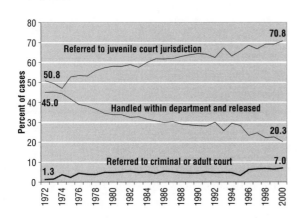

Percent distribution of juveniles taken into police custody, 1972–2000

Note: Excludes two categories: "Referred to other police agency," and "Referred to welfare agency." These categories were 1.6 and 1.3 percent respectively in 1972 and 1.1 and 0.8 percent in 2000.

SOURCE: Adapted from Ann L. Pastore and Kathleen Maguire, eds., "Table 4.26: Percent distribution of juveniles taken into police custody," in *Sourcebook of Criminal Justice Statistics 2001*, U.S. Bureau of Justice Statistics, Washington, DC, 2002 [Online] http://www.albany.edu/sourcebook/1995/wk1/t426.wk1 [accessed April 21, 2003]

FIGURE 7.6

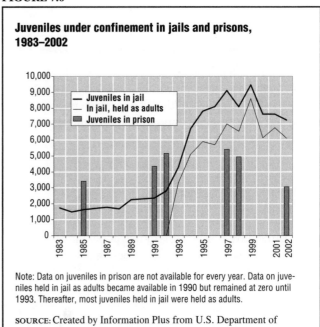

Juveniles under confinement in jails and prisons, 1983–2002

Note: Data on juveniles in prison are not available for every year. Data on juveniles held in jail as adults became available in 1990 but remained at zero until 1993. Thereafter, most juveniles held in jail were held as adults.

SOURCE: Created by Information Plus from U.S. Department of Justice, Office of Justice Programs data

The most recent survey of the characteristics of juveniles in adult confinement was conducted by the U.S. Justice Department's Office of Justice Programs in 1998, published in *Juveniles in Adult Prisons and Jails* in 2000. For purposes of this survey, juveniles were defined as those 17 and younger; the survey also collected matching data for the adult population. The federal prison system did not participate in the survey so the results are for state prisons

percent a year. The number of juveniles in jail increased in number starting in 1984—and rather steeply beginning in 1991. Numbers began to fall sharply again in 1999. (See Figure 7.6.)

TABLE 7.5

Characteristics of youths and adults in state prison, 1998

	Youths		Adults		Total
	Number	Percentage	Number	Percentage	
Offense/Crime					
Persons	2,722	57%	473,821	44%	476,544
Property	974	21%	216,756	20%	217,730
Alcohol Related	135	3%	20,457	2%	20,592
Drug Related	467	10%	210,975	20%	211,442
Public Order	185	4%	40,468	4%	40,653
Parole/Probation	79	2%	90,260	8%	90,339
Unknown	92	2%	5,676	1%	5,768
Other	85	2%	13,327	1%	13,412
Total	4,739	100%	1,071,740	100%	1,076,479
Race/Ethnicity					
Asian	65	1%	11,056	1%	11,121
Black	2,706	55%	497,343	48%	500,050
White	1,309	26%	355,960	35%	357,269
Hispanic	689	14%	156,782	15%	157,471
Native American	176	4%	9,421	1%	9,597
Total	4,945	100%	1,030,562	100%	1,035,507
Housing Type[1]					
Single Cell	1,019	30%	120,221	22%	121,240
Double Cell	670	19%	193,754	35%	194,424
Dormitory	1,757	51%	237,801	43%	239,559
Total	3,446	100%	551,776	100%	555,222

Note: Discrepancies in totals are due to rounding.
[1] Housing type statistics are reported for 21 states that house juveniles in adult correctional facilities.

SOURCE: James Austin, Kelly Dedel Johnson, and Maria Gregoriou, "Table 7. Characteristics of State Prison Inmates, 1998," in *Juveniles in Adult Prisons and Jails: A National Assessment*, U.S. Department of Justice, Office of Justice Programs, Washington, DC, October 2000

TABLE 7.6

Juvenile offenders in residential placement by offense, 1999

Most serious offense	Juvenile offenders in residential placement		Percent change 1997–99
	Number	Percent	
Total juvenile offenders	**108,931**	**100**	**3**
Delinquency	104,237	96	5
Person	38,005	35	7
Criminal homicide	1,514	1	-21
Sexual assault	7,511	7	34
Robbery	8,212	8	-13
Aggravated assault	9,984	9	5
Simple assault	7,448	7	12
Other person[a]	3,336	3	50
Property	31,817	29	-1
Burglary	12,222	11	-3
Theft	6,944	6	-5
Auto theft	6,225	6	-5
Arson	1,126	1	23
Other property	5,300	5	13
Drug	9,882	9	6
Drug trafficking	3,106	3	2
Other drug	6,776	6	9
Public order	10,487	10	8
Weapons	4,023	4	-4
Other public order	6,464	6	17
Technical violation[b]	14,046	13	12
Violent Crime Index[b]	27,221	25	3
Property Crime Index[b]	26,517	24	-3
Status offense	4,694	4	-32

[a] Offenses against other persons include kidnapping, violent sex acts other than forcible rape (e.g., incest, sodomy), custody interference, unlawful restraint, false imprisonment, reckless endangerment, harassment, and attempts to commit any such acts.
[b] Technical violations include violations of probation, parole, and valid court orders. Violent Crime Index offenses include criminal homicide, sexual assault, robbery, and aggravated assault. Property Crime Index offenses include burglary, theft, auto theft, and arson.

SOURCE: Melissa Sickmund, "More than one-third of juvenile offenders in residential placement were held for person offenses," in "Juvenile Offenders in Residential Placement: 1997–1999," *Juvenile Offenders and Victims National Report Series Fact Sheet #07*, U.S. Department of Justice, Office of Justice Programs, Office of Juvenile Justice and Delinquency Prevention, Washington, DC, March 2002

and participating local jail systems. Among juvenile offenders held in adult facilities, 3.3 percent were female, significantly lower than youths held in juvenile residential facilities (13 percent).

Table 7.5 shows the offenses for which youths and adults surveyed were incarcerated in state prison, the racial and ethnic composition of these two groups, and the manner in which they were housed. The major difference between the juvenile and the adult populations in 1998 was that only one in ten youths but one in five adults were serving time for drug offenses. Proportionally, therefore, more youths were held for offenses against persons and for property crimes than adults. A larger percentage of the juvenile population was black (55 percent versus 48 percent of adults), a smaller percentage were white (26 percent versus 35 percent), and a significantly higher percentage (4 percent versus 1 percent among adults) were Native Americans. More juveniles occupied single cells (30 percent versus 22 percent for adults) and slept in dormitories (51 percent versus 43 percent for the adult population).

JUVENILES IN RESIDENTIAL PLACEMENT

The more than 10,000 juveniles in jail and prison in 2002 were but a fraction of all juveniles in

confinement. They represented those youths transferred to the jurisdiction of adult courts, usually by waiver or under statutorily mandated rules. In 1999, the year of the last Census of Juveniles in Residential Placement (CJRP), the Office of Juvenile Justice and Delinquency Prevention counted 108,931 juvenile offenders residing in public and private juvenile detention, correctional, and shelter facilities. This category excludes prisons and jails. In 1999 approximately 13,900 juveniles were in jail and prison, bringing the total confined youth population to 122,831. Based on this number, 11 percent of all confined juveniles were in adult facilities, the rest in juvenile residential facilities. As reported by Melissa Sickmund in "Juvenile Offenders in Residential Placement: 1997–1999" (OJJDP Fact Sheet, #07, March 2002), there were 1,136 public, 1,794 private, and 9 tribally operated residential facilities in 1999.

The vast majority of juveniles in residential placement were delinquents (96 percent), the rest were confined for

TABLE 7.7

Juvenile residential facilities by state, 2000

State	Juvenile facilities			Offenders younger than 21			State	Juvenile facilities			Offenders younger than 21		
	All facilities	Public	Private	All facilities	Public	Private		All facilities	Public	Private	All facilities	Public	Private
U.S. Total*	3,061	1,203	1,848	110,284	77,662	32,464	Missouri	65	57	8	1,540	1,290	250
Alabama	46	12	34	1,583	926	657	Montana	18	8	10	260	173	65
Alaska	19	5	14	339	261	78	Nebraska	23	6	17	789	577	212
Arizona	51	16	35	2,248	1,752	398	Nevada	15	10	5	1,176	750	426
Arkansas	45	11	34	639	295	344	New Hampshire	8	2	6	193	123	70
California	285	116	169	19,286	17,551	1,735	New Jersey	57	45	12	2,274	2,171	103
Colorado	73	12	61	2,054	1,112	940	New Mexico	27	19	8	885	838	47
Connecticut	26	5	21	1,360	900	460	New York	210	59	151	5,081	2,883	2,198
Delaware	7	3	4	295	246	49	North Carolina	67	27	40	1,555	1,237	318
Dist. of Columbia	17	3	14	272	159	113	North Dakota	13	4	9	203	105	98
Florida	166	53	113	7,278	3,269	4,009	Ohio	106	71	35	4,890	4,342	548
Georgia	50	29	21	3,270	2,593	677	Oklahoma	52	14	38	1,034	535	479
Hawaii	7	3	4	122	107	15	Oregon	48	27	21	1,637	1,415	222
Idaho	22	14	8	580	470	110	Pennsylvania	163	29	134	5,085	1,241	3,844
Illinois	46	26	20	3,402	3,074	328	Rhode Island	11	1	10	360	211	149
Indiana	97	41	56	3,334	2,239	1,095	South Carolina	42	16	26	1,592	1,072	520
Iowa	76	18	60	1,166	395	771	South Dakota	22	9	13	646	365	265
Kansas	51	17	34	1,185	831	354	Tennessee	63	28	35	1,824	1,041	783
Kentucky	58	31	27	950	757	193	Texas	138	77	61	8,354	6,475	1,879
Louisiana	64	20	44	2,663	2,105	558	Utah	51	17	34	1,135	453	682
Maine	17	3	14	300	248	52	Vermont	5	1	4	158	26	132
Maryland	43	11	32	1,492	690	802	Virginia	74	62	12	2,868	2,616	252
Massachusetts	71	18	53	1,481	567	914	Washington	42	31	11	2,064	1,938	126
Michigan	108	42	66	3,896	1,782	2,114	West Virginia	27	6	21	381	241	140
Minnesota	121	22	99	1,922	986	936	Wisconsin	94	27	67	2,017	1,271	746
Mississippi	20	19	1	787	785	2	Wyoming	24	2	22	379	173	206

Note: State is the state where the facility is located. Offenders sent to out-of-state facilities are counted in the state where the facility is located, not the state where their offense occurred.
*U.S. total includes 158 offenders in 10 tribal facilities. These offenders were located in Arizona, Colorado, Montana, Oklahoma, and South Dakota.

SOURCE: Melissa Sickmund, "In October 2000, 4 in 10 juvenile facilities were publicly operated and held 70% of juvenile offenders in custody," in "Juvenile Residential Facility Census, 2000: Selected Findings," *Juvenile Offenders and Victims National Report Series Bulletin*, U.S. Department of Justice, Office of Justice Programs, Office of Juvenile Justice and Delinquency Prevention, Washington, DC, December 2002

status offenses. Status offenders are runaways, truants from school, youths who are beyond the control of their parents, curfew violators, and those who violate other non-criminal ordinances and rules. The largest number of youths in residential placement were held for burglary (11 percent), followed by two violent crime categories, aggravated assault (9 percent) and robbery (8 percent). Robbery involves the use or threat of force. Categories of offense with the greatest increase since 1997 were offenses against other persons (a 50 percent increase) and sexual assault (up 34 percent). Offenses against other persons, according to OJJDP, "include kidnapping, violent sex acts other than forcible rape (e.g., incest, sodomy), custody interference, unlawful restraint, false imprisonment, reckless endangerment, harassment, and attempts to commit any such acts" (from "Glossary of terms" [Online] http://www.ojjdp.ncjrs.org/pubs/juvctstats/glossary.html). Greatest decreases were in status offenses (down 32 percent), in criminal homicide (down 21 percent). and robbery (down 13 percent). (See Table 7.6.)

An OJJDP survey of residential facilities (rather than inmates) was conducted in 2000 (Melissa Sickmund,

"Juvenile Residential Facility Census, 2000: Selected Findings," *OJJDP Bulletin*, December 2002). It shows that the inmate population had increased to 110,284 juveniles, up 1,353. Public facilities had increased in one year by 67 to 1,203; private facilities increased by 54 to 1,848. Tribal facilities had increased by 1.

The largest populations of juveniles in residential placement were in California, Texas, Florida, Pennsylvania, and New York, in that order. They housed 40.9 percent of all juveniles in residential detention. Seventy percent of all juveniles were held in public and 30 percent in private facilities. (See Table 7.7.)

The 2000 survey of residential facilities showed that crowding is also an issue in juvenile confinement: 2,875 of 3,061 facilities reported on the availability of "standard beds," a category that excludes informal sleeping arrangements such as sofas, mattresses on the floor, and cots. Thirty-nine percent of all reporting facilities had fewer standard beds than inmates, 37 percent of public and 40 percent of private facilities. The most crowded conditions in public facilities were reported in Delaware and Rhode

TABLE 7.8

Juvenile facilities reporting bed information, 2000

State	Facilities reporting bed information			Percent of facilities with more residents than standard beds			State	Facilities reporting bed information			Percent of facilities with more residents than standard begs		
	All facilities	Public	Private	All facilities	Public	Private		All facilities	Public	Private	All facilities	Public	Private
U.S. Total*	2,875	1,164	1,704	39	37	40	Missouri	63	55	8	25	27	13
Alabama	5	11	34	38	73	26	Montana	19	8	10	26	25	20
Alaska	15	4	11	27	25	27	Nebraska	21	6	15	33	50	27
Arizona	51	15	32	39	47	41	Nevada	15	10	5	33	40	20
Arkansas	36	11	25	33	27	36	New Hampshire	8	2	6	50	50	50
California	258	115	143	56	37	71	New Jersey	54	45	9	35	38	22
Colorado	70	12	57	31	67	25	New Mexico	27	19	8	33	37	25
Connecticut	23	5	18	30	20	33	New York	208	59	149	53	37	59
Delaware	7	3	4	57	100	25	North Carolina	62	24	38	37	38	37
District of Columbia	11	3	8	18	0	25	North Dakota	13	4	9	0	0	0
Florida	147	53	94	52	47	55	Ohio	106	71	35	35	38	29
Georgia	50	29	21	42	59	19	Oklahoma	43	14	29	53	57	52
Hawaii	7	3	4	43	33	50	Oregon	44	24	20	30	25	35
Idaho	21	13	8	52	62	38	Pennsylvania	149	28	121	33	36	32
Illinois	42	25	17	19	16	24	Rhode Island	10	1	9	80	100	78
Indiana	95	41	54	23	29	19	South Carolina	37	13	24	38	38	38
Iowa	74	16	58	43	13	52	South Dakota	21	7	13	24	0	31
Kansas	47	16	31	28	25	29	Tennessee	58	27	31	52	48	55
Kentucky	57	30	27	28	30	26	Texas	125	73	52	33	37	27
Louisiana	62	20	42	35	30	38	Utah	51	17	34	39	29	44
Maine	17	3	14	41	0	50	Vermont	5	1	4	20	0	25
Maryland	43	11	32	30	36	28	Virginia	74	62	12	41	44	25
Massachusetts	69	18	51	77	89	73	Washington	42	31	11	21	19	27
Michigan	104	39	65	34	21	42	West Virginia	27	6	21	52	67	48
Minnesota	114	22	92	29	45	25	Wisconsin	91	24	67	14	13	15
Mississippi	14	13	1	29	23	100	Wyoming	23	2	21	17	0	19

Note: A single bed is counted as one standard bed and a bunk bed is counted as two standard beds. Makeshift beds (e.g., cots, rollout beds, mattresses, and sofas) are not counted as standard beds. Percents are based on facilities reporting bed information. State is the state where the facility is located. Offenders sent to out-of-state facilities are counted in the state where the facility is located, not the state where their offense occurred.

*U.S. total includes seven tribal facilities that reported bed information. These tribal facilities were located in Arizona, Colorado, Montana, and South Dakota.

SOURCE: Melissa Sickmund, "Nationwide, 39% of juvenile facilities reporting bed information held more residents than they had standard beds," in "Juvenile Residential Facility Census, 2000: Selected Findings," *Juvenile Offenders and Victims National Report Series Bulletin*, U.S. Department of Justice, Office of Justice Programs, Office of Juvenile Justice and Delinquency Prevention, Washington, DC, December 2002

Island where all public facilities had fewer beds than inmates. In Mississippi, all private facilities reported a short-fall in beds for juveniles housed. (See Table 7.8.)

Placement Status

Juveniles in residential placement are classified by the OJJDP into three categories. The largest group in 1999, 73.8 percent of the confined youths, were *committed* by juvenile courts. (See Table 7.9.) Most of the rest, 25.2 percent, were *detained* and represented a transitory population. Some of these juveniles may well have ended up in jails and prisons later. They were in residential placement awaiting their hearings, waiting for the disposition of their cases, or waiting to be transferred to some other kind of facility. The remaining 1 percent of residents were in juvenile confinement voluntarily as a consequence of so-called *diversion* agreements. Under such agreements a juvenile may opt to enter a juvenile facility voluntarily in lieu of judicial proceedings in juvenile court. The offender profiles of those committed and those detained were quite similar in most regards. A smaller percentage of detainees were being held for offenses against persons than those committed (29.1 percent versus 36.8 percent). Detainees were also proportionately less involved in property offenses (25.9 percent versus the committed population's 30.5 percent). A significantly higher proportion of detainees were being held for technical violations which involve such matters as parole violations and failure to follow court orders. Those in juvenile homes voluntarily, the diversionary group, were proportionately less delinquent than either the committed or the detained population (71.1 percent versus 95.6 percent of those committed). This small group, however, had a disproportionately high number (28.9 percent) in the "status offense" category—youths who run away, fail to attend school, are incorrigible, etc. (See Table 7.9.)

TABLE 7.9

Offense profile of juveniles by placement status, 1999

| Most serious offense | Total | Placement status | | | Percent distribution | | |
		Com-mitted	Detained	Diver-sion	Com-mitted	Detained	Diver-sion
Total	108,931	80,446	27,404	612	100.0	100.0	100.0
Delinquency	104,237	76,926	26,439	435	95.6	96.5	71.1
Person	38,005	29,625	7,986	204	36.8	29.1	33.3
Property	31,817	24,549	7,086	93	30.5	25.9	15.2
Drug	9,882	7,404	2,430	30	9.2	8.9	4.9
Public order	10,487	7,641	2,727	57	9.5	10.0	9.3
Technical violation	14,046	7,707	6,210	51	9.6	22.7	8.3
Status offense	4,694	3,519	966	177	4.4	3.5	28.9

Committed: Includes juveniles in placement in the facility as part of a court-ordered disposition. Committed juveniles may have been adjudicated and disposed in juvenile court or convicted and sentenced in criminal court.

Detained: Includes juveniles held prior to adjudication while awaiting an adjudication hearing in juvenile court, as well as juveniles held after adjudication while awaiting disposition or after adjudication while awaiting placement elsewhere. Also includes juveniles awaiting transfer to adult criminal court, or awaiting a hearing or trial in adult criminal court.

Diversion: Includes juveniles sent to the facility in lieu of adjudication as part of a diversion agreement.

To preserve the privacy of the juvenile residents, cell counts have been rounded to the nearest multiple of three. U.S. total includes 2,645 juvenile offenders in private facilities for whom the offense was not reported and 174 juvenile offenders in tribal facilities.

SOURCE: Melissa Sickmund and Yi-chun Wan, "Detailed Offense Profile by Placement Status for United States, 1999," in "Census of Juveniles in Residential Placement Databook," U.S. Department of Justice, Office of Juvenile Justice and Delinquency Prevention, National Center for Juvenile Justice, Washington, DC [Online] http://www.ojjdp.ncjrs.org/ojstatbb/cjrp [accessed April 25, 2003]

TABLE 7.10

Offenders by gender in residential facilities, 1999

| Most serious offense | Total | Male | | Female | | Female difference from male[1] |
		Number	%	Number	%	%
Total	108,931	94,370	100.0	14,561	100.0	
Delinquency	104,237	91,500	97.0	12,735	87.5	-9.5
Person	38,005	33,648	35.7	4,359	29.9	-5.7
Criminal	1,514	1,359	1.4	156	1.1	-0.4
Sexual assault	7,511	7,419	7.9	93	0.6	-7.2
Robbery	8,212	7,746	8.2	465	3.2	-5.0
Aggravated	9,984	8,562	9.1	1,422	9.8	0.7
Simple assault	7,448	5,727	6.1	1,722	11.8	5.8
Other person-related	3,336	2,835	3.0	501	3.4	0.4
Property	31,817	28,326	30.0	3,489	24.0	-6.1
Burglary	12,222	11,532	12.2	690	4.7	-7.5
Theft	6,944	5,679	6.0	1,266	8.7	2.7
Auto theft	6,225	5,412	5.7	813	5.6	-0.2
Arson	1,126	996	1.1	129	0.9	-0.2
Other property	5,300	4,707	5.0	591	4.1	-0.9
Drug	9,882	9,024	9.6	858	5.9	-3.7
Trafficking	3,106	2,964	3.1	141	1.0	-2.2
Other drug	6,776	6,060	6.4	714	4.9	-1.5
Public order	10,487	9,432	10.0	1,053	7.2	-2.8
Weapons	4,023	3,831	4.1	192	1.3	-2.7
Alcohol	328	273	0.3	54	0.4	0.1
Other public order	6,136	5,328	5.6	807	5.5	-0.1
Technical	14,046	11,070	11.7	2,976	20.4	8.7
Violent Crime[2]	27,221	25,086	26.6	2,136	14.7	-11.9
Property Crime[3]	26,517	23,619	25.0	2,898	19.9	-5.1
Status offense	4,694	2,868	3.0	1,824	12.5	9.5
Running away	1,083	483	0.5	600	4.1	3.6
Truancy	913	525	0.6	387	2.7	2.1
Incorrigibility	1,843	1,209	1.3	633	4.3	3.1
Curfew	105	72	0.1	33	0.2	0.2
Underage	378	294	0.3	84	0.6	0.3
Miscellaneous	372	285	0.3	87	0.6	0.3

Note: U.S. total includes 2,645 juvenile offenders in private facilities for whom offense was not reported and 174 juvenile offenders in tribal facilities. Technical offenses include such matters as parole violations and disobeying court orders.
[1] Female percent of total less male percent of total. Negative values mean that females are less involved than males in the activity. Numbers may not be precise because of rounding.
[2] Includes criminal homicide, violent sexual assault, robbery, and aggravated assault.
[3] Includes burglary, theft, auto theft, and arson.

SOURCE: Adapted from Melissa Sickmund and Yi-chun Wan, "Detailed Offense Profile by Sex for United States, 1999" in "Census of Juveniles in Residential Placement Databook," U.S. Department of Justice, Office of Juvenile Justice and Delinquency Prevention, National Center for Juvenile Justice, Washington, DC [Online] http://www/ojjdp.ncjrs.org/ojstatbb/cjrp [accessed April 25, 2003]

Characteristics of the Residential Placement Population

The majority of inmates in juvenile detention facilities in 1999 (86.6 percent) were male. Proportionately more males were involved in offenses against persons (35.7 percent versus the female ratio of 29.9 percent). Females, however, were more likely to have committed aggravated assault (9.8 percent of females, 9.1 percent of males) and simple assault (11.8 percent of females, 6.1 percent of males). Proportionately more males were also involved in property offenses (30 percent) than females (24 percent). As a percentage of offenses committed, females were more involved in technical and status offenses than males. (See Table 7.10.)

Racial and ethnic minorities dominated residential placement facilities in 1999. Blacks were 39 percent of the population, whites 38 percent, Hispanics (who may be of any race) were 18 percent. American Indians and Asians/Pacific Islanders represented 2 percent each. A category the OJJDP labels "Other" and describes as persons of multiple race occupied 1 percent of the beds. (See Figure 7.7.)

Also shown in the graphic is the racial/ethnic composition of juvenile facilities measured as individuals per 100,000 juveniles in each of the categories except "Other."

More black youths are in such facilities, proportionally to their presence in the population, than any other group, 1,004 individuals per 100,000 black youths. Ratios for the other groups in 1999 were 212 for whites, 485 for Hispanics, 632 for American Indians, and 182 per 100,000 for Asians/Pacific Islanders.

JUVENILES AND THE DEATH PENALTY

It is rare for the death penalty to be imposed on juveniles 17 years of age or younger. The Supreme Court, reversing the death sentence of a 16-year-old in *Eddings v. Oklahoma* (455 U.S. 104, 1982), noted that adolescents

FIGURE 7.7

Race/ethnicity of juveniles in residential placement, 1999

Percent of juveniles in residential placement

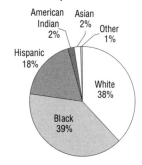

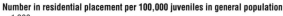

Number in residential placement per 100,000 juveniles in general population

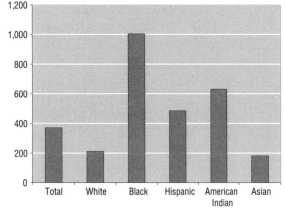

Note: The "Asian" category includes individuals who are Pacific Islanders. The "Other" category includes individuals with multiple race identifications. A rate per 100,000 juveniles is not presented for the "Other" category because there is no comparable reference population available, but the category is represented in the "Total" grouping. Hispanics may be of any race and are not included in the other racial categories.

SOURCE: Adapted from Melissa Sickmund and Yi-chun Wan, "Census of Juveniles in Residential Placement Databook," U.S. Department of Justice, Office of Justice Programs, Office of Juvenile Justice and Delinquency Programs, Washington, DC [Online] http://www.ojjdp.ncjrs.org/ojstatbb/cjrp [accessed April 25, 2003]

TABLE 7.11

Minimum age authorized for capital punishment, 2001

Age 16 or less	Age 17	Age 18	None specified
Alabama (16)	Georgia	California	Arizona
Arkansas (14) [a]	New Hampshire	Colorado	Idaho
Delaware (16)	North Carolina [b]	Connecticut [c]	Louisiana
Florida (16)	Texas	Federal system	Montana [d]
Indiana (16)		Illinois	Pennsylvania
Kentucky (16)		Kansas	South Carolina
Mississippi (16) [e]		Maryland	South Dakota [f]
Missouri (16)		Nebraska	
Nevada (16)		New Jersey	
Oklahoma (16)		New Mexico	
Utah (14)		New York	
Virginia (14) [g]		Ohio	
Wyoming (16)		Oregon	
		Tennessee	
		Washington	

Note: Reporting by states reflects interpretations by offices of state attorneys general and may differ from previously reported ages.

[a] See Arkansas Code Ann. 9-27-318(c)(2)(Sipp.2001).

[b] Age required is 17 unless the murderer was incarcerated for murder when a subsequent murder occurred; then the age may be 14.

[c] See Connecticut General Stat. 53a-46a(g)(1).

[d] Montana law specifies that offenders tried under the capital sexual assault statute be 18 or older. Age may be a mitigating factor for other capital crimes.

[e] The minimum age defined by statute is 13, but the effective age is 16 based on interpretation of U.S. Supreme Court decisions by the Mississippi Supreme Court.

[f] Juveniles may be transferred to adult court. Age can be a mitigating factor.

[g] The minimum age for transfer to adult court by statute is 14, but the effective age is 16 based on interpretation of U.S. Supreme Court decisions by the State attorney general's office.

SOURCE: Tracy L. Snell, "Table 4. Minimum age authorized for capital punishment, 2001," in *Capital Punishment 2001*, U.S. Bureau of Justice Statistics, Washington, DC, December 2002

are not mature, responsible, or self-disciplined enough to consider the long-range implications of their actions. The court also held that a defendant's young age and mental and emotional development should be considered as an important mitigating factor when deciding whether to apply the death penalty. Nonetheless, the court failed to indicate the age at which a defendant would be mature enough to receive the death penalty, indicating only that it was not 16 years.

According to the BJS, in 14 states allowing the death penalty in 2001, the minimum age authorized for capital punishment was 18 years. (See Table 7.11.) Those states include California, Colorado, Connecticut, Illinois, Kansas, Maryland, Nebraska, New Jersey, New Mexico, New York, Ohio, Oregon, Tennessee, and Washington. The federal system observes 18 years as well. However,

four states—Georgia, New Hampshire, North Carolina, and Texas—authorized the death penalty at 17 years. The minimum age for capital punishment was 16 years or less in 13 other states. Alabama, Delaware, Florida, Indiana, Kentucky, Mississippi, Missouri, Nevada, Oklahoma, and Wyoming set 16 years as the minimum, while Arkansas, Utah, and Virginia use 14 years. States without specific limits are Arizona, Idaho, Louisiana, Montana, Pennsylvania, South Carolina, and South Dakota.

From 1973 through October 31, 1998, Texas and Florida accounted for some 40 percent of the 164 offenders under a sentence of death for crimes committed before age 18. Alabama had 15 such offenders, followed by Mississippi at 10 and Louisiana at 9. From 1973 to mid-year 2000, 17 offenders were executed for crimes committed when they were under the age of 18 years. All were 17 years of age at the time of their offense—except Sean R. Sellars, executed in Oklahoma on February 4, 1999, for a crime he committed when he was 16 years old. Of the 17 offenders executed for crimes committed before their 18th birthday, 9 were put to death in Texas. Nine were white, 7 black, and 1 Latino.

ADULT SENTENCING OF JUVENILE OFFENDERS

With the passage of Proposition 21 in March 2000, Californians joined the nationwide trend to "get tough" on violent juvenile offenders. The provisions of Proposition 21 contain significant changes in the way in which juvenile offenders are dealt with in California. One of the biggest changes was that prosecutors, under certain circumstances, can have the discretion to decide whether juveniles 14 years of age or older, charged with committing certain types of murder or serious sex crimes, can be tried in adult court. Previously, judges conducted a hearing or judicial review to decide whether to try a juvenile as an adult.

That aspect as well as other tenets of the new law have come under fire from youth organizations and civil liberties groups. In a 6-1 decision on February 28, 2002, the California Supreme Court upheld the constitutionality of the increased prosecutorial powers. More court challenges to the law are in the works.

JUVENILE BOOT CAMPS

Boot camps for juvenile offenders began around 1985 when such a program was established in Orleans Parish, Louisiana. Boot camps for juveniles are typically intended for "midrange" offenders—those who have failed with lesser sanctions like probation but are not yet hardened criminals. Juvenile programs typically exclude some types of offenders, such as sex offenders, armed robbers, and youths with a record of serious violence. Definitions of terms like "nonviolent" vary from program to program.

Most juvenile boot camps share the 90–120 day duration typical of military boot camps. They employ military customs and have uniformed drill instructors, use a platoon sergeant, and subject participants to verbal harassment, summary punishment, and group punishment under some circumstances.

Besides military discipline, most juvenile boot camps include some type of work detail. Because of state-mandated education rules, programs spend a minimum of three hours daily on academic education. Most programs also include some vocational education, work-skills training, or job preparation.

Initially a popular idea, boot camps for juveniles have met with controversy. According to the Koch Crime Institute, the recidivism rate for youths attending boot camps ranged between 64 and 75 percent. "Overall, KCI researchers have found that boot camps have not been shown to reduce recidivism or deter crime. However, the recidivism rate of boot camps is only slightly higher than that of traditional juvenile facilities," according to the study *Juvenile Boot Camps: Cost and Effectiveness vs. Residential Facilities* (Brent Zaehringer, Koch Crime Institute, 1998). The National Institute of Justice also reports that recidivism rates between those attending boot camps and those undergoing traditional correctional measures show "no significant differences." Reports of neglect and physical abuse of juveniles attending some boot camps have also surfaced, bringing more controversy to the debate.

CHAPTER 8
PROBATION AND PAROLE

Any society that depends on only two sentencing options—confinement or nothing at all—is unsafe and unjust. We need a full array of effective sentencing tools that actually suit our various sentencing purposes.

— Michael Smith, Vera Institute of Justice

Most of the correctional population of the United States—those under the supervision of correctional authorities—are walking about freely. They are people on probation or people on parole. In 2001, 3.9 million people were on probation, 731,000 on parole, and 1.96 million behind the bars of prisons or of jails. For every person behind bars, more than 2 people convicted of crimes were on the street, 70 percent, all told. Probationers and parolees, however, were nonetheless under official supervision and most had to satisfy requirements placed on them as a condition of freedom or of early release from correctional facilities.

A probationer is someone who has been convicted of a crime and sentenced—but the person's sentence has been suspended on condition that he or she behave in the manner ordered by the court. Probation sometimes follows a brief period of incarceration; more often it is granted by the court immediately.

A parolee is an individual who has served a part of his or her sentence in jail and prison but, because of good behavior or by legislative mandate, has been granted freedom before the sentence is served out. The sentence remains in effect, however, and the parolee continues to be under the jurisdiction of a parole board. If the person fails to live up to the conditions of the release, the parolee may be confined again.

From the 1980s to the early 2000s, those incarcerated have increased slightly in proportion to those on probation and parole as state legislatures, prosecutors, and courts have tightened or even removed parole altogether as an option. Thus, for instance, in the 1980–2001 period (see Figure 8.1), the confined population grew most rapidly (an

FIGURE 8.1

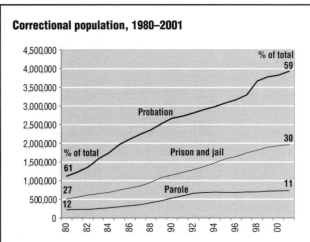

Correctional population, 1980–2001

SOURCE: Adapted from Allen Beck and Lauren Glaze, "Correctional populations of the United States," in *Key Facts at a Glance, Correctional populations,* U.S. Bureau of Justice Statistics, Washington, DC, August 20, 2002 [Online] http://www.ojp.usdoj.gov/bjs/glance/tables/corr2tab.htm [accessed April 29, 2003]

average of 6.7 percent a year)—and of this population the more severe version, incarceration in prison, grew most rapidly of all at an average rate of 7 percent a year. The probation population grew on average 6.2 percent annually; the parole population, more closely associated with prisons and jails, grew least (5.9 percent a year on average). The policy since 1980 has been to "get tough" on crime. In 1980 61 percent of the correctional population was on probation, 12 percent on parole, and 27 percent in prison and jail. Twenty-one years later, probationers were 59 percent of the population, parolees 11 percent, and those in prison and jail 30 percent.

Data since 1990 show that a change in this pattern may be taking place. (See Table 8.1.) Growth trends slowed in the 1990s in all categories, but during 2000 and 2001 (the last two years for which data are available), the probation

TABLE 8.1

Persons under adult correctional supervison, 1990, 1995–2001

Year	Total estimated correctional population[1]	Community supervision		Incarceration	
		Probation	Parole	Jail	Prison
1990	4,350,300	2,670,234	531,407	405,320	743,382
1995	5,342,900	3,077,861	679,421	507,044	1,078,542
1996	5,490,700	3,164,996	679,733	518,492	1,127,528
1997[2]	5,734,900	3,296,513	694,787	567,079	1,176,564
1998[2]	6,134,200	3,670,441	696,385	592,462	1,224,469
1999[2]	6,340,800	3,779,922	714,457	605,943	1,287,172
2000	6,445,100	3,826,209	723,898	621,149	1,316,333
2001	6,592,800	3,932,751	731,147	631,240	1,330,980
Percent change 2000-01	2.3 %	2.8 %	1.0 %	1.6 %	1.1 %
Average annual percent change 1995-2001	3.6 %	3.4 %	1.2 %	3.7 %	3.6 %

Note: Counts are for December 31, except for jail counts, which are for June 30. Jail and prison counts include inmates held in private facilities. Totals in 1998 through 2001 exclude probationers held in jail or prison.

[1] Because some offenders may have multiple statuses, totals were rounded to the nearest 100.

[2] Coverage of probation agencies was expanded. For counts based on the same reporting agencies, use 3,266,837 in 1997 (to compare with 1996); 3,417,613 in 1998 (to compare with 1997); and 3,773,624 in 1999 (to compare with 1998). The average annual percent change was adjusted for the change in coverage.

SOURCE: Lauren E. Glaze, "Persons under adult correctional supervision, 1990, 1995–2001," in *Probation and Parole in the United States, 2001*, U.S. Bureau of Justice Statistics, Washington, DC, August 2002

population increased at a more rapid rate (2.8 percent) than the jail and prison populations, possibly in response to prison crowding.

PROBATION

Characteristics of Probationers

Those whom the courts release for probation are deemed to be the least dangerous among those arrested and most likely to stay clear of the justice system in the future, although only about two-thirds of those on probation appear to succeed. (See Table 8.2.) Whereas all persons in prison serve sentences for felonies, only 53 percent of probationers were felons in 2001; 45 percent had been sentenced for misdemeanors, the rest for other infractions. A decade earlier, in 1990, the majority (52 percent) had misdemeanor sentences. Among those entering probation in 2001, 76 percent did so without any incarceration, and among those leaving this status, 62 percent had completed their probation successfully—a far higher percentage than those leaving parole (46 percent). Among those leaving this status in 2001, be it by reason of completing probation of failing to do so successfully, 13 percent returned to incarceration or were incarcerated for the first time. By contrast, 40 percent of those leaving parole were put behind bars again for failure to live up to the rules or committing a new offense. The single largest category of serious offense

committed by probationers was a drug violation (25 percent) followed by driving while intoxicated (18 percent).

In comparison with state and federal prisoners, probationers were proportionally more female (22 percent versus 6 percent of prisoners) and more white (55 percent versus 36 of those in prison) in 2001. A smaller proportion of probationers were black (31 percent of probationers, 46 percent of prisoners) and of Hispanic origin (12 percent of probationers, 16 percent of prisoners). (See Figure 8.2.)

Geographical Distribution

On average across the nation, nearly 2 people of every 100 (1,834 per 100,000 adults) were under probation, but rates varied considerably state to state and region to region. In broad terms, populations of probationers paralleled the general population with some differences. (See Figure 8.3.) The South and the Midwest had proportionally more probationers than population, especially the South, which had 41.4 percent of probationers and 35.6 percent of the population. The ratio in the Midwest was nearly the same—23.4 percent on probation versus 22.9 percent of the resident population. In the West and the Northeast, both had proportionately fewer probationers. The biggest gap in proportion was in the Northeast where 15.3 percent of the probationers but 19.0 percent of the population lived in 2001. The West claimed 19.8 percent of probationers and 22.5 percent of the population.

Table 8.3 shows these data for all states and the District of Columbia for 2001. Rankings are provided in Table 8.4. The top nine states in population are all in the top 10 for probationers, but not in rank order. Texas leads in probationer population but is second in total population. California is second in probationers, first in people. Georgia, which ranks tenth in population, does not make the top ten in probationer population. It is displaced by the state of Washington, seventh in probationers and the 15th most populous state. State rankings have remained almost unchanged since 1995.

Maine (14.8 percent), Colorado (12.1 percent), Kentucky (12.1 percent), and Virginia (11.6 percent) had the greatest increases in probationers between 2000 and 2001. Idaho (3,747 per 100,000 adult U.S. residents), Washington (3,551 per 100,000), Delaware (3,321 per 100,000), and Minnesota (3,081 per 100,000) had the highest rates of probationers to population. The top four states with the fewest probationers per 100,000 adult U.S. residents were New Hampshire (385), West Virginia (441), North Dakota (613), and Nevada (654). (See Table 8.4.)

"Community Corrections"

In the terminology of the justice system, individuals on probation participate in "community corrections"—they are undergoing correction while still in the community.

TABLE 8.2

Characteristics of adults on probation, 1990, 1995, and 2001

Characteristic	1990	1995	2001
Total	100%	100 %	100 %
Gender			
Male	82%	79 %	78 %
Female	18	21	22
Race[1]			
White	52%	53 %	55 %
Black	30	31	31
Hispanic	18	14	12
American Indian/Alaska Native	1	1	1
Asian/Pacific Islander[2]	--	--	1
Status of supervision			
Active	83%	79 %	74 %
Inactive	9	8	11
Absconded	6	9	10
Supervised out of state	2	2	2
Other	**	2	3
Adults entering probation			
Without incarceration	87%	72 %	76 %
With incarceration	8	13	17
Other types	5	15	7
Adults leaving probation			
Successful completions	69%	62 %	62%
Returned to incarceration	14	21	13
With new sentence	3	5	3
With the same sentence	9	13	7
Unknown	2	3	4

Characteristic	1990	1995	2001
Absconder[3]	7 %	**	3 %
Other unsuccessful	2	**	11
Death	--	1	1
Other	7	16	10
Type of offense of adults on probation[4]			
Felony	48 %	54%	53 %
Misdemeanor	52	44	45
Other infractions	1	2	1
Most serious offense			
Driving while intoxicated	21%	16%	18%
Drug law violations	**	**	25
Minor traffic offenses	**	**	7
Domestic violence	**	**	7
Other	79	84	43
Status of probation			
Direct imposition	38 %	48%	54%
Split sentence	6	15	9
Sentence suspended	41	26	25
Imposition suspended	14	6	10
Other	1	4	1

Note: For every characteristic there were persons of unknown status or type. Detail may not sum to total because of rounding.
**Not available.
--Less than 0.5%
[1] In 2001 race/Hispanic origin was collected as a single item. For comparison, percents were recalculated for prior years.
[2] Includes Native Hawaiians.
[3] In 1995 absconder status was reported among "other."
[4] In 2001 type of offense was limited to three categories. Driving while intoxicated was reported under the "most serious offense" category. For comparison, percents were recalculated for prior years.

SOURCE: Lauren E. Glaze, "Table 4. Characteristics of adults on probation, 1990, 1995, and 2001," in *Probation and Parole in the United States, 2001*, U.S. Bureau of Justice Statistics, Washington, DC, August 2002

The Bureau of Justice Statistics (BJS) carried out its first national survey of adults on probation in 1995. The survey has not been repeated and remains the only comprehensive view of how community corrections works in practice. A summary of highlights from 1995 follows, taken from *Characteristics of Adults on Probation, 1995* (U.S. Bureau of Justice Statistics, Washington, D.C., December 1997).

• Nearly all probationers surveyed (98.6 percent) had been released under some kind of special condition. The most common condition was a requirement to pay fines, fees, and court costs (85.3 percent). Restitution was one form of financial condition. Nearly a third of probationers (32.5 percent) were required to undergo drug testing, a higher percentage (41 percent) to take part in drug/alcohol treatment programs. Slightly more than a third had to obtain and to maintain a job. And a quarter of probationers (25.7 percent) had to perform community service.

• Most probationers had regular contact with probation officers (71.7 percent), usually by office visits but also by holding meetings in the "field" or by regular telephone conversations.

• Slightly more than half of probationers in 1995 had had a prior criminal history (50.1 percent), most as adult offenders, some as juveniles. At the time of the survey, nearly one in five had had a formal disciplinary hearing in connection with a new offense, failure to report, or failure to pay fines or to make restitution.

• The smallest number had been sentenced for violent crimes (17.3 percent), the greatest number for public order offenses (31.1 percent), the rest had been sentenced for property crimes (28.9 percent) or drug offenses (21.4 percent).

• The sentences ranged in length from less than 6 months (21.8 percent of probationers) to 36 months or more (14.1 percent of probationers).

FIGURE 8.2

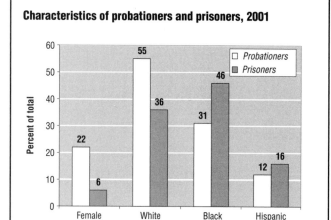

Characteristics of probationers and prisoners, 2001

Note: Other races (Asian, Pacific Islander, American Indian) are 2 percent for both groups. Whites and blacks are non-Hispanic. Hispanics may be of any race.

SOURCE: Adapted from Lauren E. Glaze, "Table 4. Characteristics of adults on probation, 1990, 1995, and 2001," in *Probation and Parole in the United States, 2001*, U.S. Bureau of Justice Statistics, Washington, DC, August 2002 and Paige M. Harrison and Allen J. Beck, "Table 15. Number of sentenced prisoners under State or Federal Juristidction, by gender, race, Hispanic origin, and age, 2001," in *Prisoners in 2001*, U.S. Bureau of Justice Statistics, Washington, DC, July 2002

FIGURE 8.3

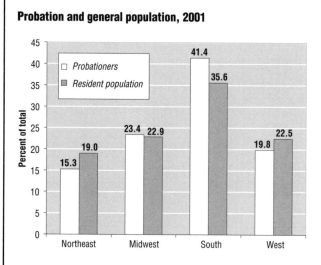

Probation and general population, 2001

SOURCE: Adapted from Lauren E. Glaze, "Table 2. Adults on probation, 2001," in *Probation and Parole in the United States, 2001*, U.S. Bureau of Justice Statistics, Washington, DC, August 2002 and "No. 18. Resident Population–States: 1980 to 2000," in *Statistical Abstract of the United States: 2001*, U.S. Census Bureau, Washington, DC, 2001

Probation Officers

Community corrections has a cost to the community—although it is lower than the cost of housing and feeding prisoners and providing them with health care. A major part of that cost is the employment of skilled probation officers to supervise probationers.

In 1975 the U.S. government employed 1,377 probation officers to supervise 64,261 federal probationers, a ratio of one officer per 47 probationers. By 1999, the last year for which an enumeration of officers is available, 3,913 officers supervised 97,190 probationers, around 25 per officer. Midway through this period, in 1987, the ratio was 39 probationers per officer. (See Table 8.5.) The federal government was expending resources to lower the ratio of probationers to officers. Between 1975 and 1987, the federal probation population grew at an average annual rate of 1.1 percent, the officer force at the rate of 2.6 percent. In the next 12 years, probationers increased at an average rate of 2.4 percent a year, officers at the rate of 6.3 percent.

Similar data for state and local probation officers are not available from the BJS, and occupational data at the level of "probation officer" are also not reported by the Bureau of Labor Statistics. One of the reports available is a New York State Senate report (Catherine M. Abate, "Putting Safety First: A Look at Probation Services in New York State," March 1998). According to that study, the national ratio of probationers to probation officers in 1994 was 258 (citing *The Corrections Yearbook of 1995:*

Probation and Parole). In New York State, in 1998, the ratio was 120 to 1, in the City of New York 230 to 1. The ideal ratio, according to the senate report, is 30 probationers per officer, a ratio the federal government reached in 1991. The availability of adequate staff to supervise probationers is a factor in reducing recidivism rates. As shown in Table 8.2 earlier, the percentage of probationers completing probation successfully declined from 69 percent in 1990 to 62 percent in 1995, the same rate as in 2001.

PAROLE

Trends in Parole

According to a survey conducted by the National Institute of Corrections, U.S. Department of Justice, *Status Report on Parole, 1995: Results of an NIC Survey* (Washington, D.C., November 1995), conflicting policy pressures were changing the manner in which parole was administered in 1995. These pressures came from "legislators seeking ways to be tougher on criminals" by making them serve all or a fixed proportion of their sentences. This had led to changes in some state laws that, in effect, "abolished parole" by taking discretion out of the hands of parole boards. These policies resulted in prison crowding in many jurisdictions sometimes managed by releasing prisoners to alleviate crowding with little or no involvement of parole boards. Prisoners thus released were often rearrested for new crimes or for violating release conditions and had to be recommitted. The situation described by the NIC in 1995 was still much the same in 2001 as reported by the Bureau of Justice Statistics. Discretionary releases of prisoners by parole boards were decreasing as a

TABLE 8.3

Adults on probation, 2001

Region and jurisdiction	Probation population, 12/31/01	Number on probation per 100,000 adult residents, 12/31/01	Region and jurisdiction	Probation population, 12/31/01	Number on probation per 100,000 adult residents, 12/31/01
U.S. total	3,932,751	1,849	Arkansas	26,558	1,319
			Delaware	19,995	3,321
Federal	31,561	15	D. of Columbia	10,468	2,291
State	3,901,190	1,834	Florida	294,626	2,304
			Georgia[2]	358,030	--
Northeast	596,189	1,462	Kentucky	21,993	716
Connecticut	49,832	1,928	Louisiana	35,744	1,101
Maine	8,939	906	Maryland	80,708	2,006
Massachusetts	44,119	904	Mississippi	15,435	741
New Hampshire[1]	3,665	385	North Carolina	110,676	1,776
New Jersey	132,846	2,075	Oklahoma[1]	30,269	1,179
New York	196,835	1,374	South Carolina	42,408	1,388
Pennsylvania	125,928	1,344	Tennessee	41,089	946
Rhode Island[1]	24,759	3,049	Texas	443,684	2,873
Vermont	9,266	1,988	Virginia	37,882	694
			West Virginia	6,176	441
Midwest	914,606	1,903			
Illinois	141,508	1,532	**West**	774,037	1,630
Indiana	112,701	2,481	Alaska	4,855	1,091
Iowa	20,797	950	Arizona	63,082	1,598
Kansas	15,250	769	California[1]	350,768	1,388
Michigan	176,406	2,385	Colorado	56,567	1,702
Minnesota	113,613	3,081	Hawaii	15,581	1,675
Missouri	55,767	1,327	Idaho[3]	35,670	3,747
Nebraska	20,847	1,651	Montana	6,258	928
North Dakota	2,901	613	Nevada	10,454	654
Ohio	195,403	2,302	New Mexico	10,335	782
South Dakota	4,462	805	Oregon[1]	46,540	1,770
Wisconsin	54,951	1,362	Utah	10,331	667
			Washington	159,119	3,551
South	1,616,358	2,117	Wyoming	4,477	1,223
Alabama	40,617	1,215			

--Not calculated

[1] All data were estimated

[2] Counts include private agency cases and may overstate the number under supervision.

[3] Counts include estimates for misdemeanors based on annual admissions.

SOURCE: Adapted from Lauren E. Glaze, "Table 2. Adults on probation, 2001," in *Probation and Parole in the United States, 2001*, U.S. Bureau of Justice Statistics, Washington, DC, August 2002

percentage of all releases; mandatory parole releases were up; and more prisoners served out their full sentences. (See Figure 8.4.) In 1995, 17 states had abolished discretionary parole according to the NIC. A more recent BJS report shows that in 2000 some 20 states had done so. (See Table 8.6.)

Discretionary parole is administered by parole boards. Their members examine the criminal history of prisoners and the candidates' prison records and reach decisions on whether to release a prisoner from incarceration now or not. In 1980, 54.8 percent of prisoners released from state institutions for any reason left prison under discretionary paroles (74.7 percent of all those paroled). By 1999, 23.7 percent left prison by the decision of parole boards (36.6 percent of all parolees). (See Figure 8.4.) The proportion had dropped again to 36 percent of all parolees by 2001.

Mandatory parole is legislatively imposed at the state level and, with some exceptions, takes away the discretion of parole boards. The following quotation from the NIC survey (*Status Report on Parole, 1995: Results of an NIC Survey*, p. 7) explains the situation:

> To ensure that offenders—especially violent or repeat offenders—are held in prison for longer periods of time, legislatures have been revising their criminal codes. The new codes often limit discretion both at the front end, at sentencing, as well as at the back end, parole. Legislatures nationwide have passed truth-in-sentencing statutes, establishing new mandatory minimum sentences, eliminating statutory and/or earned good time, and generally revised their sentencing codes in the direction of greater determinacy. These measures have, in effect, delayed parole eligibility for the offenders affected. The net result is that, in at least half of the jurisdictions studied, certain categories of offenders are required to serve substantially longer time before they can be considered for parole than they would have five years ago.

Mandatory parole provisions ensure that sentences for the same crime require incarceration for the same length of time. The prisoner can shorten his or her sentence only by good behavior—but time off for good behavior is also prohibited in some states. In some jurisdictions parole can only begin after prisoners have served 100 percent of their minimum sentences (Idaho, Nevada, and New Hampshire).

Other modes of release include release upon the expiration of the imposed sentence, medical parole, work-release, pardons, and other forms of conditional or unconditional release.

In the 1980s and 1990s, as shown in Figure 8.4, parole as a form of release diminished. In 1980, 73.4 percent of prisoners were released by parole (discretionary or mandatory), 14.3 percent because their sentences had expired, and 12.3 percent for all other reasons (which include prisoners' health conditions, work release programs, pardons, re-releases of parole violators, and other conditional or unconditional releases). In 1999, 64.8 percent of prisoners were paroled, 18.1 percent were released because they had served out their sentences, and 17.1 percent were released under other programs, some conditional, others unconditional.

Table 8.7 shows growth trends in state prisoners and state parolees from 1980 to 2000. The data highlight looser and tighter management of parole as one method of corrections. In the 1980 to 1990 period, the number of persons on parole increased 155.2 percent (an average of 9.8 percent a year). During this same time, the number of prisoners grew more slowly (131.9 percent in the period, 8.8 percent a year). From 1990 to 2000, when more and more legislative changes at the state level were taking effect, the number of persons on parole grew 29.9 percent for the period, an average of 2.6 percent a year, while the prison population grew 74.5 percent, or 5.7 percent on average a year.

TABLE 8.4

State rankings by probations functions, 2001

10 States with the largest 2001 probation populations	Number supervised	10 States with the largest percent increase	Percent increase, 2000-01	10 States with the highest rates of super-vision, 2001	Persons supervised per 100,000 adult U.S. residents*	10 States with the lowest rates of supervision, 2001	Persons supervised per 100,000 adult U.S. residents*
Texas	443,684	Maine	14.8 %	Idaho	3,747	New Hampshire	385
California	350,768	Colorado	12.1	Washington	3,551	West Virginia	441
Florida	294,626	Kentucky	12.1	Delaware	3,321	North Dakota	613
New York	196,835	Virginia	11.6	Minnesota	3,081	Nevada	654
Ohio	195,403	Wyoming	8.8	Rhode Island	3,049	Utah	667
Michigan	176,406	South Dakota	5.9	Texas	2,873	Virginia	694
Washington	159,119	Arizona	5.5	Indiana	2,481	Kentucky	716
Illinois	141,508	Utah	5.4	Michigan	2,385	Mississippi	741
New Jersey	132,846	New York	5.3	Florida	2,304	Kansas	769
Pennsylvania	125,928	Missouri	4.6	Ohio	2,302	New Mexico	782

Note: This table excludes the District of Columbia, a wholly urban jurisdiction, and Georgia probation counts, which included case-based counts for private agencies.
*Rates are computed using the estimated U.S. adult resident population on July 1, 2001.

SOURCE: Adapted from Lauren E. Glaze, "Table 1. Community corrections among the States, yearend 2001," in *Probation and Parole in the United States, 2001*, U.S. Bureau of Justice Statistics, Washington, DC, August 2002

TABLE 8.5

Persons under the supervision of the Federal Probation System and authorized probation officers, 1975–2001

Year	Number of persons under supervision	Number of probation officers	Year	Number of persons under supervision	Number of probation officers
1975	64,261	1,377	1989	77,284	2,146
1976	64,246	1,452	1990	80,592	2,361
1977	64,427	1,578	1991	83,012	2,802
1978	66,681	1,604	1992	85,920	3,316
1979	66,087	1,604	1993	86,823	3,516[1]
1980	64,450	1,604	1994	89,103	NA
1981	59,016	1,534	1995	85,822	NA
1982	58,373	1,637	1996	88,966	3,473
1983	60,180	1,574	1997	91,434	3,603
1984	63,092	1,690	1998	93,737	3,842
1985	65,999	1,758	1999	97,190	3,913
1986	69,656	1,847	2000	100,395	NA
1987	73,432	1,879	2001	104,715	NA
1988	76,366	2,046			

Note: The "number of probationers" data for 1975–87 are reported for the 12-month period ending June 30. Beginning in 1988, these data are reported for the federal fiscal year, which is the 12-month period ending September 30. The "number of probation officers" data for 1975–90 are reported as of June 30. Beginning in 1991, these data are reported as of September 30.
[1] Approximate.

SOURCE: Kathleen Maguire and Ann L. Pastore, eds. "Table 6.7: Persons under supervision of the Federal Probation System and authorized probation officers," in *Sourcebook of Criminal Justice Statistics 2001*, U.S. Bureau of Justice Statistics, Washington, DC, 2002

Characteristics of Parolees

In 2001, 12 percent of parolees were women, 39 percent were white, 41 percent were black, and 19 percent were of Hispanic origin. (See Table 8.8.) American Indians and Alaska Natives were 1 percent of parolees as were Asians, Pacific Islanders, and Native Hawaiians as a group. In general, the gender and racial/ethnic distribution of parolees more closely matched that of the prison population than the distribution of people on probation matched the prison population. (See Figure 8.2 and Figure 8.5.) There were some differences between parolees and prisoners, including proportionally more females on parole than in prison and proportionally more parolees being white and Hispanic. A lower percentage of blacks were on parole (41 percent) than in prison (46 percent).

More parolees than probationers were under the active supervision of parole officers (84 percent compared to 74 percent of those on probation). Of parolees leaving this status, fewer did so successfully in 2001 than probationers (46 versus 62 percent of probationers). (See Table 8.8.) Parolees, of course, were more serious offenders as a group, 95 percent having been sentenced to one year or more of prison for felonies. More than half of all parolees (55 percent) received this status as a consequence of mandatory parole requirements. Thirty-six percent were granted parole at the discretion of parole boards. Some parolees (7 percent) abscond—fail to report as required. Some are reinstated every year after disciplinary hearings. In 2000, 7 percent of those entering parole did so through reinstatement. Another 2 percent were given parole by other means not spelled out by the BJS.

Parole Geography

The fewest parolees in the nation were in Maine in 2001, 3 per 100,000 of population. The highest number proportionally to population occurred in Pennsylvania (921 per 100,000 adult residents) and in the District of Columbia (974 per 100,000 adult residents). The U.S. average was 350, a value that also includes those on parole from federal institutions. (See Table 8.9.) California and Texas, first and second in total population in the nation,

FIGURE 8.4

Percent of releases from state prison by method, 1980–99

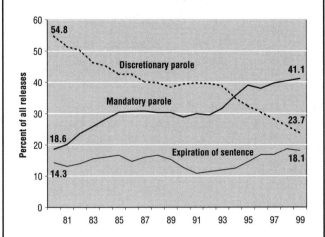

Note: Excludes releases for all other reasons, including prisoner's health condition, work release programs, pardons, re-releases of parole violators, and other conditional or unconditional releases.

SOURCE: Adapted from Timothy Hughes and Doris James Wilson, "Percent of releases from State prison by method, 1980–99," in *Reentry Trends in the U.S.,* U.S. Bureau of Justice Statistics, Washington, DC, October 8, 2002 [Online] http://www.ojp.usdoj.gov/bjs/reentry/tables/methodtab.htm [accessed April 30, 2003]

TABLE 8.7

Number of persons in state prison and on parole, yearend 1980, 1985, and 1990–2000

Year	State prisoners[1] Number	State prisoners[1] Percent change	State parolees[2] Number	State parolees[2] Percent change
1980	305,458		196,786	
1985	462,284		283,139	
1990	708,393		502,134	
1991	753,951	6.4%	568,887	13.3%
1992	802,241	6.4	618,689	8.8
1993	879,714	9.7	620,390	0.3
1994	959,668	9.1	628,941	1.4
1995	1,025,624	6.9	627,960	-0.2
1996	1,076,375	4.9	620,498	-1.2
1997	1,127,686	4.8	631,275	1.7
1998	1,176,055	4.3	629,216	-0.3
1999	1,228,455	4.5	643,452	2.3
2000	1,236,476	0.7	652,199	1.4
Percent change,				
1980-90		131.9%		155.2%
1990-2000		74.5%		29.9%
Average annual change,				
1980-90		8.8%		9.8%
1990-2000		5.7%		2.6%

Note: Counts are for December 31 of each year and may have been revised based on the most recently reported counts.
[1] Based on prisoners under the jurisdiction of state correctional authorities.
[2] Adult state parolees only.

SOURCE: Timothy A. Hughes, Doris James Wilson, and Allen J. Beck, "Table 1. Number of persons in State prison and on parole, yearend 1980, 1985, and 1990–2000," in *Trends in State Parole, 1990–2000,* U.S. Bureau of Justice Statistics, Washington, DC, October 2001

TABLE 8.6

States that have abolished discretionary parole, 2000

All offenders		Certain violent offenders
Arizona	Minnesota	Alaska
California[1]	Mississippi	Louisiana
Delaware	North Carolina	New York
Florida[2]	Ohio[4]	Tennessee
Illinois	Oregon	
Indiana	Virginia	
Kansas[3]	Washington	
Maine	Wisconsin	

[1] In 1976 the Uniform Determinate Sentencing Act abolished discretionary parole for all offenses except some violent crimes with long sentence or a sentence to life.
[2] In 1995 parole eligibility was abolished for offenses with a life sentence and a 25-year mandatory term.
[3] Excludes a few offenses, primarily 1st-degree murder and intentional 2nd-degree murder.
[4] Excludes murder and aggravated murder.

SOURCE: Timothy A. Hughes, Doris James Wilson, and Allen J. Beck, "States that have abolished discretionary parole, 2000," in *Trends in State Parole, 1990–2000*, U.S. Bureau of Justice Statistics, Washington, DC, October 2001

were also first and second in number of people on parole. (See Table 8.10.) In the 2000 to 2001 period, parole population grew most in Oklahoma. The population nearly doubled, growing at 86.6 percent. The next three states leading growth were Idaho (19.7 percent), Arkansas (19 percent), and Montana (14.3 percent).

Comparing the distribution of parole populations to the general population, data for 2001 show a pattern roughly similar to that for probationers, but inverted. (See Figure 8.6.) The Midwest and the South had proportionately more probationers than resident population. In the case of parolees, these regions had lower percentages of parolees than population in 2001, most pronouncedly in the Midwest, where the spread was 6.9 percent—16 percent of parolees, 22.9 percent of population. At the same time, the Northeast and the West, which had proportionately fewer probationers, had more parolees, especially in the Northeast, where the spread was 5.6 percent—24.6 percent of all parolees, 19 percent of the population.

Parole Violation and Rearrest Trends

As shown in Table 8.8, some 50 percent of individuals on parole completed their sentences successfully in 1990. By 2001, only 46 percent of paroles ended successfully. Another view of failed parole is presented by statistics collected by the BJS which track admissions to state prison. In 1980, 83 percent of those admitted to prison were new court commitments; 17 percent were parole violators. By 1999, 65 percent of new admissions were new commitments; admissions due to parole violations had increased to 35 percent of all admissions. (See Figure 8.7.)

TABLE 8.8

Characteristics of adults on parole, 1990, 1995, and 2001

Characteristic	1990	1995	2001		Characteristic	1990	1995	2001
Total	100%	100%	100%		**Adults entering parole**			
					Discretionary parole	59%	50%	36%
Gender					Mandatory parole	41	45	55
Male	92%	90%	88%		Reinstatement	**	4	7
Female	8	10	12		Other	**	2	2
Race[1]					**Adults leaving parole**			
White	36%	34%	39%		Successful completion	50%	45%	46%
Black	46	45	41		Returned to			
Hispanic	18	21	19		incarceration	46	41	40
American Indian/Alaska Native	1	1	1		With new sentence	17	12	9
Asian/Pacific Islander[2]	--	--	1		Other	29	29	30
Status of supervision					Absconder[3]	1	**	9
Active	82%	78%	84%		Other unsuccessful	1	**	2
Inactive	6	11	4		Transferred	1	2	1
Absconded	6	6	7		Death	1	1	1
Supervised out of state	6	4	5		Other	**	10	1
Other	**	--	--					
Sentence length								
Less than 1 year	5%	6%	5%					
1 year or more	95	94	95					

Note: For every characteristic there were persons of unknown status or type. Detail may not sum to total because of rounding.

** Not available.

-- Less than 0.5%

[1] In 2001 race/Hispanic origin was collected as a single item. For comparison, percents were recalculated for prior years.

[2] Includes Native Hawaiians.

[3] In 1995 absconder status was reported among "other."

[4] In 2001 type of offense was limited to three categories. Driving while intoxicated was reported under the "most serious offense" category. For comparison, percents were recalculated for prior years.

SOURCE: Lauren E. Glaze, "Table 7. Characteristics of adults on parole, 1990, 1995, and 2001," in *Probation and Parole in the United States, 2001*, U.S. Bureau of Justice Statistics, Washington, DC, August 2002

FIGURE 8.5

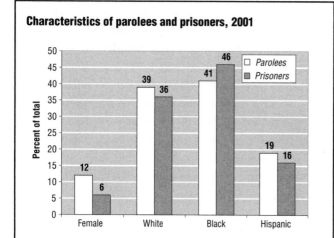

Characteristics of parolees and prisoners, 2001

Note: Other races (Asian, Pacific Islander, American Indian) are 2 percent for both groups. Whites and blacks are non-Hispanic. Hispanics may be of any race.

SOURCE: Adapted from Lauren E. Glaze, "Table 7. Characteristics of adults on parole, 1990, 1995, and 2001," in *Probation and Parole in the United States, 2001*, U.S. Bureau of Justice Statistics, Washington, DC, August 2002 and Paige M. Harrison and Allen J. Beck, "Table 15. Number of sentenced prisoners under State or Federal juristidcction, by gender, race, Hispanic origin, and age, 2001," in *Prisoners in 2001*, U.S. Bureau of Justice Statistics, Washington, DC, July 2002

These data are from the same period during which discretionary paroles granted by parole boards declined from 54.8 to 23.7 percent of all releases and mandatory paroles, set by law, increased from 18.6 percent to 41.1 percent of all releases. (See Figure 8.4.) The BJS does not report a causal link between methods of granting parole and parole violation/rearrest trends. Data on the most serious offenses of parole violations, published for 1991 and 1997 (*Trends in State Parole, 1990–2000*, U.S. Bureau of Justice Statistics, Washington, D.C., 2001) indicate that those with violent offenses declined from 35.9 to 33.7 percent of parole violators, 1991 to 1997, those with property offenses declined from 35.8 to 30.1 percent, but drug violators increased as a proportion of parole violators from 19.3 to 22.1, and those with public order violations (which include serious cases of drunken driving) increased 8.7 to 12.9 percent. More recent data at this level of detail were not available in mid-2003.

In 1999, 14 states experienced prison admissions for parole violation at a higher rate than the national average of 34.8 percent of all admissions. (See Table 8.11.) The highest rates were experienced in California (67.2 percent), Utah (55.3 percent), and Louisiana (53.1 percent). In these states, in effect, more prisoners were admitted for violating parole than individuals who were committed for

TABLE 8.9

Adults on parole, 2001

Region and jurisdiction	Parole population, 12/31/01	Number on parole per 100,000 adult residents, 12/31/01	Region and jurisdiction	Parole population, 12/31/01	Number on parole per 100,000 adult residents, 12/31/01
U.S. total	723,898	350	Arkansas	8,659	517
			Delaware	579	90
Federal	76,069	37	D. of Columbia	5,332	974
State	647,829	312	Florida	5,982	48
			Georgia[2]	21,556	346
Northeast	159,653	402	Kentucky	4,614	171
Connecticut	1,868	83	Louisiana	22,860	718
Maine	28	3	Maryland	13,666	340
Massachusetts	3,703	77	Mississippi[2]	1,596	86
New Hampshire[1]	944	103	North Carolina	3,352	49
New Jersey	11,709	189	Oklahoma[1]	1,825	133
New York	57,858	397	South Carolina	4,378	137
Pennsylvania	82,345	921	Tennessee	8,093	188
Rhode Island[1]	331	47	Texas[1]	111,719	720
Vermont	867	195	Virginia	5,148	91
			West Virginia	1,112	67
Midwest	103,331	220			
Illinois	30,196	329	**West**	158,890	351
Indiana[2]	4,917	118	Alaska	525	120
Iowa	2,763	140	Arizona[2]	3,474	94
Kansas[2]	3,829	202	California[2]	117,647	479
Michigan	15,753	225	Colorado	5,500	179
Minnesota	3,072	87	Hawaii	2,504	285
Missouri	12,563	309	Idaho	1,409	182
Nebraska	476	42	Montana[2]	621	106
North Dakota	110	24	Nevada	4,056	304
Ohio	18,248	211	New Mexico	1,670	133
South Dakota[1]	1,481	277	Oregon	17,579	729
Wisconsin	9,923	242	Utah	3,231	229
			Washington[1]	160	4
South	225,955	299	Wyoming	514	153
Alabama	5,484	170			

-- Not calculated.

[1] All data were estimated.

[2] Data do not include parolees in one or more of the following categories: absconder, out of state, or inactive.

SOURCE: Adapted from Lauren E. Glaze, "Table 5. Adults on parole, 2001," in *Probation and Parole in the United States, 2001*, U.S. Bureau of Justice Statistics, Washington, DC, August 2002

new violations by the courts. Among the 36 states with lower than the national average, those with the lowest were Florida (6.9 percent), Alabama (9.3 percent), Indiana (9.6 percent), and Mississippi and West Virginia (both with 9.7 percent).

TABLE 8.10

State rankings by parole functions, 2001

10 States with the largest 2001 parole populations	Number supervised	10 States with the largest percent increase	Percent increase, 2000-01	10 States with the highest rates of supervision, 2001	Persons supervised per 100,000 adult U.S. residents*	10 States with the lowest rates of supervision, 2001	Persons supervised per 100,000 adult U.S. residents*
California	117,904	Oklahoma	86.6 %	Pennsylvania	921	Maine	3
Texas	107,688	Idaho	19.7	Oregon	729	Washington	4
Pennsylvania	86,238	Arkansas	19.0	Texas	720	North Dakota	24
New York	56,719	Montana	14.3	Louisiana	718	Nebraska	42
Illinois	30,157	Connecticut	13.8	Arkansas	517	Rhode Island	47
Louisiana	23,330	Rhode Island	13.3	California	479	Florida	48
Georgia	20,809	Kentucky	12.7	New York	397	North Carolina	49
Oregon	18,761	Mississippi	12.0	Georgia	346	West Virginia	67
Ohio	17,885	Nevada	11.4	Maryland	340	Massachusetts	77
Michigan	16,501	Nebraska	11.3	Illinois	329	Connecticut	83

Note: This table excludes the District of Columbia, a wholly urban jurisdiction.
*Rates are computed using the estimated U.S. adult resident population on July 1, 2001.

SOURCE: Adapted from Lauren E. Glaze, "Table 1. Community corrections among the States, yearend 2001," in *Probation and Parole in the United States, 2001*, U.S. Bureau of Justice Statistics, Washington, DC, August 2002

FIGURE 8.6

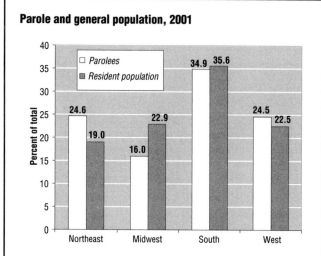

SOURCE: Adapted from Lauren E. Glaze, "Table 5. Adults on parole, 2001," in *Probation and Parole in the United States, 2001*, U.S. Bureau of Justice Statistics, Washington, DC, August 2002 and "No. 18. Resident Population–States: 1980 to 2000," in *Statistical Abstract of the United States: 2001*, U.S. Census Bureau, Washington, DC, 2001

FIGURE 8.7

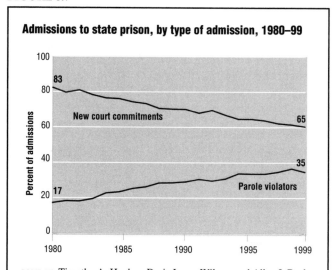

SOURCE: Timothy A. Hughes, Doris James Wilson, and Allen J. Beck, "Figure 4. Admissions to State prison, by type of admission, 1980–99," in *Trends in State Parole, 1990–2000*, U.S. Bureau of Justice Statistics, Washington, DC, October 2001

TABLE 8.11

Percent parole violators among admissions to state prison, 1990 and 1999

Region and jurisdiction	Percent of admissions that were parole violators		Region and jurisdiction	Percent of admissions that were parole violators	
	1990	1999		1990	1999
All States[1]	28.8%	34.8%	Florida	5.3	6.9
			Georgia	21.1	20.5
Northeast			Kentucky	27.5	31.9
Connecticut	43.4%	17.4%	Louisiana	14.7	53.1
Maine	21.3	40.9	Maryland	13.8	32.6
Massachusetts	31.4	22.7	Mississippi	13.9	9.7
New Hampshire	19.3	31.6	North Carolina	13.0	12.8
New Jersey	20.8	35.5	Oklahoma	3.4	14.1
New York	18.1	31.5	South Carolina	22.8	24.1
Pennsylvania	26.1	36.1	Tennessee	32.9	36.2
Rhode Island	24.9	19.0	Texas	37.1	21.0
Vermont	14.5	17.0	Virginia	10.2	11.1
			West Virginia	13.0	9.7
Midwest					
Illinois	25.4%	27.3%	**West**		
Indiana	5.3	9.6	Alaska	14.0%	44.2%
Iowa	26.7	19.3	Arizona	14.0	23.0
Kansas	35.0	38.2	California	58.1	67.2
Michigan	23.2	36.8	Colorado	20.9	37.1
Minnesota	23.1	32.1	Hawaii	27.7	49.1
Missouri	26.2	38.8	Idaho	20.4	32.2
Nebraska	16.3	16.1	Montana[2]	19.9	--
North Dakota	13.8	18.7	Nevada	18.6	17.7
Ohio	12.9	17.6	New Mexico	28.4	35.7
South Dakota	17.7	20.7	Oregon	48.0	25.1
Wisconsin	19.2	31.2	Utah	51.0	55.3
			Washington	13.0	10.5
South			Wyoming	6.4	34.5
Alabama	25.9%	9.3%			
Arkansas	22.4	25.3			
Delaware	6.2	25.3			

Note: Based on data from the National Prisoner Statistics (NPS-1) series.
-- Not reported.
[1] Excludes the District of Columbia.
[2] Parole violators comprised 9.5% of admissions in 1999; however, data on other persons returned after post-custody supervision were not available.

SOURCE: Timothy A. Hughes, Doris James Wilson, and Allen J. Beck, "Table 19. Percent parole violators among admissions to State prison, 1990 and 1999," in *Trends in State Parole, 1990–2000*, U.S. Bureau of Justice Statistics, Washington, DC, October 2001

CHAPTER 9
SENTENCING

Sentencing reform policies have paralleled the mood of the country on crime and punishment, shifting between requiring a fixed prison time prior to release or allowing discretionary release of offenders by judges, parole boards, or corrections officials. Over the last two decades, sentencing requirements and release policies have become more restrictive, primarily in response to widespread "get tough on crime" attitudes in the Nation.

—Paula M. Ditton and Doris James Wilson, *Truth in Sentencing in State Prisons*, Bureau of Justice Statistics, January 1999

Sentencing policies have changed since the 1980s in response to rising crime rates. Prison populations began increasing in 1973 from a rate of 96 prisoners per 100,000 adult residents in the United States to 470 per 100,000 in 2001. (See Table 9.1.) The 96 per 100,000 rate was one of the lowest, matched, for instance, by the rate in 1928. The average imprisonment rate during the 1925–73 period was 107 prisoners per 100,000 people. The highest rate in this time period was reached in 1939 when 137 people were incarcerated in state and federal prisons per 100,000 residents. The average in the period 1974–2001 was 271. The rate increased every year in this later period from 102 in 1974 to 470 in 2001.

The period of expanding incarceration also coincided with emphasis at state and federal levels on controlling the use and distribution of drugs. The first legislation against drugs was the Harrison Act enacted in 1914; it outlawed opiates and cocaine. The "war" was declared in the early 1970s when the National Commission on Marihuana and Drug Abuse (also known as the Shafer Commission) published its recommendation that marijuana be legalized (*Marihuana: A Signal of Misunderstanding*, Report of the National Commission on Marihuana and Drug Abuse, March 1972 [Online] http://www.cognitiveliberty.org/news/schafer.htm [accessed May 6, 2003]). The commission was appointed by President Richard Nixon, who later rejected the commission's recommendation and declared war on drugs.

TABLE 9.1

Sentenced state and federal prisoners per 100,000 residents, 1925–2001

Rate per 100,000 resident population					
Year	Rate	Year	Rate	Year	Rate
1925	79	1951	107	1977	129
1926	83	1952	107	1978	132
1927	91	1953	108	1979	133
1928	96	1954	112	1980	139
1929	98	1955	112	1981	154
1930	104	1956	112	1982	171
1931	110	1957	113	1983	179
1932	110	1958	117	1984	188
1933	109	1959	117	1985	202
1934	109	1960	117	1986	217
1935	113	1961	119	1987	231
1936	113	1962	117	1988	247
1937	118	1963	114	1989	276
1938	123	1964	111	1990	297
1939	137	1965	108	1991	313
1940	131	1966	102	1992	332
1941	124	1967	98	1993	359
1942	112	1968	94	1994	389
1943	103	1969	97	1995	411
1944	100	1970	96	1996	427
1945	98	1971	95	1997	444
1946	99	1972	93	1998	461
1947	105	1973	96	1999	473
1948	106	1974	102	2000	469
1949	109	1975	111	2001	470
1950	109	1976	120		

Note: Prison population data are compiled by a yearend census of prisoners in state and federal institutions. Data for 1925 through 1939 include sentenced prisoners in state and federal prisons and reformatories whether committed for felonies or misdemeanors. Data for 1940 through 1970 include all adult felons serving sentences in state and federal institutions. Since 1971, the census has included all adults or youthful offenders sentenced to a state or federal correctional institution with maximum sentences of over 1 year.

SOURCE: Adapted from Kathleen Maguire and Ann L. Pastore, eds., "Table 6.23: Number and rate (per 100,000 resident population in each group) of sentenced prisoners under jurisdiction of State and Federal correctional authorities on December 31," in *Sourcebook of Criminal Justice Statistics 2001*, U.S. Bureau of Justice Statistics, Washington, DC, 2002

TABLE 9.2

Truth-in-sentencing requirements, by state, 1999

Meet federal 85% requirement		50% requirement	100% minimum requirement	Other requirements
Arizona	Missouri	Indiana	Idaho	Alaska[3]
California	New Jersey	Maryland	Nevada	Arkansas[4]
Connecticut	New York	Nebraska	New Hampshire	Colorado[5]
Delaware	North Carolina	Texas		Kentucky[6]
D. of Columbia	North Dakota			Massachusetts[7]
Florida	Ohio			Wisconsin[8]
Georgia	Oklahoma[2]			Montana[9]
Illinois[1]	Oregon			
Iowa	Pennsylvania			
Kansas	South Carolina			
Louisiana	Tennessee			
Maine	Utah			
Michigan	Virginia			
Minnesota	Washington			
Mississippi				

[1] Qualified for federal funding in 1996 only.
[2] Effective July 1, 1999, offenders will be required to serve 85% of the sentence.
[3] Two-part sentence structure (2/3 in prison; 1/3 on parole); 100% of prison term required.
[4] Mandatory 70% of sentence for certain violent offenses and manufacture of methamphetamine.
[5] Violent offenders with 2 prior violent convictions serve 75%, 1 prior violent conviction, 56.25%.
[6] Effective July 15, 1998, offenders are required to serve 85% of the sentence.
[7] Requires 75% of a minimum prison sentence.
[8] Effective December 31, 1999, two-part sentence: offenders serve 100% of the prison term and a sentence of extended supervision at 25% of the prison sentence.
[9] Added based on William J. Sabol et al., *The Influences of Truth-in-Sentencing Reforms on Changes in States' Sentencing Practices and Prison Populations*, The Urban Institute, Washington, DC, April 2002.

SOURCE: Adapted from Paula M. Ditton and Doris James Wilson, "Table 1. Truth-in-sentencing requirements, by State," in *Truth in Sentencing in State Prisons*, U.S. Bureau of Justice Statistics, Washington, DC, January 1999 and William J. Sabol et al., "Table 1.4. State truth-in-sentencing laws," in *The Influences of Truth-in-Sentencing Reforms on Changes in States' Sentencing Practices and Prison Populations*, The Urban Institute, Washington, DC, April 2002

As reported on the web page of the Bureau of Justice Statistics (BJS) (Allen Beck and Paige Harrison, "Number of persons in custody of State correctional authorities by most serious offense, 1980–2000," [Online] http://www.ojp.usdoj.gov/bjs/glance/tables/corrtyptab.htm [accessed May 7, 2003]) in 1980 prisoners in state systems incarcerated for drug offenses were 6.5 percent of the prison population. By 2000 they represented 20.9 percent of prisoners. In the 1980–2000 period, individuals serving felony sentences for drug violations increased 1,222 percent, five times as fast as prisoners serving time for violent crimes. Drug related incarcerations as well as violent crime incarcerations began to grow more sharply in the late 1980s after the introduction of crack cocaine.

It is against this background that new sentencing policies developed. Paula M. Ditton and Doris James Wilson (*Truth in Sentencing in State Prisons*, Bureau of Justice Statistics, Washington, D.C., January 1999) summarize the situation beginning with the 1970s as follows:

In the early 1970's, States generally permitted parole boards to determine when an offender would be released from prison. In addition, good-time reductions for satisfactory prison behavior, earned-time incentives for participation in work or educational programs, and other time reductions to control prison crowding resulted in the early release of prisoners. These policies permitted officials to individualize the amount of punishment or leniency an offender received and provided means to manage the prison population. Such discretion in sentencing and release policies led to criticism that some offenders were punished more harshly than others for similar offenses and to complaints that overall sentencing and release laws were too soft on criminals. By the late 1970's and early 1980's, States began developing sentencing guidelines, enacting mandatory minimum sentences and adopting other sentencing reforms to reduce disparity in sentencing and to toughen penalties for certain offenses, specifically drug offenses (as part of the "war on drugs"), offenses with weapons, and offenses committed by repeat or habitual criminals.

TRUTH-IN-SENTENCING

Sentence reforms enacted by states came to be known as "truth-in-sentencing" statutes. The first such statute was enacted by the state of Washington in 1984. According to the most recent tally conducted by the Urban Institute (William J. Sabol, et al., *The Influences of Truth-in-Sentencing Reforms on Changes in States' Sentencing Practices and Prison Populations*, Washington, D.C., April 2002) 42 states and the District of Columbia had enacted some type of truth-in-sentencing statute.

Also in 1984, Congress established the U.S. Sentencing Commission (USSC) in the Sentencing Reform Act. Congress charged this new federal agency with developing sentencing guidelines for federal courts. The Sentencing Reform Act was the federal enactment of truth-in-sentencing.

"Truth-in-sentencing," abbreviated as TIS, is intended to tell the public that a sentence announced by the court will actually be served—rather than the criminal serving only some small fraction of the sentence, the prisoner being released on parole, or the individual having the sentence commuted to probation and serving no time at all. Under TIS statutes, offenders are required to spend substantial portions of their sentences in prison. The federally recommended portion is 85 percent of the sentence. Twenty-nine states required such time to be served as of 2002.

With TIS came the distinction between indeterminate and determinate sentencing. Indeterminate sentencing gives parole boards the authority to release offenders at their option after a process of review. Determinate sentencing takes parole boards "out of the loop," fixes the term to be served, and provides or denies the means to shorten the sentence by good behavior or other "earned"

TABLE 9.3

Federal sentencing guidelines on kidnapping

§2A4.1. Kidnapping, Abduction, Unlawful Restraint

(a) Base Offense Level: **24**
(b) Specific Offense Characteristics

   (1) If a ransom demand or a demand upon government was made, increase by **6** levels.

   (2) (A) If the victim sustained permanent or life-threatening bodily injury, increase by **4** levels; (B) if the victim sustained serious bodily injury, increase by **2** levels; or (C) if the degree of injury is between that specified in subdivisions (A) and (B) increase by **3** levels.

   (3) If a dangerous weapon was used, increase by **2** levels.

   (4) (A) If the victim was not released before thirty days had elapsed, increase by **2** levels.

      (B) If the victim was not released before seven days had elapsed, increase by **1** level.

      (C) If the victim was released before twenty-four hours had elapsed, decrease by **1** level.

   (5) If victim was sexually exploited, increase by **3** levels.

   (6) If the victim is a minor and, in exchange for money or other consideration, was placed in the care or custody of another person who had no legal right to such care or custody of the victim, increase by **3** levels.

   (7) If the victim was kidnapped, abducted, or unlawfully restrained during the commission of, or in connection with, another offense or escape therefrom; or if another offense was committed during the kidnapping, abduction, or unlawful restraint, increase to --

      (A) the offense level from the Chapter Two offense guideline applicable to that other offense if such offense guideline includes an adjustment for kidnapping abduction, or unlawful restraint, or otherwise takes such conduct into account; or

      (B) **4** plus the offense level from the offense guideline applicable to that other offense, but in no event greater than level **43**, in any other case, if the resulting offense is greater than that determined above.

SOURCE: "4. Kidnapping, Abduction, or Unlawful Restraint," in *2002 Federal Sentencing Guideline Manual*, United States Sentencing Commission, Washington, DC, 2002

time. Part of the truth-in-sentencing statutes are mandatory minimum sentences specified by law for specific offenses and circumstances. Mandatory minima are published in sentencing guidelines, which judges are required to use. Guidelines define the range of sentences the judge may apply, again governed by the offense and the prior history of the offender, e.g., first-time or repeat-offender, severity of the offense, etc.

Setting uniform sentences for offenses and requiring that fixed proportions of them be served by those convicted put pressure on prison and jail capacities. In response, Congress passed the Violent Crime Control and Law Enforcement Act of 1994, known as the 1994 Crime Act. Its grant program provisions set as a requirement for funding that states have in place truth-in-sentencing statutes. Thus, the federal government provided incentives to states for enacting truth-in-sentencing laws or to conform such laws to the federal sentencing guidelines published by the USSC. Eleven states passed truth-in-sentencing laws in 1995 in response to the federal initiative.

A tabulation of states with TIS statutes is shown as Table 9.2. These data are from 1999 and show the minimum sentence required to be served in each state. Table 9.2, compiled mainly from BJS data, was amended to include Montana as of 2002 per a study issued by the Urban Institute.

The net effect of federal guidelines, the 1994 Crime Act and its financial incentives, and state actions before and after federal legislation has been to make sentencing more uniform across the nation and, at the state level, to extend the time convicted felons spend in prison.

FEDERAL SENTENCING GUIDELINES

Federal sentencing guidelines illustrate how the truth-in-sentencing approach—determinate sentencing—works in practice. The federal guidelines were originally developed by the U.S. Sentencing Commission. USSC continues to update the guidelines as laws administered by the federal courts are changed or new laws are passed. The guidelines are published as the *United States Sentencing Commission Guidelines Manual*, a 580-page document in its most recent edition (November 2002). Supplemental volumes are also issued by the USSC. All are accessible online at the USSC's web site, http://www.ussc.gov.

At the core of the guidelines are offenses as defined by federal statutes. The USSC assigns an "offense level" to each offense, known as the Base Offense Level. Levels are numbered from 1 to 43. The lowest actual offense for which the USSC has a level is Trespass. Trespass is level 4. First-degree murder has a Base Offense Level of 43. Based on various circumstances associated with an offense, additional levels may be added or taken away until a particular offense has been precisely defined by level. Levels are abstract numbers. Their purpose is to enable the judge or prosecutor to find a particular sentence, in months of imprisonment, in the federal Sentencing Table.

An illustration is provided for kidnapping, abduction, and unlawful restraint. (See Table 9.3.) The table reproduces the USSC's guideline for this offense. The offense has a Base Offense Level of 24. But additional levels can be added. Thus, for instance, if the victim sustained serious bodily injury, the level is increased by 2 to 26. If the victim was also sexually exploited, the level is increased by 3 levels to 29. But if the victim was released before 24 hours had passed, the level is decreased by 1 to 28.

In the USSC's Sentencing Table, presented as Table 9.4, level 28 points to 6 columns of sentence ranges indicating a minimum and a maximum sentence in each column. In the first column, where the sentence range is 78 to 97 months, the offender either has no prior convictions or has one prior conviction. In the sixth column, where the sentence is 140 to 175 months, the offender has 13 or more prior convictions. A single level thus provides six different levels of confinement, and, within each level, there is a range from minimum to maximum. Judges are not entirely deprived of discretion by determinate sentencing.

TABLE 9.4

Federal sentencing table, 2002

In months of imprisonment

	Offense level	I (0 or 1)	II (2 or 3)	III (4, 5, 6)	IV (7, 8, 9)	V (10, 11, 12)	VI (13 or more)
				Criminal History Category (Criminal History Points)			
Zone A	1	0-6	0-6	0-6	0-6	0-6	0-6
	2	0-6	0-6	0-6	0-6	0-6	1-7
	3	0-6	0-6	0-6	0-6	2-8	3-9
	4	0-6	0-6	0-6	2-8	4-10	6-12
	5	0-6	0-6	1-7	4-10	6-12	9-15
	6	0-6	1-7	2-8	6-12	9-15	12-18
	7	0-6	2-8	4-10	8-14	12-18	15-21
	8	0-6	4-10	6-12	10-16	15-21	18-24
Zone B	9	4-10	6-12	8-14	12-18	18-24	21-27
	10	6-12	8-14	10-16	15-21	21-27	24-30
Zone C	11	8-14	10-16	12-18	18-24	24-30	27-33
	12	10-16	12-18	15-21	21-27	27-33	30-37
Zone D	13	12-18	15-21	18-24	24-30	30-37	33-41
	14	15-21	18-24	21-27	27-33	33-41	37-46
	15	18-24	21-27	24-30	30-37	37-46	41-51
	16	21-27	24-30	27-33	33-41	41-51	46-57
	17	24-30	27-33	30-37	37-46	46-57	51-63
	18	27-33	30-37	33-41	41-51	51-63	57-71
	19	30-37	33-41	37-46	46-57	57-71	63-78
	20	33-41	37-46	41-51	51-63	63-78	70-87
	21	37-46	41-51	46-57	57-71	70-87	77-96
	22	41-51	46-57	51-63	63-78	77-96	84-105
	23	46-57	51-63	57-71	70-87	84-105	92-115
	24	51-63	57-71	63-78	77-96	92-115	100-125
	25	57-71	63-78	70-87	84-105	100-125	110-137
	26	63-78	70-87	78-97	92-115	110-137	120-150
	27	70-87	78-97	87-108	100-125	120-150	130-162
	28	78-97	87-108	97-121	110-137	130-162	140-175
	29	87-108	97-121	108-135	121-151	140-175	151-188
	30	97-121	108-135	121-151	135-168	151-188	168-210
	31	108-135	121-151	135-168	151-188	168-210	188-235
	32	121-151	135-168	151-188	168-210	188-235	210-262
	33	135-168	151-188	168-210	188-235	210-262	235-293
	34	151-188	168-210	188-235	210-262	235-293	262-327
	35	168-210	188-235	210-262	235-293	262-327	292-365
	36	188-235	210-262	235-293	262-327	292-365	324-405
	37	210-262	235-293	262-327	292-365	324-405	360-life
	38	235-293	262-327	292-365	324-405	360-life	360-life
	39	262-327	292-365	324-405	360-life	360-life	360-life
	40	292-365	324-405	360-life	360-life	360-life	360-life
	41	324-405	360-life	360-life	360-life	360-life	360-life
	42	360-life	360-life	360-life	360-life	360-life	360-life
	43	life	life	life	life	life	life

Note: Zones indicate whether or not the individual is eligible for probation. Terms that fall into Zone A are eligible for straight probation. Terms that fall into Zone B are eligible for a split sentence in which a portion of the sentence is served in prison, a portion under probation. The person may receive less than the minimum sentence but must serve the remaining time under probation, intermittent confinement, community confinement, or home detention. Terms that fall into Zone C are eligible for probation, but at least half of the guideline sentence must be served in prison. Terms that fall into Zone D require that the minimum term must be served in prison. The criminal history columns refer to prior offenses. Under Category II, for instance, the person to be sentenced has had 2 or 3 prior convictions. This note is not part of the official Sentencing Table; it has been adapted from Lucien B. Cambell and Henry J. Bemporad, *An Introduction to Federal Guideline Sentencing*, United States Sentencing Commission, Washington, DC, March 2003.

SOURCE: "Sentencing Table," in *2002 Federal Sentencing Guideline Manual*, United States Sentencing Commission, Washington, DC, 2002

TABLE 9.5

Sentences within and departing from U.S. Sentencing Commission guidelines, fiscal year 2000

Primary offense	Total number of cases	Within guideline range	Substantial assistance departure[1]	Other downward departure	Upward departure
			Downward departures		
			Percent of total –		
Total	54,569	64.5%	17.9%	17.0%	0.7%
Murder	74	66.2	13.5	10.8	9.5
Manslaughter	47	70.2	2.1	14.9	12.8
Kidnaping, hostage-taking	66	54.5	27.3	15.2	3.0
Sexual abuse	228	68.9	1.3	24.6	5.3
Assault	416	77.6	2.4	16.6	3.4
Robbery	1,596	71.1	13.1	14.5	1.3
Arson	71	66.2	22.5	11.3	-
Drug offenses					
Trafficking	22,253	56.6	27.8	15.3	0.2
Communication facility	392	67.3	22.7	9.4	0.5
Simple possession	430	93.0	3.5	2.6	0.9
Firearms	3,288	75.6	10.9	12.5	1.1
Burglary, breaking/entering	49	79.6	8.2	8.2	4.1
Auto theft	210	77.6	16.2	4.3	1.9
Larceny	2,154	84.4	6.9	7.9	0.8
Fraud	5,775	68.6	18.8	11.6	1.1
Embezzlement	874	81.2	5.5	13.0	0.2
Forgery, counterfeiting	1,242	79.6	11.5	7.8	1.0
Bribery	235	57.0	25.1	17.0	0.9
Tax	706	71.2	14.4	14.0	0.3
Money laundering	926	56.8	28.2	13.9	1.1
Racketeering, extortion	778	58.1	30.6	9.5	1.8
Gambling, lottery	91	59.3	34.1	6.6	-
Civil rights	79	67.1	17.7	15.2	-
Immigration	9,938	63.5	3.6	32.5	0.4
Pornography, prostitution	490	68.0	6.9	20.6	4.5
Prison offenses	288	82.6	5.6	11.5	0.3
Admin. of justice offenses	946	73.9	12.4	12.6	1.2
Environmental, wildlife	185	60.0	16.8	22.2	1.1
National defense	15	40.0	26.7	33.3	-
Antitrust	38	44.7	47.4	7.9	-
Food and drug	74	83.8	8.1	6.8	1.4
Other	615	80.3	11.4	8.0	0.3

Note: A case is determined to involve no departure if the sentence imposed is within the guideline range. If a sentence imposed by the court falls outside the guideline range, the court provides reasons for the departure. Of the 59,846 guideline cases, 5,277 cases were excluded due to one or both of the following conditions: missing offense type, 257; or missing/inapplicable departure information, 5,229.

[1] Cases departed downward based on motion by the government for a reduced sentence due to the defendant's substantial assistance to authorities.

SOURCE: Adapted from Kathleen Maguire and Ann L. Pastore, eds., "Table 5.34. Sentences within and departing from U.S. Sentencing Commission guidelines," in *Sourcebook of Criminal Justice Statistics 2001*, U.S. Bureau of Justice Statistics, Washington, DC, 2002 [Online] http://www.albany.edu/sourcebook/1995/wk1/t534.wk1 [accessed May 8, 2003]

Level 28 falls into the Sentencing Table's Zone D. This means that the individual may not receive any probation and must serve at least the minimum sentence shown in the applicable column. A three-time offender would be minimally sentenced to 87 months in prison and, under the USSC guidelines, could receive, maximally, 54 days off per year for good behavior and would therefore serve at least 85 percent of the minimum sentence. In the case illustrated earlier, where sexual exploitation is involved, the individual would also be charged for criminal sexual abuse (a Base Offense Level of 24) or for sexual abuse of a minor (Level 18 to 24 depending on whether the abuse was attempted or committed). Parole is not available in any of the guideline cases.

Property crimes are handled in the USSC guidelines in a similar manner. The base level is increased with the amount of property involved. With larceny, embezzlement, and other forms of theft, for instance, the Base Offense Level is 6 in cases where the loss to the victim is $5,000 or less. If the loss is greater than $5,000 but less than $10,000, the level rises to 8 and continues to rise as the amount of the loss rises. If the loss is more than $200,000 but less than $400,000, the level is 18. If the loss is greater than $100 million, the level is 32—which will result in a mandatory sentence of at least 10 years in prison for a first-time offender. A person who earned the maximum days for good behavior could expect to be out in eight years and six months if he or she received the minimum sentence. Fines and restitution of stolen money or property would be required in addition.

"Departures" from the Guidelines

Application of the Federal Sentencing Guidelines has not increased the average length of sentences. Based on data published in the *Sourcebook of Criminal Justice Statistics Online* http://www.albany.edu/sourcebook/1995/wk1/t523.wk1 [accessed May 8, 2003]) the average sentence imposed in 1990 was 59.2 months, excluding life sentences. The average length peaked at 66.4 months in 1995 and then declined to 56.5 months in 2001. This is due, in part, to stipulations in the guidelines for so-called "departures" from the guidelines' own provisions. Departures may be "upward" for cases where special circumstances merit longer incarceration than the guideline provides for the maximum sentence; "downward" departures authorize lesser than guideline sentences either for extenuating circumstances or because the defendant provided "substantial assistance" to federal authorities, typically in the form of helping a broader investigation or providing testimony against other suspects. Table 9.5 reports that in 2000 only 64.5 percent of sentences rendered by federal courts were within the guideline range; 0.7 percent of sentences were upward departures and 34.9 percent were downward departures, slightly more than half of those for "substantial assistance." Data from 1996 indicate that in that year a slightly higher percentage of cases were within the guideline, 65.5 percent.

Departures mean that the guidelines are applied to a majority but not to all persons charged with federal offenses—and also variably by category of offense. In 2000 the two highest categories under guidelines were simple possession of drugs (93 percent under guideline) and larceny (84.4 percent). The two lowest categories were offenses related to national defense (40 percent) and antitrust violations (44.7 percent). Those charged with antitrust violations were most likely to get lower sentences

TABLE 9.6

Sentence length and time served for first releases from state prison, 1990 and 1999

	Mean sentence length[1]		Mean time served in –				Total time served[3]		Percent of sentence served[4]	
			Jail[2]		Prison					
	1990	1999	1990	1999	1990	1999	1990	1999	1990	1999
All offenses	69 mo	65 mo	6 mo	5 mo	22 mo	29 mo	28 mo	34 mo	38.0%	48.7%
Violent offenses	99 mo	87 mo	7 mo	6 mo	39 mo	45 mo	46 mo	51 mo	43.8%	55.0%
Murder[5]	209	192	9	10	83	96	92	106	43.1	53.1
Manslaughter	88	102	5	6	31	49	37	56	41.0	52.5
Rape	128	124	7	6	55	73	62	79	45.5	58.3
Other sexual assault	77	76	5	6	30	42	36	47	43.8	57.0
Robbery	104	97	7	6	41	48	48	55	42.8	51.6
Assault	64	62	6	6	23	33	30	39	43.9	58.7
Property offenses	65 mo	58 mo	6 mo	5 mo	18 mo	25 mo	24 mo	29 mo	34.4%	45.6%
Burglary	79	73	6	5	22	31	29	36	33.9	44.3
Larceny/theft	52	45	6	4	14	19	20	24	35.5	46.9
Motor vehicle theft	56	44	7	5	13	20	20	25	33.1	52.5
Fraud	56	49	6	4	14	19	20	23	33.2	41.7
Drug offenses	57 mo	59 mo	6 mo	5 mo	14 mo	22 mo	20 mo	27 mo	32.9%	42.8%
Possession	61	56	6	5	12	20	18	25	29.0	42.4
Trafficking	60	64	6	5	16	24	22	29	34.8	42.0
Public-order offenses	40 mo	42 mo	5 mo	4 mo	14 mo	19 mo	18 mo	23 mo	42.6%	51.1%

Note: Based on prisoners with a sentence of more than 1 year who were released for the first time on the current sentence. Excludes prisoners released from prison by escape, death, transfer, appeal, or detainer.

[1] Maximum sentence length for the most serious offense. Excludes sentences of life, life without parole, life plus additional years, and death.

[2] Time served in jail and credited toward the current sentence.

[3] Based on time served in jail and in prison. Detail may not add to total because of rounding.

[4] Based on total sentence length (not shown) for all consecutive sentences.

[5] Includes nonnegligent manslaughter.

SOURCE: Timothy A. Hughes, Doris James Wilson, and Allen J. Beck, "Table 5. Sentence length and time served for first releases from State prison, 1990 and 1999," in *Trends in State Parole, 1990–2000*, U.S. Bureau of Justice Statistics, Washington, DC, October 2001

for cooperating with prosecutors; those charged with manslaughter were the most likely to get higher than guideline sentences for unusual violence.

STATE SENTENCES AND TIME SERVED

The adoption of truth-in-sentencing statutes appears to have resulted, at the state level, in a decrease in the *length* of sentences imposed but an increase in the total *time served*, including percent of the sentence imposed actually being spent in prison. (See Table 9.6.)

Average sentence lengths can decline while time served can stay the same or increase if mandatory time in prison, as a percent of the sentence, increases. Thus, for instance, a person sentenced to 5 years serving 60 percent of his sentence serves as long as a person sentenced to 4 years who serves 75 percent of her sentence. In both cases time served will be 3 years.

Data in Table 9.6, the most recent comprehensive statistical measurement available, show that sentence lengths are down almost uniformly. Between 1990 and 1999, average sentence lengths in state institutions were up only for manslaughter, drug trafficking, and public-order offenses. Average time served in jail in this period was also down in all categories except manslaughter and

sexual offenses, other than rape. Average prison time served, however, was up across the board, 31.8 percent overall between 1990 and 1999. Measured in percentage increase, the three most rapidly growing categories were drug possession (up 66.7 percent), manslaughter (up 58 percent), and motor vehicle theft (up 53.8 percent). By broader categories, the biggest increase in this period was for drug offenses (up 57.1 percent), followed by public order offenses (which include drunken driving and weapons possession—up 35.7 percent), property crime (up 38.9 percent), and violent crime (15.4 percent). These results are largely a consequence of increases in the percent of sentences actually served, shown in the last two columns of the table, which are directly related to changes in sentencing statutes. In this measure motor vehicle theft showed the biggest increase (58.6 percent), followed by possession of drugs (up 46.2 percent).

THREE STRIKES, YOU'RE OUT

Nine years after passing the first truth-in-sentencing law, the State of Washington passed the first of the so-called "three-strikes" laws in December 1993. The measure took effect in the wake of a voter initiative, which passed by a three-to-one margin. Three-strikes laws are the functional equivalent of sentencing guidelines in that they

TABLE 9.7

Comparison of Washington and California three-strikes laws

Type	Washington	California
Homicide	Murder 1 or 2 Controlled substance homicide Homicide by abuse Manslaughter 1 or 2	Murder
Sexual offenses	Rape 1 or 2 Child molestation Incest of child Sexual exploitation	Rape Lewd act on child Continual sexual abuse of child Penetration by foreign object Sexual penetration by force Sodomy by force Oral copulation by force
Robbery	Robbery 1 or 2	Robbery
Felony assault	Attempt murder Assault 1 or 2	Attempt murder Assault with a deadly weapon on a peace officer Assault with a deadly weapon by an inmate Assault with intent to rape or rob
Other crimes against persons	Explosion with threats to humans Extortion Kidnaping 1 or 2 Vehicular assault	Any felony resulting in bodily harm Arson causing bodily injury Carjacking Exploding device with intent to injure Exploding device with intent to murder Kidnaping Mayhem
Property crimes	Arson 1 Attempt arson 1 Burglary	Arson Burglary of occupied dwelling Grand theft with firearm
Drug offenses		Drug sales to minors
Weapons offenses	Any felony with deadly weapon Possession of incendiary device Possession of prohibited explosive device	Any felony with deadly weapon Any felony where firearm used
Other	Treason Promoting prostitution Leading organized crime	

SOURCE: John Clark, James Austin, and D. Alan Henry, "Exhibit 1. Comparison of Washington and California Strikes Laws," in "'Three Strikes and You're Out': A Review of State Legislation," *Research Briefs*, National Institute of Justice, Washington, DC, 1997

TABLE 9.8

Three-strikes laws at the state and federal level as of 1997

Jurisdiction	Enacted	Consequence
Alaska[1]	1996	40 to 99 years
Arkansas	1995	Murder: at least 40 without parole
California	1994	Indeterminate, at least 25
Colorado	1994	Life, at least 40 without parole
Connecticut	1994	Up to life at court's discretion
Florida	1995	10 to life depending on crime
Georgia[2]	1995	Life without parole
Indiana	1994	Life without parole
Kansas	1994	Triple of guideline sentence
Louisiana	1994	Life without parole
Maryland[3]	1994	Life without parole
Montana	1995	Life without parole
Nevada	1995	25 to life
New Jersey	1995	Life without parole
New Mexico	1994	Life, at least 30 without parole
North Carolina	1994	Life without parole
North Dakota[2]	1995	10 to life depending on crime
Pennsylvania	1995	Enhanced sentence of up to 25 years
South Carolina[2]	1995	Life without parole
Tennessee[2]	1995	Life without parole
Utah	1995	5 up to life at court's discretion
Vermont	1995	Up to life at court's discretion
Virginia	1994	Life without parole
Washington	1993	Life without parole
Wisconsin	1994	Life without parole
Federal Government	1995	Life in prison

Note: In all jurisdictions, "strikeable" offenses must be serious violent or drug crimes. In California, only the first two offenses need to be violent; the "triggering" crime may be any felony.
[1] From Walter Dickey and Pam Stiebs Hollenhorst, "Data on Use of 'Three-Strikes' Type Laws," in "Three-Strikes Laws: Massive Impact in California and Georgia, Little Elsewhere," *Overcrowded Times*, Vol. 9, No. 6, December 1998.
[2] Law applies after two strikes.
[3] Law applies after four strikes.

SOURCE: Adapted from John Clark, James Austin, and D. Alan Henry, "Exhibit 9. Variations in State Strikes Laws" and "Exhibit 10. Comparison of New Strikes Laws with Preexisting Sentencing Provisions," in "'Three Strikes and You're Out': A Review of State Legislation," *Research Briefs*, National Institute of Justice, Washington, DC, 1997

mandate a fixed length of sentence for repeat offenders for specified crimes or a mix of crimes—but their formulation in public debate, using the baseball analogy, is much easier to understand than the complexities of thick books of codes and sentencing tables. In three-strikes laws, the offender receives a mandatory sentence upon conviction for the third offense—life imprisonment without parole (the case in Washington state), 25 years without parole (as in California), or some variant of a long sentence. The purpose behind such laws is to remove the criminal from society for a long period of time or in some instances, for life. Such criminals have been convicted repeatedly of serious offenses or felonies.

The Washington law identifies specific offenses which are "strikable." California, which passed its own (and more famous) three-strikes law just months after Washington passed its measure, specifies the categories of offenses which must precede the third conviction, but the third offense can be any felony. This is the feature of California's law which brought it into such prominence and, in 2003, caused review of the legislation by the U.S. Supreme Court in the case of *Ewing v. California*. Table 9.7 compares the three-strikes laws in Washington and California.

Strike Zone

A strike zone refers to the crimes that constitute a strike and under what conditions those crimes become a strike. A strike generally is a serious offense, such as a violent felony, including murder, rape, robbery, arson, aggravated assault, and carjacking. The strike zone is intended to deter offenders convicted repeatedly of such crimes, usually violent or career criminals.

States with Three-Strike Laws

The last authoritative compilation of states with three-strikes measures was published in September 1997 by the National Institute of Justice (NIJ), U.S. Department of Justice (John Clark et al., "Three Strikes and You're Out: A Review of State Legislation," *Research in Brief*, Washington, D.C., September 1997). (See Table 9.8.) The NIJ showed 24 states with such laws all passed in the 1993–95 period. A tabulation published a year later by Walter Dickey and Pam Stiebs Hollenhorst ("Three-Strikes Laws: Massive Impact in California and Georgia, Little Elsewhere," *Overcrowded Times*, December 1998) showed the same listing with Alaska added (as of 1996) and Kansas omitted, possibly because the Kansas measure changes what judges may do under the state's sentencing guidelines. No similar tabulation appears to have been published since, and the Supreme Court, in its 2003 ruling on the California statute, cited only the NIJ report. Thus, it appears that 25 states have such laws, sometimes known as "habitual offender" rather than as three-strikes laws.

As of 1998 (the Dickey, Hollenhorst tabulation), the only states in which significant numbers of offenders had been sentenced under three-strikes measures were California (40,511), Georgia (942), South Carolina (825), Nevada (304), Washington (121), and Florida (116). California had convicted 18 times more offenders under its three-strikes law than all other states combined as of 1998.

California's law is unique in that the third offense may be any felony or even a misdemeanor. This is possible because certain classes of offenses are known under California law as "wobblers." Depending on the circumstances of the offense and the history of the offender, some offenses may be prosecuted as misdemeanors or as felonies. In virtually all other states with three-strikes laws, all three offenses must be violent crimes—murder, rape, robbery, arson, aggravated assault, and vehicular assault. In some states other crimes are also specified. These include the sale of drugs (Indiana), drug offenses punishable by five years or more of incarceration (Louisiana), escape from prison (Florida), treason (Washington), and embezzlement and bribery (South Carolina). California includes the sale of drugs to minors as one of the crimes that qualify as strike one or strike two offenses.

Tightening Preexisting Statutes

In all but one of the states with three-strikes statutes (Kansas is the exception), legislation was already on the books when the popularity of three-strikes laws caused half the states—and the Federal Government as well (in 1995)—to enact laws pioneered on the West Coast. California, for instance, had a law on its books which was very similar to those that were later passed *as* three-strikes statutes in other states. As reported by the NIJ ("'Three Strikes and You're Out': A Review of State Legislation," Washington, D.C., September 1997), California required, pre-three-strikes:

Life with no parole eligibility before 20 years for third violent felony conviction where separate prison terms were served for the first two convictions; life without parole for fourth violent felony convictions.

California's statute, therefore, represented a *tightening* of existing law and a modification of it so that the triggering offense for life imprisonment was the *third* felony—which did not have to be violent.

Much the same pattern, with variations, characterized the introduction of three-strikes laws in other states. In Louisiana a mandatory life term was required for the *fourth* felony conviction if two previous convictions had been violent or drug offenses. The new law imposed the sentence after the *third* offense. In Tennessee, the preexisting law was mandatory life without parole for the third violent felony conviction. Tennessee's new law imposed the same requirement for the *second* violent felony. In Vermont, also, a "four strikes" law was modified and made into a three-strikes law as in Louisiana. In some states, the tightening was more stringent. Thus in New Mexico, the preexisting law imposed an increased sentence of 1 year for the second, an increase of 4 years for the third, and an add-on of 8 years for the fourth felony. The new law imposed a life sentence after the third violent felony but permitted parole after 30 years. For a view of laws as they were in 1997, and the preexisting laws they replaced, please see http://www.ncjrs.org/pdffiles/165369.pdf. Many laws may have been modified since, but they have not been surveyed in recent years.

Impact and Effectiveness

In a NIJ-sponsored report, E. Chen (*Impacts of Three Strikes and Truth in Sentencing on the Volume and Composition of Correctional Populations*, National Institute of Justice, Rockville, MD, 2000) states: "This study of Three Strikes and You're Out … and Truth in Sentencing … laws found in general [that] they had only a few short term impacts on the dynamics of prison populations in all States except Washington and for one variable in California." The impact of three-strikes in Washington indicates "some reductions in the growth of parole entries and exits associated with three strikes laws." In California three-strikes laws and truth-in-sentencing, in combination, increased the percentage of prisoners older than 50 years. The author attributes the absence of effects for three-strikes laws elsewhere to their minimal use in other states.

More significant effects are reported for California in the U.S. Supreme Court's judgment in the case of *Ewing v. California*, authored by Justice Sandra Day O'Connor (538 U.S., 2003). Citing a statement issued by the Office of the Attorney General, California Department of Justice, *"Three Strikes and You're Out"—Its Impact on the California Criminal Justice System After Four Years*, 1998, the Justice writes: "Four years after the passage of

California's three strikes law, the recidivism rate of parolees returned to prison for the commission of a new crime dropped by nearly 25 percent." She continues to cite from the statement as follows:

> [a]n unintended but positive consequence of "Three Strikes" has been the impact on parolees leaving the state. More California parolees are now leaving the state than parolees from other jurisdictions entering California. This striking turnaround started in 1994. It was the first time more parolees left the state than entered since 1976. This trend has continued and in 1997 more than 1,000 net parolees left California.

The statement suggests that a three-strikes law with severe penalties, energetically enforced, appears at least to cause the net export of offenders to other jurisdictions.

Constitutional Test

California's statute, the most stringent, was upheld by the U.S. Supreme Court in *Ewing v. California* on March 5, 2003. The case involved Gary Ewing, who was on parole from a 9-year prison term when he stole three golf clubs from a pro shop in El Segundo, California. He had hidden the clubs in his trousers and consequently walked a little strangely as he left. An employee of the shop called the police after seeing Ewing limp out. The police arrested Ewing in the parking lot outside. Each of the stolen clubs was worth $399. Ewing had a long record of offenses going back to 1982. He had been sentenced for theft and given a suspended sentence. A series of offenses followed: grand theft auto (1988), petty theft (1990), battery and theft on separate occasions (1992), burglary (January 1993), possession of drug paraphernalia (February), appropriating lost property (July), unlawful firearms possession and trespassing (September), and three burglaries and one robbery (October and November). During the last of these episodes, he threatened a victim, claiming to have a gun. When the victim resisted, Ewing pulled a knife, forced the victim into an apartment, and rifled through the victim's bedroom. The victim managed to escape, raised the alarm, and Ewing fled with the victim's money and credit cards. He was arrested in December 1993 and sentenced to prison. He was released in 1999 on parole. Ten months after his release came his arrest for stealing the golf clubs. Ewing was sentenced under the three-strikes statute to 25 years to life. After the California Court of Appeals upheld his conviction, Ewing appealed to the U.S. Supreme Court claiming grossly disproportionate punishment under the Eighth Amendment's protection against cruel and unusual punishment.

The Supreme Court upheld Ewing's conviction basing itself on an earlier case, *Harmelin v. Michigan* (501 U.S. 957, 996–997), which states in part that the "Eighth Amendment does not require strict proportionality between crime and sentence [but] forbids only extreme sentences that are 'grossly disproportionate' to the crime." The Court also affirmed the right of the state legislature to set policy for the purposes of protecting public safety, and, quoting from *Harmelin*, stated that "The Constitution 'does not mandate adoption of any one penological theory.'" The Court recognized that among the justifications for a sentence, alongside deterrence, retribution, and rehabilitation, incapacitation—making the offender incapable of preying on the public—could also be used.

Justice Stephen Breyer, joined by Justices John Stevens, David Souter, and Ruth Bader Ginsburg, dissented. Justice Breyer, author of the dissenting opinion, held that Ewing's sentence had been disproportionate to the offense. Justice Breyer based himself on a similar 1983 case (*Solem v. Helm*, 463 U.S. 277) in which the Court ruled in the petitioner's favor. In *Solem* a recidivist offender (Jerry Helm) received a longer sentence (a life sentence) for a lesser crime (passing a bad check for $100). All of Helm's offenses were committed in South Carolina under laws which predated South Carolina's three-strikes law but nevertheless mandated life without parole for third offenses.

The Court's five to four decision in *Ewing* leaves open the possibility that, in some future case, the Supreme Court may look at California's three-strikes law again and reach a different decision. For the present, however, three-strikes laws have been upheld by the highest court in the United States.

ALTERNATIVE SENTENCING

Forms of sentencing other than probation, prison, or a combination of the two (split sentences) also exist and are widely used in virtually every state. The most recent compilation of such approaches was published by the Bureau of Justice Statistics in 2000 in cooperation with the Conference of State Court Administrators (David B. Rottman, et al., *State Court Organization 1998*, BJS, Washington, D.C., June 2000).

The BJS identified 11 forms of distinct alternative sentences, although some of these are functionally similar. With the exception of boot camps for young or adult offenders, they all provide offenders more freedom than incarceration but less freedom than ordinary probation. Alternative sentencing is, in part, a response to calls by penal reformers for a "continuum of punishments with probation at one end, more severe community-based sanctions in the middle, and incarceration at the most restrictive end" (*Americans Behind Bars*, The Edna McConnell Clark Foundation, New York City, New York, 1993) and in part a response to crowding in prisons. Thus, for instance, according to the BJS, many states use halfway houses as a way of relieving crowding. Alternative sentencing is, of course, applied to offenders whose absence of prior criminal history or general characteristics indicate that they can be trusted not to abuse their greater freedom. Opponents, however, see prison sentencing as the only "real punishment" for criminals.

State Departments of Correction, the District of Columbia, and the Federal Bureau of Prisons offer a range of alternative sentencing options for criminal offenders. Although programs can vary among regions, those options include work release and weekend sentencing, shock incarceration (sometimes called boot camp), community service programs, day fines, day reporting centers, electronic monitoring and house arrest, residential community corrections, and diversionary treatment programs. There is also more variation in the availability of other types of alternative sentencing options, such as mediation and restitution.

Client-Specific Planning

In 1980 the National Center on Institutions and Alternatives proposed the idea of client-specific planning. In these programs independent sentencing specialists provide judges with background information on offenders and assess their potential for meeting the requirements of a community-based punishment plan. Based on this information, the specialist recommends penalties that can include probation, treatments, payment of restitution, or other conditions. The judge may use the plan, change it, or reject it.

Mediation and Restitution

Mediation began in Canada in 1974 and spread to the United States, where more than 20 states were using mediation by the beginning of the 21st century. In mediation, the victim and the offender meet under the auspices of a community worker and work out a "reconciliation" between them, usually involving some type of restitution and requiring offenders to take responsibility for their actions. This technique is used mainly for minor crimes and often involves private organizations; therefore, the judiciary does not always accept its resolution. Most often restitution is not considered the complete punishment but part of a wider punishment, such as probation or working off the restitution dollar amount while in prison.

Work Release and Weekend Sentencing

Work-release programs permit selected prisoners nearing the end of their terms to work in the community, returning to prison facilities or community residential facilities in nonworking hours. Such programs are designed to prepare inmates to return to the community in a relatively controlled environment while they are learning how to work productively. Work release also allows inmates to earn income, reimburse the state for part of their confinement costs, build up savings for their eventual full release,

and acquire more positive living habits. Those on weekend sentencing programs spend certain days in prison, usually weekends, but are free the remainder of the time. Both of these types of sentences are known as "intermittent incarceration." Violent offenders and those convicted of drug offenses are usually excluded from such programs by the courts.

Shock Incarceration (Boot Camps)

Shock incarceration is a modern phrase for reformatories or "boot camps" operated under military discipline for juveniles and adults. The name comes from William Whitelaw, British Home Secretary (1979–1983), who called for a "short, sharp shock" that would end teenagers' criminal careers. Boot camps established in Great Britain attracted youths who liked the challenge, but the facilities did not lower the recidivism rate according to testimony presented to the British Parliament by corrections officials (http://www.parliament.the-stationery-office.co.uk/pa/cm200102/cmselect/cmpubacc/619/2021110.htm). The prototype of such a facility in the United States was established at the Elmira Reformatory in New York as far back as 1876 (Alexander W. Pisciotta, *Benevolent Repression*, New York University Press, New York, 1994). The first modern, correctional boot camp was established in Georgia in 1983. Faced with unprecedented overcrowding in its prisons and jails, Georgia was looking for alternatives to incarceration for adult offenders. Oklahoma began its program in 1984 and, by the end of 1988, 15 programs were operating in 9 states. The majority of programs started in 1990. In 1998, 33 correctional agencies (state and federal) operated 49 camps for adult inmates. Sentences are usually short (three to five months) and intended to be rehabilitative by instilling self-respect and discipline in the offender.

Boot camps are intended to be both punitive in their rigid discipline and rehabilitative in the self-esteem they claim to confer upon successful completion of the program. Shock incarceration is intended to motivate prisoners, teach respect for oneself and others, and break the destructive cycles of behavior. Virtually all work on the assumption that a military regimen is beneficial.

The major selling points for boot camps have been saving money and reducing prison crowding. However, the major factor contributing to reduced costs and less overcrowding is that the boot camp programs are shorter in duration than traditional sentences, and thus participants are released earlier. In addition, a few studies of boot camps have found that the facilities have not had a major effect on recidivism.

Many adult boot camps claim to be positively oriented toward developing programs aimed at offender rehabilitation. Typically, boot camp programs include physical training and regular drill-type exercise, housekeeping and maintenance of the facility, and often hard labor. Some programs include vocational, educational, or treatment programs. Drug and alcohol counseling, reality therapy, relaxation therapy, individual counseling, and recreation therapy are often incorporated into such programs. Some offenders in boot camps have drug problems, and many programs devote time to drug treatment each week. Programs closely regulate dress, talking, movement, eating, hygiene, etc. Obedience to rules reinforces submission to authority and forces the prisoners to handle a challenge that is both tedious and demanding.

Community Service Programs

Begun in the United States in Alameda County, California, in 1966 as a penalty for traffic offenses, community service has spread throughout the United States. The penalty is most often a supplement to other penalties and mainly given to "white collar" criminals, juvenile delinquents, and those who commit nonserious crimes. Offenders are usually required to work for government or private nonprofit agencies cleaning parks, collecting roadside trash, setting up chairs for community events, painting community projects, and helping out at nursing homes.

Individuals sentenced to community service are expected to work without pay to pay society back for their offenses. The BJS labels community service "an exception to unconstitutional servitude" indirectly referring to the Thirteenth Amendment to the Constitution which states, in Section 1: "Neither slavery nor involuntary servitude, except as a punishment for crime whereof the party shall have been duly convicted, shall exist within the United States, or any place subject to their jurisdiction." By exempting the involuntary servitude of convicted criminals, the Constitution makes both community service and chain gangs possible.

Day Fines

Under this type of alternative sentence, the offender pays out a monetary sum rather than spending time in jail or prison. Most judges assess fixed, flat-fee fines sparingly. The fees are tied to the seriousness of the crimes and the criminal records of the offenders, and they bear no relationship to the wealth of the offender. As a result, judges often think the fixed fines are too lenient on wealthy offenders and too harsh on poor ones. Using the day fine alternative, however, permits judges to first determine how much punishment an offender deserves, which is defined in some unit other than money.

For example, a judge decides that the gravity of the offense is worth 15, 60, or 120 punishment units, without regard to income. Then the value of each unit is set at a percentage of the offender's daily income, and the total fine amount is determined by simple multiplication. The fine is paid into the jurisdiction's treasury. Day fines are also used in Europe.

Day Reporting Centers

These centers, known as DRCs, were developed in Great Britain and first appeared in the United States in the 1980s. Intended to allow offenders to reside in the community, such programs require participants to report daily or less frequently. In 1994 the National Institute of Justice reported DRCs operating in 22 states. In the most recent BJS survey of state court systems (*State Court Organization 1998, June 2000*) seven states specifically reported using DRCs.

These programs, designed for persons on pretrial release, probation, or parole, require participants to appear at day reporting centers on a frequent and regular basis in order to partake in services or activities provided by the center or other community agencies. Those sentenced to report to DRCs are often in need of treatment or counseling for drug or alcohol abuse, and most centers provide a wide array of on-site treatment and services. Failure to adhere to program requirements or to report at stated intervals can lead to commitment in prison or jail. Participation at the DRC can also be terminated if the subject is charged with a new crime.

DRCs monitor offenders on the road to rehabilitation. They are also intended to relieve jail or prison overcrowding. Many DRCs operate in distinct phases in which offenders move from higher to lower levels of control based on their progress in treatment and compliance with supervisory guidelines. Most programs run five or six months. DRCs do not generally exclude serious offenders, although many programs appear to select nonserious drug- and alcohol-using offenders. Some DRCs require offenders to perform community service, but the level and type of community service performed varies from jurisdiction to jurisdiction.

Intensive Probation Supervision (IPS)

IPS is another implementation of close supervision of offenders while they reside in the community. Offenders on probation are increasingly people convicted of felonies (rather than misdemeanors), who are sentenced to intensively supervised probation because prisons are crowded but the offenders require close monitoring. Routine probation, however, was neither intended nor structured to handle this type of high-risk probationer. Therefore, IPS was developed as an alternative to prison or routine probation, with the additional aim of reducing the risk to public safety.

Caseloads of officers assigned to IPS offenders are kept low. In typical programs, the offender must make frequent contacts with a supervising officer, pay restitution to victims, participate in community service, have and keep a job, and, if appropriate, undergo random and unannounced drug testing. Offenders are often required to pay a probation fee. All states had IPS programs by 1998.

House Arrest and Electronic Monitoring Program (EMP)

Some nonviolent offenders are sentenced to house arrest in which they are legally ordered to remain confined in their own homes. They are allowed to leave only for medical purposes or to go to work, although some curfew programs permit offenders to work during the day and have a few hours of free time before returning home at a specified time.

The most severe type of house arrest is home incarceration, where the offender's home is actually a prison that he or she cannot leave except for very special reasons, such as medical emergencies. Home-detention programs require the offender to be at home when he or she is not working. Some offenders are required to perform a certain number of hours of community service and, if they are employed, to repay the cost of probation and/or pay restitution.

Electronic monitoring works in tandem with house arrest. Electronic monitoring can consist of a small radio transmitter attached to the offender in a nonremovable bracelet or anklet. Some systems send a signal to a small monitoring box, which is programmed to phone a Department of Corrections computer if the signal is broken; other systems randomly call probationers, and the computer makes a voice verification of the prisoner. In some cases, a special device in the electronic monitor sends a confirmation to the computer. More advanced technologies are being applied to electronic monitoring of probationers and parolees, including Global Positioning Systems (GPS) technologies, which use satellite imagery to keep track of subjects. GPS can help corrections officers ensure that the subject is not violating any territorial restrictions.

Electronic monitoring is often used to monitor the whereabouts of those under house arrest and permitted to be only at home or at work. EMP is sometimes used to ensure that child molesters stay a specified distance from schools. Individuals under house arrest must remain in their residences at all times unless at work or attending approved treatment programs. Electronic monitoring costs states much less than building new prison cells or housing more inmates.

Residential Community Corrections (Halfway Houses)

These facilities are known less formally as "halfway houses" because they are intended to serve as places where prisoners spend their pre-release time becoming reintegrated into community life. Offenders may also be sentenced to halfway houses directly in lieu of incarceration if their offenses and general profile indicate that they will benefit from the structure and counseling available in such facilities. According to the BJS, halfway houses are frequently used in many states to relieve prison overcrowding.

Residential programs house offenders in a structured environment. Offenders work full time, maintain the residence center, perform community service, and can attend educational or counseling programs. They may leave the centers only for work or approved programs such as substance-abuse treatment. One type of residential program, called the restitution center, allows the offender to work to pay restitution and child-support payments. Centers also regularly test the residents for drugs.

Diversionary Treatment Programs

Probation combined with mandatory treatment programs is an alternative sentence for non-violent offenders convicted of drug offenses, alcohol abuse, or sex offenses. Sentenced individuals are free on probation but typically are required to attend sessions of group therapy and supervised professional treatment.

CHAPTER 10
SPECIAL FACILITIES AND POPULATIONS

The correctional facilities of the United States are categorized as jails for short-term offenders and prisons for offenders incarcerated for one year or longer. Some juvenile offenders are held in adult jails or prisons; the majority are confined in residential placement facilities. Corrections are under local, state, or federal jurisdiction and all are operated under their own legislative mandates. Yet special facilities do exist to handle specific prisoner populations, such as military prisoners. The U.S. military operates under its own legal system, the Uniform Code of Military Justice, and runs its own prisons. In this chapter, data are presented on prison populations in U.S. Territories and Commonwealths. American Indian nations exercise authority over their own populations; the Bureau of Justice Statistics (BJS) collects information on jails in what the bureau calls "Indian Country." Also, in the aftermath of the September 11, 2001 terrorist attacks on the United States, immigrants have come under close scrutiny. Data are presented on their rates of confinement before and after 9/11. Finally, death row inmates form a special population in the nation's prisons. Many spend a decade or more as their cases are decided. A look at trends in death row populations concludes this chapter.

MILITARY INCARCERATION

The U.S. military has always operated under laws of its own. Today, that is the Uniform Code of Military Justice (UCMJ), enacted by Congress on May 5, 1950 (U.S. Court of Appeals for the Armed Forces, "History" [Online] http://www.armfor.uscourts.gov/History.htm [accessed May 14, 2003]). Congress created the U.S. Court of Appeals for the Armed Forces as the final appellate court under the UCMJ, but an amendment of the code on August 1, 1984, provided for U.S. Supreme Court review of judgments in a limited number of cases. Before UCMJ, a military Board of Review adjudicated, with the president having final authority to decide conflicts. The UCMJ's

FIGURE 10.1

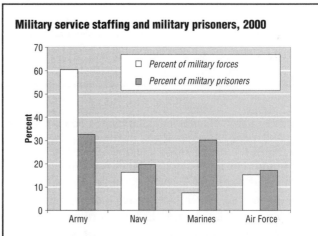

Military service staffing and military prisoners, 2000

Note: The U.S. Coast Guard was approximately 0.6 percent of military manpower and 0.5 percent of military prisoners in 2000.

SOURCE: Created by Information Plus from "No. 500. Department of Defense Manpower: 1950 to 2000," in *Statistical Abstract of the United States 2001*, U.S. Census Bureau, Washington, DC, 2001 and Paige M. Harrison and Allen J. Beck, "Table 13. Prisoners under military jurisdiction, by branch of service, yearend 2000 and 2001," in *Prisoners in 2001*, U.S. Bureau of Justice Statistics, Washington, DC, 2002

Articles 77 through 134 define offenses equivalent to felonies. Article 118, for instance, deals with murder. Offenses are tried in general court-martials and may result in the imprisonment of offenders. The most serious cases are incarcerated at the military's Fort Leavenworth Penitentiary in Kansas, established in 1875 as a military prison.

In 2000 more than 2.3 million men and women served in the U.S. military. That same year, according to the BJS (Paige M. Harrison and Allen J. Beck, *Prisoners 2001*, Washington, D.C., July 2002), 2,420 military personnel were held in military prisons. The overall incarceration rate in the United States was 4.5 times higher than in the military services. In the services, the rate was 104 per

TABLE 10.1

Prisoners under jurisdiction of United States military authorities, 1996–2001

Branch of service	Number[1]						Percent change 2000 to 2001
	1996	1997	1998	1999	2000	2001	
To which prisoners belonged							
Total	2,747	2,772	2,426	2,279	2,420	2,436	0.7%
Air Force	487	575	484	409	413	480	16.2
Army	1,106	1,063	862	761	789	804	1.9
Marine Corps	685	628	682	565	730	628	-14.0
Navy	455	490	389	523	474	516	8.9
Coast Guard	14	16	9	21	14	8	-42.9
Holding prisoners							
Total	2,747	2,772	2,426	2,279	2,420	2,436	0.7
Air Force[2]	NA	103	128	92	102	126	23.5
Army	1,486	1,494	1,115	1,026	994	981	-1.3
Marine Corps	650	571	617	480	563	428	-24.0
Navy	611	604	526	681	761	901	18.4

[1] Detail may not add to total because of rounding.
[2] Data for 1996 exclude prisoners confined in Air Force facilities.

SOURCE: Kathleen Maguire and Ann L. Pastore, eds., "Table 6.57. Prisoners under jurisdiction of U.S. military authorities," in *Sourcebook of Criminal Justice Statistics 2001*, U.S. Bureau of Justice Statistics, Washington, DC, 2002 [Online] http://www.albany.edu/sourcebook/1995/wk1/t534.wk1 [accessed May 15, 2003]

100,000 military personnel in 2000 compared with 478 per 100,000 residents in the U.S. civilian population.

Proportionally to military manpower levels, the U.S. Marines had the highest level of prisoners and the U.S. Army the lowest. (See Figure 10.1.) With 60.5 percent of military personnel, the Army had 32.6 percent of military prisoners. The Marines, with 7.5 percent of personnel, had 30.2 percent of the military prisoners in 2000. The U.S. Navy had 16.3 percent of total military manpower and 19.6 percent of the military prison population; the U.S. Air Force had 15.3 percent of personnel and 17.1 percent of military prisoners. The closest proportionality was in the U.S. Coast Guard (not shown on the figure). The Coast Guard had 0.6 percent of the military personnel, representing 0.5 percent of military prisoners. Percentages add to slightly more than 100 percent due to rounding.

Data for 2000 are a snapshot. Levels can shift rapidly, as shown in Table 10.1. The table tracks military incarceration rates from 1996 to 2001. Total prisoners were down by 311 prisoners between 1996 and 2001. Between 2000 and 2001, the U.S. Air Force showed a 16.2 percent gain in prisoners and the U.S. Marines a 14.0 percent decline. The U.S. Army prison population increased by 1.9 percent and the Navy added 8.9 percent between 2000 and 2001. The Coast Guard prison rate, however, dropped 42.9 percent. In 2000, 55 percent of all military prisoners were serving terms of 1 year or longer.

All four of the combat services maintain correctional facilities. In 2001, the Army's six facilities, among them the Disciplinary Barracks at Fort Leavenworth, housed 40.3 percent of prisoners. (See Table 10.1.) The Navy's 11 prisons housed 37 percent, the Air Force's 36 facilities housed 5.2 percent, and the Marines' 6 facilities housed 17.6 percent of all military convicts. Military prisons were much less crowded than state or federal prisons. In 2001 they were at 54 percent of total capacity compared with 101 percent for state prisons and 131 percent for federal prisons.

U.S. TERRITORIES AND COMMONWEALTHS

The reach of crime and of corrections extends even to tiny islands in the Caribbean or in the Pacific Ocean—two watery regions where U.S. territories and commonwealths are located. Table 10.2 provides population figures, location and geographical information, and employment data for those territories and commonwealths.

The largest of the U.S. possessions, the Commonwealth of Puerto Rico, is an island just shy of being three times the size of Rhode Island in land area. Puerto Rico had a population of nearly 4 million people in 2002. The smallest territory is American Samoa, two islands inhabited by just short of 69,000 people. U.S. territories and associated commonwealths had a combined total population in 2002 of 4.39 million. The commonwealths are self-governing entities. The territories are administered by the U.S. Department of the Interior, but these territories also have self-governing political bodies; their judicial officials are named by the Secretary of the Interior.

Nearly 15,900 people were in the custody of correctional authorities in the territories/commonwealths in 2001. (See Table 10.3.) Of these 11,900 had been sentenced to serve more than 1 year. The incarceration rate in the territories/commonwealths for 2001 was 271 per 100,000 persons in the resident population compared to 470 per 100,000 in the United States. The lowest incarceration rate was experienced by the Northern Mariana Islands, 93 per 100,000; some 14 small islands provide this commonwealth with a territory about 2.5 times the size of Washington, D.C. The highest rate was experienced by the U.S. Virgin Islands, 339 per 100,000. Puerto Rico's figure, 278 per 100,000, dominated results for all U.S. possessions in 2001 because of Puerto Rico's large population.

According to the Bureau of Justice Statistics, the prison population of the possessions has grown more rapidly than in the states—up 28 percent since 1995 compared with a 21-percent increase for states (*Prisoners 2001*).

JAILS IN INDIAN COUNTRY
Tribal Jurisdiction

In its management of American Indian nations, Congress reserved for federal jurisdiction 14 crimes

TABLE 10.2

United States territories and commonwealths

Territory/commonwealth	2002 population	Location and geographical relationship		Approximate land area	Labor force	Percent unemployed
American Samoa	68,688	South Pacific	Halfway between Hawaii and New Zealand	About size of Washington, DC	14,000 (1996)	6.0 (2000)
Guam	160,796	North Pacific	1/4 distance between Hawaii and Philippines	3 times Washington, DC	60,000 (2000)	15.0 (2000)
Commonwealth of the Northern Mariana Islands	77,311	North Pacific	3/4 distance beween Hawaii and Philippines	2.5 times Washington, DC	6006 (1995)[1]	44.9 (1995)[2]
Commonwealth of Puerto Rico	3,957,988	Caribbean	East of Dominican Republic at level of Cuba	About 3 times Rhode Island	1,300,000 (2000)	9.5 (2000)
U.S. Virgin Islands	123,498	Caribbean	East of Puerto Rico	2 times Washington, DC	48,356 (1999)	4.9 (1999)

[1] Source reports 6,006 indigenous members of the labor force and the presence in 1995 of 28,717 foreign workers.
[2] Of 6,006 indigenous workers, 2,699 were unemployed in 1995.

SOURCE: Compiled by Information Plus from *The World Factbook 2002*, U.S. Central Intelligence Agency, Washington, DC, March 2003

TABLE 10.3

Prisoners in the United States territories, 2000 and 2001

U.S. territory	Advance 2001	Total Final 2000	Percent change, 2000-01	Advance 2001	Final 2000	Percent change, 2000-01	Incar- ceration rate, 2001*
				Sentenced to more than 1 year			
Total	15,852	16,130	-1.7%	11,910	11,916	-0.1%	271
American Samoa	155	140	10.7	125	114	9.6	182
Guam	585	684	-14.5	297	323	-8.0	185
Commonwealth of the Northern Mariana Islands	102	97	5.2	72	51	41.2	93
Commonwealth of Puerto Rico	14,516	14,691	-1.2	10,997	11,075	-0.7	278
U.S. Virgin Islands	494	518	-4.6	419	353	18.7	339

* The number of prisoners with a sentence of more than 1 year per 100,000 persons in the resident population. Midyear population estimates were provided by the U.S. Bureau of the Census, International Data Base.

SOURCE: Paige M. Harrison and Allen J. Beck, "Table 14. Prisoners in custody of correctional authorities in the U.S. Territories, yearend 2000 and 2001," in *Prisoners in 2001*, U.S. Bureau of Justice Statistics, Washington, DC, July 2002

TABLE 10.4

American Indians and Alaska Natives under correctional supervision, 2000–01

	Number	Percent of category	Percent of total[1]
Total	49,673	100.0	100.0
In custody, midyear 2001	21,286	100.0	42.9
Local jails[2]	6,000	28.2	12.1
Jails in Indian country	1,912	9.0	3.8
State prisons	11,419	53.6	23.0
Federal prisons	1,955	9.2	3.9
Under community supervision	28,387	100.0	57.1
State/Federal, 12/31/00			
Probation	23,889	84.2	48.1
Parole	4,380	15.4	8.8
Indian country, midyear 2001	118	0.4	0.2

[1] Subtotals do not sum to totals because of rounding.
[2] Estimated from the 2001 Annual Survey of Jails.

SOURCE: Adapted from Todd D. Minton, "Number of American Indians and Alaska Natives under correctional supervision, 2001," in *Jails in Indian Country, 2001*, U.S. Bureau of Justice Statistics, Washington, DC, May 2002

committed by or against Indians in Indian Country (Indian lands and reservations). The relevant provisions of the Major Crimes Act of 1885, codified as 18 USC 1153, read as follows (http://uscode.house.gov/usc.htm):

(a) Any Indian who commits against the person or property of another Indian or other person any of the following offenses, namely, murder, manslaughter, kidnapping, maiming, a felony under chapter 109A, incest, assault with intent to commit murder, assault with a dangerous weapon, assault resulting in serious bodily injury (as defined in section 1365 of this title), an assault against an individual who has not attained the age of 16 years, arson, burglary, robbery, and a felony under section 661 of this title within the Indian country, shall be subject to the same law and penalties as all other persons committing any of the above offenses, within the exclusive jurisdiction of the United States.

(b) Any offense referred to in subsection (a) of this section that is not defined and punished by Federal law in force within the exclusive jurisdiction of the United States shall be defined and punished in accordance with the laws of the State in which such offense was committed as are in force at the time of such offense.

In other words, under 18 USC 1153 serious crimes must be tried in federal court if federal criminal code can be brought to apply—and if not, it falls to the states to try such crimes.

In Public Law 280, passed in 1953 and codified as 18 USC 1162, Congress made the state responsibility clearer:

(a) Each of the States or Territories listed in the following table [table lists Indian jurisdictions within Alaska, California, Minnesota, Nebraska, Oregon, and Wisconsin] shall have jurisdiction over offenses committed by or

TABLE 10.5

Indian country jail inmates and capacity, 1998–2001

	1998	1999	2000	2001
Number of inmates				
Midyear	1,479	1,621	1,775	1,912
Peak day in June	2,306	2,289	2,441	2,656
Rated capacity	1,945	2,065	2,076	2,101
Percent of capacity occupied*				
Midyear	76%	78%	86%	91%
Peak day in June	119	111	118	126

*Number of inmates in custody divided by rated capacity.

SOURCE: Adapted from Todd D. Minton, "Indian country jails operated at 126% of capacity," in *Jails in Indian Country, 2001*, U.S. Bureau of Justice Statistics, Washington, DC, May 2002

FIGURE 10.2

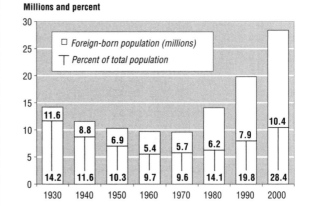

Foreign-born population in the United States, 1930–2000

Note: Percents are above the T-shaped bar. In 2000, 10.4 percent of the U.S. population was foreign-born and the foreign-born population was 28.4 million.

SOURCE: Adapted from A. Dianne Schmidley, "Figure 1-1. Foreign-Born Population and Percent of Total Population for the United States: 1850 to 2000," in *Profile of the Foreign-Born Population in the United States: 2000*, Current Population Reports, U.S. Census Bureau, Washington, DC, December 2001

against Indians in the areas of Indian country listed opposite the name of the State or Territory to the same extent that such State or Territory has jurisdiction over offenses committed elsewhere within the State or Territory, and the criminal laws of such State or Territory shall have the same force and effect within such Indian country as they have elsewhere within the State or Territory.

This provision of U.S. Code gives states authority over criminal prosecutions taking place on reservations. Offenses left over for tribal jurisdiction are, in effect, petty offenses and misdemeanors. In the Indian Civil Rights Act of 1968 (ICRA), Congress spelled out the limitation under which tribal courts could operate. The relevant provision was codified as 25 USC 1302 (7):

> No Indian tribe in exercising powers of self-government shall (7) require excessive bail, impose excessive fines, inflict cruel and unusual punishments, and in no event impose for conviction of any one offense any penalty or punishment greater than imprisonment for a term of one year and a fine of $5,000, or both.

Indian Offenders under Tribal Jurisdiction

The American Indian population, including Alaska Natives, was just under 2.5 million in 2000. Around that time, 49,673 Indians and Alaska Natives were under correctional supervision, 42.9 percent in custody (midyear 2001 figure) and 57.1 percent under community supervision (yearend 2000 figure). (See Table 10.4.)

Of the 21,286 in custody, 9 percent were held in jails in Indian Country. Most (53.6 percent) were in state prisons; 28.2 percent were held in local jails in cities, towns, and counties; and 9.2 percent were in federal prisons. (See Table 10.4.) Similarly, 99.6 percent of those under community supervision were under state or federal control, most on probation (84.2 percent), the rest on parole (15.4 percent).

Based on U.S. Census Bureau definitions, American Indians lived either inside or outside of "identified areas," these being reservations, trust lands, tribal designated statistical areas, tribal jurisdiction statistical areas, and Alaska Native village statistical areas. Following the 1990 Census, the bureau published data showing that, as of April 1990, 37.7 percent of American Indians, Eskimos, and Aleuts lived "inside" these areas; the majority lived "off the reservation" (*Statistical Abstract of the United States 1993*, Washington, D.C., 1993). Similar data for the 2000 Census have not as yet been tabulated. Proportionally more American Indians live in Indian Country than are tried and held in tribal facilities when they commit offenses because the legal structure governing offenses favors federal and state jurisdictions.

Tribal jails are crowded much like state and federal facilities—and appear to be growing more crowded. (See Table 10.5.) In 1998, 76 percent of jail beds were in use in midyear, and 119 percent of capacity was used on the peak day, in June. Capacity increased more slowly than incarcerations so that by 2001 some 91 percent of capacity was in use in midyear and jails in Indian Country operated at 126 percent above capacity on the peak day in June.

IMMIGRANTS IN CONFINEMENT

Since the passage of the Immigration and Nationality Act of 1965, which eliminated a quota system based on country of origin, immigration has risen in the United States. In 1960 the foreign-born population of the United States stood at 9.7 million, and the foreign-born

FIGURE 10.3

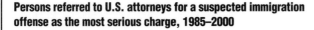

Persons referred to U.S. attorneys for a suspected immigration offense as the most serious charge, 1985–2000

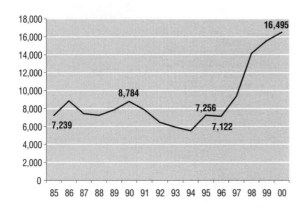

SOURCE: John Scalia and Marika F. X. Litras, "Highlights," in *Immigration Offenders in the Federal Criminal Justice System, 2000*, U.S. Bureau of Justice Statistics, Washington, DC, August 2002

TABLE 10.6

Number of detainees under INS jurisdiction, 1995, 2000, and 2001

Facility type	Number of detainees			Percent change, 2000-01	Percent of all detainees	
	1995	2000	2001		1995	2001
Total*	8,177	19,528	19,137	-2.0%	100.0%	100.0%
INS-operated facilities	3,776	4,785	4,550	-4.9	46.2	23.8
Private facilities under exclusive contract to INS	652	1,829	1,947	6.5	8.0	10.2
Federal Bureau of Prisons	1,282	1,444	1,276	-11.6	15.7	6.7
Other federal facilities	181	178	162	-9.0	2.2	0.8
Intergovernmental agreements	2,286	11,281	11,201	-0.7	28.0	58.5
State prisons	8	369	419	13.6	0.1	2.2
Local jails	1,984	8,886	8,681	-2.3	24.3	45.4
Other facilities	294	2,026	2,101	3.7	3.6	11.0

Note: INS stands for Immigration and Naturalization Service.
*Detail does not sum to total due to unknown facility type for 1 detainee in 2000 and 2001.

SOURCE: Paige M. Harrison and Allen J. Beck, "Table 12. Number of detainees under the jurisdiction of the Immigration and Naturalization Service (INS), by type of facility, yearend 1995, 2000, and 2001," in *Prisoners in 2001*, U.S. Bureau of Justice Statistics, Washington, DC, July 2002

---

comprised 5.4 percent of the U.S. population. By 2000 the foreign-born numbered 28.4 million and represented 10.4 percent of the population. (See Figure 10.2.) In 1960, 75 percent of the foreign born were of European origin with another 9.8 percent from Canada. By 2000 people born in Latin America represented 51 percent of the foreign-born and Asians 25.5 percent; those of European origin had slipped to 15.3 percent of all foreign-born (A. Dianne Schmidley, *Profile of the Foreign-Born Population in the United States: 2000*, Current Population Reports, U.S. Census Bureau, Washington, D.C., 2000).

As legal immigration increased, so did illegal entry, mostly from Latin America. As an example of what had been seen through the 1980s and 1990s, in 2000, according to the Immigration and Naturalization Service, 68.7 percent of illegal aliens were from Mexico ("Estimates of the Unauthorized Immigrant Population Residing in the United States: 1990 to 2000," U.S. Immigration and Naturalization Service [Online] http://www.immigration.gov/graphics/shared/aboutus/statistics/Ill_Report_1211.pdf [accessed May 21, 2003]). One response to this phenomenon was the Immigration Reform and Control Act of 1986 which enabled some illegal aliens to obtain lawful permanent residence. The Immigration Act of 1990 increased the overall number of legal immigrants admitted. Midway through the 1990s, opposition to immigration, particularly to the presence of illegal aliens, began to focus around the issues of jobs taken by illegal aliens and tax dollars expended on the education, health care, and maintenance (through welfare expenditures) of illegal aliens. Since 1996 Congress has generally pursued a policy of immigration reform ranging from beefing up border controls to stripping illegal aliens of legal rights. The Illegal Immigration

Reform and Immigration Responsibility Act of 1996 signaled the turn in policy. According to the Bureau of Justice Statistics (John Scalia and Marika F. X. Litras, *Immigration Offenders in the Federal Criminal Justice System, 2000*, BJS, Washington, D.C., August 2002):

> The 1996 act authorized increases in law enforcement by the U.S. Immigration and Naturalization Service (INS). Following enactment, the number of INS law enforcement officers increased from 12,403 to 17,654. The Border Patrol received almost two-thirds of the additional officers. About 75% of the increase in referrals to U.S. attorneys for immigration offenses between 1996 and 2000 was observed in the five States that received the greatest number of new INS officers.

The number of persons referred to U.S. attorneys for suspected immigration offenses began to increase sharply in 1997. (See Figure 10.3.) Such referrals rose from 7,122 in 1996 to 16,495 in 2000. Referrals averaged 7,298 in the 12-year period 1985–1996 during a period of liberal immigration policy—and then averaged 13,886 during the 4-year period 1997–2000. One of the aims of Congress in the 1996 act was to remove illegal immigrants from the country rapidly and without long processes of judicial review—a policy that would later be reaffirmed in the USA Patriot Act of 2001. The 1996 act's chief focus was on the entry of illegal aliens, not terrorism, and also on U.S. citizens engaged in smuggling aliens into the country. From 1985 to 2000, among those charged with immigration offenses, 87 percent of Mexicans and 93 percent of Chinese were held on charges of illegal entry or reentry and 64 percent of U.S. citizens charged were held for smuggling people.

FIGURE 10.4

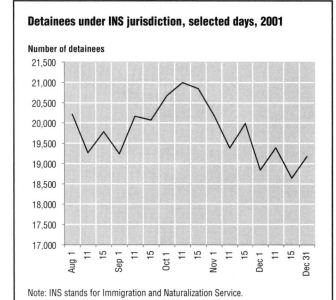

Detainees under INS jurisdiction, selected days, 2001

Note: INS stands for Immigration and Naturalization Service.

SOURCE: Adapted from Paige M. Harrison and Allen J. Beck, "Figure 2. Daily counts of detainees under INS jurisdiction, August 1 to December 31, 2001," in *Prisoners in 2001*, U.S. Bureau of Justice Statistics, Washington, DC, July 2002

FIGURE 10.5

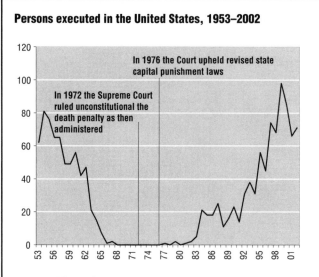

Persons executed in the United States, 1953–2002

SOURCE: Adapted from Tracy L. Snell, "Number of persons executed in the United States, 1930–2002," in *Key Facts at a Glance*, U.S. Bureau of Justice Statistics, Washington, DC, December 2002 [Online] http://www.ojp.usdoj.gov/bjs/glance/tables/exetab.htm [accessed May 7, 2003]

A shift in emphasis occurred after the terrorist attacks of September 11, 2001. The change is evident in data that record persons detained under INS auspices (rather than referred to U.S. attorneys, although these numbers overlap). In the category of detained persons, also, numbers had increased dramatically. In 1995, 8,177 persons were detained. By year-end 2001 the number had increased to 19,137. (See Table 10.6.) The number of detained persons reached a historic high on October 11, 2001 (20,997). (See Figure 10.4.) This occurred after the INS changed its regulations on September 18, 2001, following the 9/11 terror attacks. The new policy was announced by Attorney General John Ashcroft in a September 18 press briefing ("Attorney General Remarks"). Ashcroft announced that the 24-hour detention rule, in place before the policy changed, would be doubled to 48 hours, "or to an additional reasonable time if necessary under an emergency or in other extraordinary circumstances." This policy, later formalized as part of the USA Patriot Act, has enabled the government to hold terrorist suspects, or those suspected of aiding terrorists, in detention for lengthy periods of time.

The data presented in Table 10.6 show that even before the "war on terror," the ability of the federal government to hold INS detainees was becoming strained. In 1995 the INS housed 2,286 detainees under intergovernmental agreements in state prisons, local jails, and other facilities. By 2000 such state and local facilities held 11,281 immigrants whereas those held by the INS itself or other federal facilities had not increased significantly.

Figure 10.4 shows that the 9/11 terrorist attacks produced a temporary bulge in those detained for a two-month period. Thereafter the number of immigrants detained once more dropped to levels similar to those experienced in the pre-9/11 period. Meanwhile, however, the USA Patriot Act, signed into law on October 26, 2001, gives the government power to hold immigrant terror suspects or those immigrants suspected of aiding terrorists for longer periods.

The Patriot Act is controversial because it gives the government powers of surveillance that some people believe violates their right of privacy. In the context of prisons and jails, the act's Section 412 concerns mandatory detention of suspected terrorists. (A copy of the act is available on the INS Web site at http://www.immigration.gov/graphics/lawsregs/patriot.pdf.) Section 412 gives the Attorney General the power to "certify" that an alien is engaged in an activity that endangers the national security of the United States. The intent of the legislation is that a certified person be held until removed from the United States. The Attorney General must either charge the person with a crime or place the person "in removal procedures." But if removal is "unlikely in the reasonably foreseeable future, [the person] may be detained for additional periods of up to six months only if the release of the alien will threaten the national security of the United States or the safety of the community or any person." The act provides for judicial review of the Attorney General's actions by the U.S. Supreme Court or federal district courts. Unless courts overrule the Attorney General's judgment, circumstances can arise under which

FIGURE 10.6

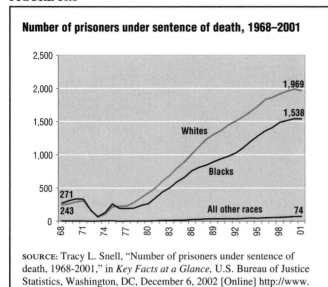

Number of prisoners under sentence of death, 1968–2001

SOURCE: Tracy L. Snell, "Number of prisoners under sentence of death, 1968-2001," in *Key Facts at a Glance,* U.S. Bureau of Justice Statistics, Washington, DC, December 6, 2002 [Online] http://www.ojp.usdoj.gov/bjs/glance/tables/drracetab.htm [accessed May 7, 2003]

an alien can be held indefinitely, always for successive 6-month periods.

Other Foreigners Under Detention

A related issue of detention is the federal government's confinement of persons at the U.S. military base in Guantanamo Bay, Cuba, as "unlawful combatants." These persons, captured during the conflict in Afghanistan, are held under a presidential order issued November 13, 2001 ("President Issues Military Order," The White House [Online] http://www.whitehouse.gov/news/releases/2001/11/20011113-27.html [accessed May 19, 2003]). According to the order, such individuals are in the custody of the Department of Defense and are to be tried, when tried, by military commissions rather than in U.S. district courts. The lengthy detention of such prisoners has also been the subject of much controversy and debate. Amnesty International's 2003 annual report, issued in May 2003, charged that more than 600 such individuals were still being held at Guantanamo. As unlawful combatants, these detainees are not guaranteed legal assistance and do not have to be charged with a crime. They may be held indefinitely for interrogation.

DEATH ROW INMATES

In 1972 the U.S. Supreme Court ruled that the death penalty was "cruel and unusual punishment" in three cases the Court agreed to hear—two for rape and one for murder, each involving a black offender. The Court's ruling was based on the manner in which the death penalty was then administered by the states; the states left sentencing to juries with little or no guidance; juries could impose the death penalty or a lesser sentence. The Court reasoned

that this left open the possibility that minorities might be more severely punished than members of the white majority. The Court discussed but did not rule, in the abstract, on the constitutionality of the death penalty per se. The case is known as *Furman v. Georgia* (408 US 238—1972) in which the Court also decided *Jackson v. Georgia* and *Branch v. Texas*, two similar cases.

Executions reached a peak of 199 in 1935 and then began declining. When *Furman v. Georgia* was decided, the last execution had occurred six years before in 1966, the only execution in that year. No person was executed between 1967 and 1976. One execution occurred in 1977, a year after the Supreme Court in effect reinstated the death penalty in another case, *Gregg v. Georgia* (428 US 453—1976). After that, executions began to grow year by year and reached a new peak of 98 executions in 1999. (See Figure 10.5).

Between 1972 and 1976, states passed new legislation implementing sentencing guidelines and provided procedural safeguards for defendants in response to the Supreme Court's guidance contained in *Furman v. Georgia*. In *Gregg v. Georgia*, the Court held that as implemented under revised laws in Georgia, the death sentence was legal. The Court went further and stated that it was not cruel and unusual punishment per se and argued that the 8th Amendment's prohibition of such punishment did not outlaw the death penalty. It was widely used at the time when the amendment passed; the Constitution also mentioned capital punishment in other contexts.

The number of prisoners on death row has grown dramatically since the 1970s in part because the Supreme Court's 1972 and 1976 rulings set new boundaries for the administration of capital punishment. Since that time, states have been engaged in a process of modifying their laws. In 2001 alone, according to the Bureau of Justice Statistics (Tracy L. Snell and Laura M. Maruschak, *Capital Punishment 2001*, Washington, D.C., December 2002), 10 states revised their statutes regarding capital punishment; in eight of these states, provisions were enacted to exempt certain individuals or types of cases from the death penalty or to raise the threshold to be met before the death penalty could be applied.

In 1973 prisoners on death row numbered 134, the lowest number in the 1968–2001 period. The highest number was reached in 2000—3,601. The most recently available count, for 2001, was 3,581. Blacks on death row exceeded whites in 1968, 271 to 243, showing why the Supreme Court, in its 1972 decision, felt that discrimination may have been present in the administration of the death penalty. (See Figure 10.6.) Beginning in 1976, whites began to outnumber blacks on death row consistently. In 2001, 1,969 of death row inmates were white, 1,538 were black, and 74 were of all other races. Proportionally whites

TABLE 10.7

Demographic characteristics of prisoners under sentence of death, 2001

Characteristic	Prisoners under sentence of death, 2001		
	Yearend	Admissions	Removals
Total number under sentence of death	3,581	155	175
Gender			
Male	98.6 %	100 %	98.3 %
Female	1.4	0	1.7
Race			
White	55.0 %	57.4	62.3
Black	42.9	39.4 %	36.6 %
All other races*	2.1	3.1	1.1
Hispanic origin			
Hispanic	11.2 %	16.2 %	3.8 %
Non-Hispanic	88.8	83.8	96.3
Education			
8th grade or less	14.5 %	15.8 %	12.3 %
9th-11th	37.2	32.5	36.1
High school graduate/GED	38.4	47.5	41.9
Any college	9.9	4.2	9.7
Median	11th	12th	12th
Marital status			
Married	22.1 %	19.9 %	31.7 %
Divorced/separated	21.0	15.4	16.8
Widowed	2.6	0.7	3.7
Never married	54.3	64.0	47.8

Note: Calculations are based on those cases for which data were reported. Missing data by category were as follows:

	Yearend	Admissions	Removals
Hispanic origin	381	13	15
Education	501	35	20
Marital status	335	19	14

* At yearend 2000, other races consisted of 30 American Indians, 29 Asians, and 12 self-identified Hispanics. During 2001, 4 Asians and 1 self-identified Hispanic were admitted; 2 American Indians were removed.

SOURCE: Tracy L. Snell and Laura M. Maruschak, "Table 7: Demographic characteristics of prisoners under sentence of death, 2001," in *Capital Punishment 2001*, U.S. Bureau of Justice Statistics, Washington, DC, December 2002

TABLE 10.8

Age at time of arrest for capital offense and age of prisoners under sentence of death, yearend 2001

Age	Prisoners under sentence of death			
	At time of arrest		On December 31, 2001	
	Number*	Percent	Number	Percent
Total number under sentence of death on 12/31/01	3,311	100 %	3,358	100 %
17 or younger	77	2.3	0	0.1
18–19	358	10.8	4	5.4
20–24	882	26.6	192	13.2
25–29	742	22.4	471	17.5
30–34	548	16.6	628	17.9
35–39	364	11.0	640	18.8
40–44	178	5.4	675	11.8
45–49	98	3.0	424	8.5
50–54	41	1.2	304	4.1
55–59	14	0.4	148	1.5
60–64	4	0.1	55	1.1
65 or older	5	0.2	40	1.1
Mean age	28 years		39 years	
Median age	27 years		39 years	

Note: The youngest person under sentence of death was a black male in North Carolina, born in December 1982 and sentenced to death in November 2001. The oldest person under sentence of death was a white male in Arizona, born in September 1915 and sentenced to death in June 1983.
* Excludes 270 inmates for whom the date of arrest for capital offense was not available.

SOURCE: Tracy L. Snell and Laura M. Maruschak, "Table 8: Age at time of arrest for capital offense and age of prisoners under sentence of death at yearend 2001," in *Capital Punishment 2001*, U.S. Bureau of Justice Statistics, Washington, DC, December 2002

(55 percent of death row inmates) were under- and blacks (42.9 percent) were over-represented relative to their share of the population in 2001. In 2000, whites were 72 percent and blacks 11 percent of the general population. All other races were 2 percent of death row inmates and 6 percent of the population. (Population data are from the Census Bureau.)

Death Row Demographics

During 2001, 155 new prisoners were put on death row while 175 were removed. (See Table 10.7.) Among those removed, 66 were executed, 19 died (17 of natural causes, 2 by suicide), and the remaining 90 had their convictions overturned or vacated or changed to life imprisonment. At the end of 2001, 3,581 persons were on death row, down from 3,601 in 2000.

According to *Capital Punishment 2001*, 51 of the 3,581 death row inmates at the end of 2001 were women. Of these, 31 were white, 17 were black, and 3 were of other races. California had the largest number (12) followed by Texas (7) and North Carolina (6). The overwhelming majority of prisoners on death row were men (98.6 percent). Among men, 1,938 were white, 1,521 were black, and 71 were of other races. The three states with the greatest number of males on death row as of December 31, 2001 were California with 591, Texas with 446, and Florida with 369. Among all prisoners sentenced to death, 88.8 percent were non-Hispanic, 11.2 percent were of Hispanic origin.

Total death row populations mirror the general population up to a point. California had the most inmates, 603, at the end of 2001, followed by Texas (453) and Florida (372). These states ranked 1, 2, and 4 in general population in the 2000 Census. New York, the third-largest state, had 6 death row inmates, the same number as Montana, the eighth smallest state by size of population.

By educational attainment, more than half of inmates (51.7 percent) had less than a high school education, 38.4 percent had a high school diploma or equivalent certification, 9.9 had attended or had graduated from college.

The majority of inmates at the end of 2001 had never been married (54.3 percent), 22.1 percent were married, 21 percent were divorced, 2.6 percent were widowed.

Age of Inmates and Time on Death Row

In 2001 nearly half of death row inmates, 49 percent, had been between 20 and 29 years of age at the time of arrest. (See Table 10.8.) As of December 31, 2001, the two age groups with the largest population under sentence of death were 35 to 39 and 40 to 44. The youngest inmate was 19 years of age, the oldest 86. The average age of those at sentencing was 28. The average age of all death row inmates in 2001 was 39.

Substantial time elapses between sentencing and the resolution of cases on death row, be it by execution or other forms of "removal." The prisoners on death row in 2001 had spent on average 8 years and 7 months in prison since sentencing. Those executed in 2001 had been in prison 11 years and 10 months. The time between sentencing and execution has been lengthening. It was 4 years and 3 months between 1977 and 1983 and 6 years and 2 months in 1984. For this reason, the age of prisoners at sentencing is about 10 years lower than the average age of the population on death row.

Executed Prisoners

Fifteen states executed 64 prisoners in 2001; the federal government executed 2. Of the 66 executed prisoners, 63 were men, 3 were women. In terms of race, 48 were white, 17 were black, and 1 was an American Indian. Three of the whites executed were Hispanics. All executions were by lethal injection.

Preliminary data reported by BJS in *Capital Punishment 2001* for 2002 (January 1 through December 11) indicate that 13 states executed 68 prisoners, 2 of whom were women. Within this group, 51 were white and 17 were black. Sixty-seven were executed by lethal injection; one prisoner was electrocuted.

Thirty-eight states provide capital punishment for murder and, in some instances, for other offenses. California authorizes capital punishment for train wrecking, treason, and perjury that leads to someone else's execution. Florida and New Jersey have capital punishment for drug trafficking. Louisiana provides for capital punishment for rape of a person under 12 and also punishes treason by death. Mississippi includes aircraft piracy. Twelve states and the District of Columbia do not have the death penalty. States with no death penalty provisions in their laws as of December 31, 2001 were Alaska, Hawaii, Iowa, Maine, Massachusetts, Michigan, Minnesota, North Dakota, Rhode Island, Vermont, West Virginia, and Wisconsin.

The federal government has 41 laws imposing the death penalty, including espionage, genocide, terrorist murder of a U.S. national in another country, and treason.

CHAPTER 11
PRISONERS' RIGHTS UNDER LAW

In 1871 a Virginia court, in *Ruffin v. Commonwealth* (62, Va. 790, 1871), commented that a prisoner "has, as a consequence of his crime, not only forfeited his liberty, but all his personal rights except those which the law in its humanity accords to him. He is for the time being the slave of the state." Eighty years later, in *Stroud v. Swope* (187 F. 2d. 850, 9th Circuit, 1951), a federal circuit judge asserted: "We think it well settled that it is not the function of the courts to superintend the treatment and discipline of persons in penitentiaries, but only to deliver from imprisonment those who are illegally confined." Correctional administrators held that prisoners lost all of their constitutional rights after conviction. Prisoners had privileges, not rights, and privileges could be taken away arbitrarily. (William C. Collins, *Legal Responsibility and Authority of Correctional Officers,* American Correctional Association, Laurel, Maryland, 1982.)

A significant change in the legal view came in the 1960s. In *Cooper v. Pate* (378 U.S. 546, 1964) the U.S. Supreme Court held that the Civil Rights Act of 1871 (42 USC 1983) granted protection to prisoners. The code states that:

> Every person who, under color of any statute, ordinance, regulation, custom, or usage, of any State or Territory or the District of Columbia, subjects, or causes to be subjected, any citizen of the United States or other person within the jurisdiction thereof to the deprivation of any rights, privileges, or immunities secured by the Constitution and laws, shall be liable to the party injured in an action at law, suit in equity, or other proper proceeding for redress.

With the *Cooper* decision, the Supreme Court announced that prisoners, "persons," had rights guaranteed by the U.S. Constitution and could ask the judicial system for help in challenging the conditions of their imprisonment. Cases brought later came to be known as Section 1983 lawsuits because the Court had based itself on

Section 1983 of Title 42 of the U.S. Code. Prisoners' suits in federal courts skyrocketed from 218 in 1966 to 26,824 in 1992. After 1992 new laws made it more difficult for prisoners to sue.

Observers differ about the nature of the lawsuits, how the federal courts process them, and the manner in which they are resolved. Many consider some of the lawsuits to be frivolous and undeserving of the limited resources of the federal courts. Others assert that some lawsuits have merit, but that the federal courts tend to treat all section 1983 lawsuits in an assembly line fashion with little or no individual attention.

PRODUCE THE BODY

In *Cooper v. Pate* the Supreme Court relied upon civil rights. Another source of prisoners' rights arose from the Court's reliance on habeas corpus. The Latin phrase is an imperative meaning "Have the body ..." with the rest of the phrase, "brought before me," implied. A writ of habeas corpus is therefore the command issued by one court to another court (or lesser authority) to produce a person and to explain why that person is being detained. Habeas corpus dates back to an act of the British Parliament passed in 1679. The U.S. Congress enacted the Judiciary Act of 1789 and gave federal prisoners the right to habeas corpus review. The Habeas Act of 1867 later protected the rights of newly freed slaves and also extended habeas corpus protection to state prisoners. The effective meaning of habeas corpus for prisoners is that it enables them to petition federal courts to review any aspect of their cases.

The Court also revisited habeas corpus in the 1960s. In *Smith v. Bennett* (365 U.S. 708, 1961), the Court ruled that states could not deny a writ of habeas corpus to prisoners who could not pay a filing fee. In *Long v. District Court* (385 U.S. 192, 1966), the Court ruled that a state must furnish prisoners, not otherwise able to obtain them, with transcripts of prior hearings. In *Johnson v. Avery* (393 U.S. 483, 1969) the Court emphasized the basic purpose of the writ of habeas corpus in enabling those unlawfully imprisoned to obtain their freedom. The case concerned whether the state could prevent inmates from helping each other file petitions. The Justices held that "it is fundamental that access of prisoners to the courts for the purpose of presenting their complaints may not be denied or obstructed." They ruled that until the state provides some reasonable alternative to assist inmates in the preparation of petitions for postconviction relief, it "may not validly enforce a regulation which absolutely bars inmates from furnishing such assistance to other prisoners." In *Bounds v. Smith* (430 U.S. 817, 1977) the Court further asserted that prison authorities must "assist inmates in the preparation and filing of meaningful legal papers by providing prisoners with adequate law libraries or adequate assistance from persons trained in the law."

Bounds did not create an abstract, free-standing right to a law library or legal assistance; rather it acknowledged the right of access to the courts. Inmates have to prove that the alleged shortcomings in the prison library or legal assistance program hindered their efforts to pursue a non-frivolous legal claim. In addition, the Court relied on a constitutional principle that:

> ...prevents courts of law from undertaking tasks assigned to the political branches.... It is the role of courts to provide relief to claimants, in individual or class actions, who have suffered, or will imminently suffer, actual harm; it is not the role of courts, but that of the political branches to shape the institutions of government in such fashion as to comply with the laws and the Constitution.... If—to take another example from prison life—a healthy inmate who had suffered no deprivation of needed medical treatment were able to claim violation of his constitutional right to medical care..., simply on the ground that prison medical facilities were inadequate, the essential distinction between judge and executive would have disappeared: it would have become the function of the courts to assure adequate medical care in prisons.

Bounds did not guarantee prison law libraries and legal assistance programs. They are only "one constitutionally acceptable method to assure meaningful access to the courts." There can be "alternative means to achieve that goal." An inmate has to show that access to the courts was so "stymied by inadequacies of the law library that he or she was unable even to file a complaint."

Some 24 years after *Bounds*, in *Shaw v. Murphy* (532 U.S. 223, 2001), a more conservative Court ruled that Kevin Murphy, incarcerated in a Montana state prison, did not "possess a special First Amendment right to provide legal assistance to fellow inmates." Murphy was punished after he attempted to intervene in a process in which a fellow prisoner was charged with assaulting a guard. Much had changed since the 1970s. Murphy himself was employed

as an "inmate law clerk" and provided legal assistance to other inmates. Murphy had applied to assist another prisoner, Pat Tracy, but the prison had denied the request because Murphy, a high-security inmate, could not meet with Tracy, a maximum-security inmate. Murphy persisted nonetheless, investigated the case on his own, and wrote a letter to Tracy offering his help. Murphy's punishment arose from this action.

CONSTITUTIONAL RIGHTS

Prisoners can also bring their cases to the federal courts by accusing the prison systems of violating the First, Fourth, and Eighth Amendments and the due process clauses of the Fifth and Fourteenth Amendments of the U.S. Constitution. The Fifth Amendment provides that no person should be deprived of life, liberty, or property by the federal government "without due process of the law."

The Fourteenth Amendment observes that no state should "deprive any person of life, liberty, or property without due process of law." Constitutional rights have been claimed by prisoners and asserted or denied by the courts. Selected cases illustrate the evolution of prisoners' rights.

FIRST AMENDMENT CASES

The First Amendment of the U.S. Constitution guarantees that:

> Congress shall make no law respecting an establishment of religion, or prohibiting the free exercise thereof; or abridging the freedom of speech, or of the press; or the right of the people peaceably to assemble; and to petition the government for a redress of grievances.

Censorship

In *Procunier v. Martinez* (416 U.S. 396, 1973) the Supreme Court ruled that prison officials cannot censor inmate correspondence unless they:

> ...show that a regulation authorizing mail censorship furthers one or more of the substantial governmental interests of security, order, and rehabilitation. Second, the limitation of First Amendment freedom must be no greater than is necessary or essential to the protection of the particular governmental interest involved.

Prison officials can refuse to send letters that detail escape plans or encoded messages but cannot censor inmate correspondence simply to "eliminate unflattering or unwelcome opinions or factually inaccurate statements." Because prisoners retain rights, when "a prison regulation or practice offends a fundamental constitutional guarantee, federal courts will discharge their duty to protect constitutional rights."

However, the Court recognized that it was "ill-equipped to deal with the increasingly urgent problems of prison administration." Running a prison takes expertise and planning, all of which, said the Court, is part of the responsibility of the legislative and executive branches. The task of the judiciary, however, is to establish a standard of review for prisoners' constitutional claims that is responsive to both the need to protect inmates' rights and the policy of judicial restraint.

The Court ruled in 1974 (*Pell v. Procunier*, 417 U.S. 817) that federal prison officials could prohibit inmates having face-to-face media interviews. The Court reasoned that judgments regarding prison security "are peculiarly within the province and professional expertise of corrections officials, and in the absence of substantial evidence in the record to indicate that the officials have exaggerated their response to these considerations, courts should ordinarily defer to their expert judgement in such matters." Prisoners had other means by which to communicate with the media.

In 1985, in *Nolan v. Fitzpatrick* (451 F. 2d 545), the First Circuit Court ruled that inmates had the right to correspond with newspapers. The prisoners were limited only in that they could not write about escape plans or include contraband material in their letters.

The Missouri Division of Corrections permitted correspondence between immediate family members who were inmates at different institutions and between inmates writing about legal matters, but allowed other inmate correspondence only if each prisoner's "classification/treatment team" thought it was in the best interests of the parties.

Another Missouri regulation permitted an inmate to marry only with the superintendent's permission, which can be given only when there were "compelling reasons" to do so, such as a pregnancy. In *Turner v. Safley* (482 U.S. 78, 1987) the Supreme Court found the first regulation constitutional and the second one unconstitutional.

The Court held that the "constitutional right of prisoners to marry is impermissibly burdened by the Missouri marriage regulation." The Supreme Court had ruled earlier that prisoners had a constitutionally protected right to marry (*Zablocki v. Redhail*, 434 U.S. 374, 1977), subject to restrictions due to incarceration such as time and place and prior approval of a warden. However, the Missouri regulation practically banned all marriages.

The findings in *Turner v. Safley* have become a guide for prison regulations in the United States. The High Court observed that:

> When a prison regulation impinges on inmates' constitutional rights, the regulation is valid if it is reasonably related to legitimate penological interests.... First, there must be a "valid, rational connection" between the prison regulation and the legitimate government interest put forward to justify it.... Moreover, the government objective must be a legitimate and neutral one.... A second factor

relevant in determining the reasonableness of a prison restriction ... is whether there are alternative means of exercising the right (sic) that remain open to prison inmates. A third consideration is the impact accommodation of the asserted constitutional right will have on guards and other inmates, and on the allocation of prison resources generally.

Religious Beliefs

While inmates retain their First Amendment freedom to practice their religions, the courts have upheld restrictions on religious freedom when corrections departments need to maintain security, when economic considerations are involved, and when the regulation is reasonable.

The District of Columbia jail allowed, at public expense, interdenominational services, as well as services by Catholics, Jews, Protestants, Unitarians, the Salvation Army, and other religious groups. Public funds paid for Protestant and Catholic chaplains and for religious medals. An honorarium was paid to a rabbi when needed.

Several times in 1959 a group of Muslims requested permission to hold religious services. The Director of Corrections of the District of Columbia, Donald Clemmer, refused the requests because he believed that "Muslims teach racial hatred." The director also confiscated a religious medal from the petitioner, William Fulwood, because Clemmer deemed the medal was symbolic of a doctrine of hate and wearing it would promote racial tension in the prison. The jail administration also did not allow Furwood to correspond with Elijah Muhammad, the leader of the Black Muslims, or subscribe to the Los Angeles *Herald Dispatch* because it carried a column by Muhammad.

In 1962 the U.S. District Court of the District of Columbia in *Fulwood v. Clemmer*, 206 F. Supp 370) ruled that, by allowing some religious groups to hold religious services and by conducting such services a public expense while denying that right to Muslims, the jail officials had discriminated against the Muslim inmates. These acts violated the "Order of the Commissioners of the District of Columbia No. 6514-B, dated Nov. 25, 1953, which requires prison officials to make facilities available without regard to race or religion."

The court held the same opinion on the distribution and wearing of religious medals. However, on the issue of correspondence and the newspaper subscription, the court stated that the judiciary "lacked general supervisory powers over prisons, and in absence of ... abuse of discretion by prison officials, courts should not interfere."

In 1972 in *Cruz v. Beto* (405 U.S. 319), Fred A. Cruz, a Buddhist serving in a Texas prison, claimed that while other prisoners were allowed use of the prison chapel, officials refused Buddhists the right to hold religious services. Cruz was placed in solitary confinement on a diet of bread and water for two weeks for sharing religious materials with other prisoners.

The Supreme Court stated that prison officials are "accorded latitude in the administration of prison affairs, and prisoners necessarily are subject to appropriate rules and regulations." However, prisoners have the right to petition the government for "redress of grievances," and the federal courts, while they do not sit to supervise prisons, must "enforce constitutional rights of all 'persons,' including prisoners." The Court concluded that "reasonable opportunities must be afforded to all prisoners to exercise the religious freedom guaranteed by the First and Fourteenth Amendments without fear of penalty."

A five-to-four split Supreme Court in *O'Lone v. Shabazz* (482 U.S. 340, 1987) declared that "state prison officials acted in a reasonable manner" and were not violating First Amendment freedoms when they did not allow inmates who were members of the Islamic faith to attend religious services held on Friday afternoons. "Prison policies were related to legitimate security and rehabilitative concerns, alternative means of exercising religious faith with respect to other practices were available, and placing Islamic prisoners into work groups so as to permit them to exercise religious rights would have adverse impact" on the running of the prison.

In the opinion of the four dissenters, however, when:

...exercise of the asserted right is not presumptively dangerous ... and where the prison has completely deprived an inmate of that right, then prison officials must show that "a particular restriction is necessary to further an important governmental interest...." The prison in this case has completely prevented respondent inmates from attending the central religious service of their Moslem faith....

The State has neither demonstrated that the restriction is necessary to further an important objective nor proved that less extreme measures may not serve its purpose.... If a Catholic prisoner were prevented from attending Mass on Sunday, few would regard that deprivation as anything but absolute, even if the prisoner were afforded other opportunities to pray, to discuss the Catholic faith with others, and even to avoid eating meat on Friday if there were a preference.

Cases in lower courts have also dealt with religious food preferences, the wearing of religious jewelry, religious hairstyles and dress, and compulsory attendance in programs that use religious thematics. For instance, courts have ordered pork-free diets for groups whose religion forbids them from eating pork, although they must make up a significant portion of the inmate population. There are also limits to what a prison administrator is reasonably expected to do. In New York the federal court upheld the prison's refusal to meet the food requirements of Rastafarians, a religion of Jamaican origin (*Benjamin v.*

Coughlin, 708 F. Suppl. 570, 1989) because the complex requirements would have burdened the prison administratively and financially. Depending on the sect of the religion, the group wanted no meats, no canned foods or dairy products, no foods grown with inorganic pesticides or fertilizers, and foods cooked in natural materials, such as clay pots.

In 1996, the U.S. 7th Circuit Court of Appeals held that Wisconsin could not prohibit the wearing of religious jewelry (*Sasnett v. Sullivan*, 91 F.3d 1018), according to the Religious Freedom Restoration Act. Prison officials had claimed that such jewels could be used as weapons but had permitted the use of rosary beads which, the Circuit held, could be used in strangulating others. The state was held to be inconsistent.

The courts themselves can be inconsistent, as well. Michael G. Gallahan, a Cherokee, practiced his religious beliefs, including having worn long hair since the age of five. Tenets of his religion recognize hair as a "sense organ" and taught that loss of hair was equated to losing part of the body. Prison officials had established hair-length regulations because of the belief that long hair was a convenient place for hiding weapons, could obscure facial identification, and could cause sanitary problems.

In *Gallahan v. Hollyfield* (516 F. 2d 1004, 1981) a U.S. District Court in Virginia ruled that "a prisoner is not stripped of all rights on incarceration; specifically he retains those First Amendment rights that are not inconsistent with his status as a prisoner or with the legitimate penological objectives of the corrections system." The judges found that Gallahan "established a sincere belief in his religion" and that the state's reasons were "insufficient" to enforce the hair-length regulation, especially since Gallahan had agreed to wear his hair tied back in a ponytail.

However, in 1992 the appellate court upheld haircut rules in a case involving a Rastafarian hairstyle (*Scott v. Mississippi Department of Corrections*, 961 F.2d 77) arguing that the "loss of absolute freedom of religious expression is but one sacrifice required by ... incarceration."

The Sixth Circuit Court of Appeals, in *Abdullah v. Kinnison* (769 F. 2d 345, 1985), ruled that a prison directive requiring practicing Muslims to keep white prayer robes in the institutional chapel rather than in cells was justified by security reasons and did not violate the First Amendment.

In 1996 the New York Court of Appeals ruled on *Griffin v. Coughlin* (NY CtApp, No 73), a case involving 12-step programs. As a precondition to his continued participation in a family reunion program, David Griffin had been required to participate in a substance abuse program modeled after Alcoholics Anonymous (AA), which makes references to "God" and a "Higher Power." He claimed that the requirement to participate in such a program violated his right to practice atheism under the First Amendment. The court ruled that the prison could not compel an inmate to attend a substance abuse program in which references to "God" and a "Higher Power" were made. The court concluded that the program violated the Establishment clause of the Constitution and "the state has exercised coercive power to advance religion by denying benefits of eligibility for the family reunion problem to atheist and agnostic inmates who object and refuse to participate in religious activity."

The dissenters thought that, although the 12-step program may be perceived as:

...somewhat religious, [it] remains overwhelmingly secular in philosophy, objective, and operation.... The inmate was not compelled to participate in the ... program. He voluntarily chose the course of action that placed his agnosticism and nonbeliefs at risk because he wished to receive something he is not unqualifiably entitled to from the state.

FOURTH AMENDMENT

The Fourth Amendment guarantees the "right of the people to be secure ... against unreasonable searches and seizures ... and no warrants shall issue, but upon probable cause...." The courts have not been as active in protecting prisoners under the Fourth Amendment as under the First and Eighth Amendments. In *Bell v. Wolfish* (441 U.S. 520, 1979) the U.S. Supreme Court asserted that:

...simply because prison inmates retain certain constitutional rights does not mean that these rights are not subject to restrictions and limitations.... Maintaining institutional security and preserving internal order and discipline are essential goals that may require limiting or retraction of the retained constitutional rights of both convicted prisoners and pretrial detainees. Since problems that arise in the day-to-day operation of a corrections facility are not susceptible to easy solutions, prison administrators should be accorded wide-ranging deference in the adoption and execution of policies and practices that, in their judgment, are needed to preserve internal order and discipline and to maintain institutional security.

Based on this reasoning the Court ruled that body searches did not violate the Fourth Amendment. "Balancing the significant and legitimate security interest of the institution against the inmates' privacy interest, such searches can be conducted on less than probable cause and are not unreasonable."

In another Fourth Amendment case (*Hudson v. Palmer*, 46 U.S. 517, 1984), the Supreme Court upheld the right of prison officials to search a prisoner's cell and seize property.

The recognition of privacy rights for prisoners in their individual cells simply cannot be reconciled with the concept of incarceration and the needs and objectives of penal institutions.... [However, the fact that a prisoner does not have a reasonable expectation of privacy] does not mean he is without a remedy for calculated harassment unrelated to prison needs. Nor does it mean that prison attendants can ride roughshod over inmates' property rights with impunity. The Eighth Amendment always stands as a protection against "cruel and unusual punishments."

Sexual Misconduct

Sexual misconduct by corrections personnel refers to any type of improper conduct of a sexual nature directed at prisoners. Given the control and power imbalance inherent between a corrections officer and a prison inmate, there is widespread consensus within society that this sort of misconduct should not be tolerated.

Due to the incidence of sexual misconduct involving correctional staff and inmates, by 1996 some 31 states, the District of Columbia, and the federal government had passed legislation criminalizing such behavior in a correctional setting. According to *Sexual Misconduct in Prisons: Laws, Remedies and Incidence* (National Institute of Corrections, 2000), since 1996 additional legislation had been passed in 15 states. (See Table 11.1.)

In a paper prepared by the General Accounting Office (GAO) (*Women in Prison, Sexual Misconduct by Correctional Staff*, June 1999) a summary of sexual misconduct allegations in the 3 largest prison jurisdictions—Federal Bureau of Prisons, California, and Texas—is presented. The allegations summarized were those made by female inmates during the period 1995–1998. There were a collective 506 such allegations of which 18 percent (92 cases) were sustained resulting in staff resignations or employment terminations. Officials in these jurisdictions cited lack of evidence as the primary reason why more allegations were not sustained. They reported that most of the allegations involved verbal harassment, improper visual surveillance, improper touching, and/or consensual sex. Allegations involving rape and other forms of forced sexual assault were relatively rare. Generally, however, the jurisdictions studies did not have readily available, comprehensive data on the number, nature, and outcomes of sexual misconduct allegations. As a result, the GAO report highlighted the need for more formalized systems of monitoring, analyzing, and reporting allegations of staff-on-inmate sexual misconduct.

EIGHTH AMENDMENT

The Eighth Amendment guarantees that "cruel and unusual punishment [not be] inflicted." The Eighth Amendment has been used to challenge the death penalty, three-strikes laws, crowded prisons, lack of health or safety in prisons, and excessive violence by the guards.

TABLE 11.1

Statutes prohibiting sexual misconduct involving correctional staff and inmates as of May 2000

	Legislation Passed 1996 or Earlier	New or Supplemental Legislation Passed Since 1996	Level of Offense
Alabama	None	No response to this question	
Alaska	4		Felony
Arizona	4		Misdemeanor
Arkansas	4	4	Misdemeanor
California	4		Felony or misdemeanor
Colorado	4		Felony (if coercive)
Connecticut	4		Felony or misdemeanor
Delaware	4		Felony
District of Columbia	4		Felony
Florida	4	4	Felony
Georgia	4		Felony
Hawaii	4		Felony
Idaho	4		Felony
Illinois		4	Felony
Indiana	4		Felony
Iowa	4		Aggravated misdemeanor
Kansas	4		Felony
Kentucky	None		
Louisiana	4		Felony
Maine	4		Felony
Maryland		4	Misdemeanor
Massachusetts		4	(Not specified)
Michigan	4		Misdemeanor
Minnesota	None		
Mississippi		4	Felony
Missouri	4		Felony
Montana	None		
Nebraska		4	Felony
Nevada	4		(Not available)
New Hampshire		4	Felony
New Jersey	4		(Not available)
New Mexico	4		Felony
New York	4		Felony or misdemeanor
North Carolina	4		Felony
North Dakota	4		Misdemeanor
Ohio	4		Felony
Oklahoma	4		Felony
Oregon	None		
Pennsylvania		4	Misdemeanor
Rhode Island	4		Felony
South Carolina		4	Felony
South Dakota	4	4	Felony
Tennessee		4	Misdemeanor
Texas	4	4	Felony (if coercive)
Utah	None		
Vermont	None		
Virginia		4	Felony or misdemeanor
Washington		4	Felony or misdemeanor
West Virginia	None		
Wisconsin	4		Felony
Wyoming	4	No 1999 survey response	Felony (if coercive)
U.S. Bureau of Prisons	4		Felony or misdemeanor (criminal if coercive)
Guam	None		
Puerto Rico	None		

SOURCE: "Table 1. Statutes prohibiting sexual misconduct involving correctional staff and inmates" in *Sexual Misconduct in Prisons: Laws, Remedies and Incidence,* National Institute of Corrections, U.S. Department of Justice, Longmont, CO, May 2000

The Supreme Court has established several tests to determine whether conditions or actions violated the Eighth Amendment:

- Did the actions or conditions offend concepts of "decency and human dignity and precepts of civilization which Americans profess to possess"?

- Was it "disproportionate to the offense"?

- Did it violate "fundamental standards of good conscience and fairness"?

- Was the punishment unnecessarily cruel?

- Did the punishment go beyond legitimate penal purposes?

Isolation

Several landmark cases changed the way prisoners can be held in isolation. In *Holt v. Sarver* (300 F. Supp 82, 1969) a U.S. district court in Arkansas found "solitary confinement or close confinement in isolation units of prisons not unconstitutional per se, but, depending on circumstances, it may violate the Eighth and Fourteenth Amendments." Isolation cells in an Arkansas prison were used for prisoners who broke rules, those who needed protective custody to separate them from other inmates, and those who were:

> ...general escape or security risks or who were awaiting trial on additional charges.... Confinement in isolation cells was not "solitary confinement" in the conventional sense of the term. On the contrary, the cells are substantially overcrowded.... The average number of men confined in a single cell seems to be four, but at times the number has been much higher (up to ten and eleven).

While the judges agreed that "if confinement of that type is to serve any useful purpose, it must be rigorous, uncomfortable, and unpleasant. However, there are limits to the rigor and discomfort of close confinement which a state may not constitutionally exceed."

The court found that the confinement of inmates in these isolation cells, which were "overcrowded, dirty, unsanitary, and pervaded by bad odors from toilets, constituted cruel and unusual punishment." The court also asserted that "prolonged confinement" of numbers of men in the same cell under unsanitary, dangerous conditions was "mentally and emotionally traumatic as well as physically uncomfortable. It is hazardous to health. It is degrading and debasing; it offends modern sensibilities, and, in the Court's estimation, amounts to cruel and unusual punishment."

In addition, those inmates who were not in isolation slept together in barracks where many of the inmates had weapons and attacked each other. While the court recognized that assaults, fights, and killings occurred in all penal institutions, the Arkansas Farm had not taken reasonable precautions. Prisoners should at least be "able to fall asleep at night without fear of having their throats cut before morning, and the state has failed to discharge a constitutional duty in failing to take steps to enable them to do so."

Another landmark case involving isolation occurred in the late 1970s, again in Arkansas. The state sentenced inmates to punitive isolation in extremely small cells for an indeterminate period, with their status being reviewed at the end of each 14-day period. While most were released within 14 days, many remained in that status for weeks or months, depending on their attitudes as appraised by prison personnel. Usually the inmates shared a cell with one other inmate, and at times three or four were together, causing them to sleep on the floor. Considering that these were violent men filled with "frustration and hostility," and that some were "dangerous and psychopaths," confining them together caused threatening situations that produced "a forcible response from prison personnel."

The lower courts found that the force used by the guards was excessive and declared that "confinement of prisoners in punitive isolation for more than 30 days constituted cruel and unusual punishment and was impermissible." In *Finney v. Hutto* (548 F. 2d. 740, 1977) the U.S. Court of Appeals agreed.

The Death Penalty

Three Supreme Court cases, all decided in the 1970s, have produced the current interpretation of the Eighth Amendment relative to the death penalty. In *Furman v. Georgia* (408 U.S. 238, 1972), the Court held that the death penalty in three cases under review was "cruel and unusual" because under the then prevailing statutes juries had "untrammeled discretion to impose or withhold the death penalty." Due process required procedural fairness, including consideration of the severity of the crime and the circumstances. In the three cases decided in *Furman*, three individuals were condemned to die, two for rape and one for murder. All three of the offenders were black.

In response to *Furman* states modified their statutes. North Carolina imposed a mandatory death sentence for first degree murder. This law was tested in the Supreme Court as *Woodson v. North Carolina* (428 U.S. 980, 1976). The Court held that while the death penalty was not cruel and unusual punishment in every circumstance, it ruled that a mandatory death sentence did not satisfy the requirements laid down in *Furman*. The Court said: "North Carolina's mandatory death penalty statute for first-degree murder departs markedly from contemporary standards respecting the imposition of the punishment of death and thus cannot be applied consistently with the Eighth and Fourteenth Amendments' requirement that the State's power to punish 'be exercised within the limits of civilized standards.'" The Court overturned the North Carolina law.

Woodson was decided on July 2, 1976. On the same day the Court rendered its judgment in the case of *Gregg v. Georgia*, the case of a man sentenced to death for murder and robbery committed under new legislation passed in Georgia following *Furman*. In this case the Court upheld the death penalty saying, in part:

The Georgia statutory system under which petitioner was sentenced to death is constitutional. The new procedures on their face satisfy the concerns of *Furman*, since before the death penalty can be imposed there must be specific jury findings as to the circumstances of the crime or the character of the defendant, and the State Supreme Court thereafter reviews the comparability of each death sentence with the sentences imposed on similarly situated defendants to ensure that the sentence of death in a particular case is not disproportionate. Petitioner's contentions that the changes in Georgia's sentencing procedures have not removed the elements of arbitrariness and capriciousness condemned by *Furman* are without merit.

Since that time the death penalty has been constitutional if imposed within the implicit guidelines laid down in these three Supreme Court cases.

Three-Strikes

In 2003 the Supreme Court ruled on the constitutionality of the California three-strikes law, the nation's most severe. The case involved a defendant, Gary Albert Ewing, who had been sentenced to 25 years to life for a third offense, the theft of three golf clubs each valued at $399. His previous offenses included (among others) a burglary and a robbery while threatening his victim with a knife. *Ewing v. California* (538 U.S., 2003) was a good test of the California statute because neither one of Ewing's first two offenses were of a seriously violent character and the third, the triggering offense, was what under California law is known as a "wobbler," namely an offense that can be tried, at the prosecutor's option, as either a felony or a misdemeanor.

The petition in *Ewing* argued that the punishment was "cruel and unusual" and disproportionate to the offense committed. In effect Ewing had the profile of a habitual but petty criminal whose theft of golf clubs should have been tried as a misdemeanor. In this case the Court dismissed the proportionality argument and, instead, affirmed the state's right to set policy for the protection of the public. Quoting from another case, the Court said that "The Eighth Amendment does not require strict proportionality between crime and sentence [but] forbids only extreme sentences that are 'grossly disproportionate' to the crime." California had the right to incapacitate repeat offenders by incarcerating them. According to the Court, the Constitution did not mandate that the states apply any one penological theory.

Prison Conditions and Medical Care

In *Rhodes v. Chapman* (452 U.S. 337, 1981) the Supreme Court ruled that housing prisoners in double cells was not cruel and unusual punishment. The justices maintained that:

> ...conditions of confinement, as constituting the punishment at issue, must not involve the wanton and unnecessary infliction of pain, nor may they be grossly disproportionate to the severity of the crime warranting imprisonment. But conditions that cannot be said to be cruel and unusual under contemporary standards are not unconstitutional. To the extent such conditions are restrictive and even harsh, they are part of the penalty that criminals pay for their offenses against society.

The Court concluded that the Constitution "does not mandate comfortable prisons," and only those "deprivations denying the 'minimal civilized measure of life's necessities'" violate the Eighth Amendment.

In two later cases as well, the Supreme Court held that unpleasant or inadequate prison conditions and poor medical care did not constitute cruel and unusual punishment unless deliberate indifference by the authorities could be established. The Court established this principle in *Wilson v. Seiter* (501 U.S. 294, 1991) when it upheld the judgment of a lower court that prisoners "claiming that conditions of confinement constituted cruel and unusual punishment were required to show deliberate indifference on the part of prison officials." Wilson "alleged overcrowding, excessive noise, insufficient locker storage space, inadequate heating and cooling, improper ventilation, unclean and inadequate restrooms, unsanitary dining facilities and food preparation, and housing with mentally and physically ill inmates" proved "at best" that the authorities were negligent. However, the Court found that Wilson had insufficient grounds for claiming Eighth Amendment protection.

An earlier case, *Estelle v. Gamble* (429 U.S. 97, 1976) had paved the way for *Wilson*. On November 9, 1973 J. W. Gamble, an inmate of the Texas Department of Corrections, was injured while performing a prison work assignment. Although he complained numerous times about his back injury and received some pills, the guards accused him of malingering. In January the disciplinary committee placed Gamble in solitary confinement for refusing to work. On February 4 he asked to see a doctor for chest pains and blackouts. Almost 12 hours later a medical assistant saw him and had him hospitalized.

The next morning, after an electrocardiogram, he was placed on Quinidine for treatment of irregular cardiac rhythm and moved to administrative segregation. On February 7, after experiencing pain in his chest, left arm, and back, Gamble asked to see a doctor and was refused. The next day he was refused again. After finally seeing the doctor again on February 9 and being given Quinidine, Gamble swore out a complaint that the staff had "subjected him to cruel and unusual punishment in violation of the Eighth Amendment."

In *Estelle v. Gamble*, the Court concluded that deliberate indifference to serious medical needs of prisoners constitutes "unnecessary and wanton infliction of pain," whether the indifference is displayed by prison doctors in their response to the prisoner's need or by prison guards who deny or delay access to treatment or interfere with the treatment. The Court, however, ruled that "every claim by a prisoner that he has not received adequate medical treatment" does not mean a violation of the Eighth Amendment. An "inadvertent failure to provide adequate medical care" is not "an unnecessary and wanton infliction of pain" or "repugnant to the conscience of mankind.... Medical malpractice does not become a constitutional violation merely because the victim is a prisoner." Only deliberate indifference "can offend 'evolving standards of decency' in violation of the Eighth Amendment." Because Gamble saw medical personnel 17 times over three months, the court did not find this a violation of the Eighth Amendment. "A medical decision not to order an X ray or like measures does not represent cruel and unusual punishment."

In another case, *Helling v. McKinney* (509 U.S. 25, 1993), the Court ruled that a Nevada inmate had the right to bring a court action because he had been assigned to a cell with another prison who smoked five packs of cigarettes daily, and he had not been informed of the health hazards that he could incur from second-hand smoke. Quoting its earlier decision in *DeShaney v. Winnebago County Dept. of Social Services* (489 U.S. 189, 1989), the Court declared:

> [W]hen the state takes a person into its custody and hold him there against his will, the Constitution imposes upon it a corresponding duty to assume some responsibility for his safety and general well being.... The rationale for this principle is simple enough: when the state by the affirmative exercise of its power so restrains an individual's liberty that it renders him unable to care for himself, and, at the same time fails to provide for his basic human needs—e.g., food, clothing, shelter, medical care, and reasonable safety—it transgresses the substantive limits on state action set by the Eight Amendment.

The justices asserted that prison administrators could not:

> ...ignore a condition of confinement that is sure or very likely to cause serious illness and needless suffering the next week or month or year. In *Hutto v. Finney* (437 U.S. 678, 1978) we noted that inmates in punitive isolation were crowded into cells and that some of them had infectious maladies such as hepatitis and venereal disease. This was one of the prison conditions for which the Eighth Amendment required a remedy, even though it was not alleged that the likely harm would occur immediately and even though the possible infection might not affect all of those exposed.... Nor can we hold that prison officials may be deliberately indifferent to the

exposure of inmates to a serious, communicable disease on the ground that the complaining inmate shows no serious current symptoms.

The Supreme Court sent the case back to the district court for retrial, where McKinney had to prove his allegations to show that the Eighth Amendment was violated and that "society considers the risk that the prisoner complains of to be so grave that it violates contemporary standards of decency to expose anyone unwillingly to such a risk." However, in 1992, the director of the Nevada State Prisons had adopted a smoking policy restricting smoking to specified areas, which made McKinney's case virtually moot (a hypothetical case—only cases involving real injury can be considered by the courts).

Guards Using Force

In *Whitney v. Albers* (475 U.S. 372, 1986) the Supreme Court ruled that guards, during prison disturbances or riots, must balance the need "to maintain or restore discipline" through force against the risk of injury to inmates. Those situations require prison officials "to act quickly and decisively" and allow guards and administrators leeway in their actions. In *Whitney* a prisoner was shot in the knee during an attempt to rescue a hostage. The Court found that the injury suffered by the prisoner was not cruel and unusual punishment under the circumstances.

In 1983 Keith Hudson, an inmate at the state penitentiary in Angola, Louisiana, argued with Jack McMillian, a guard. McMillian placed the inmate in handcuffs and shackles to take him to the administrative lockdown area. On the way, according to Hudson, McMillian punched him in the mouth, eyes, chest, and stomach. Another guard held him while the supervisor on duty watched. Hudson sued accusing the guards of cruel and unusual punishment.

A magistrate found that the guards used "force when there was no need to do so" and the supervisor allowed their conduct, thus violating the Eighth Amendment. The Court of Appeals for the Fifth Circuit, however, reversed the decision, ruling that:

...inmates alleging use of excessive force in violation of the Eighth Amendment must prove: (1) significant injury; (2) resulting "directly and only from the use of force that was clearly excessive to the need"; (3) the excessiveness of which was objectively unreasonable; and (4) that the action constituted an unnecessary and wanton infliction of pain.

The court agreed that the use of force was unreasonable and was a clearly excessive and unnecessary infliction of pain. However, the Court of Appeals found against Hudson because his injuries were "minor" and "required no medical attention."

The Supreme Court heard this case in 1992 (*Hudson v. McMillian* (503 U.S. 1) and disagreed that the inmate

had to suffer serious injury before the Eighth Amendment could be invoked. In *Whitney*, the Court argued, the "extent of injury suffered by an inmate is one factor" considered to determine whether the use of force was unnecessary. However, the absence of serious injury, while "relevant ... does not end" the Eighth Amendment inquiry. The question must be asked whether the force applied was a "good faith effort to maintain or restore discipline, or maliciously and sadistically [applied] to cause harm." Although the circuit court termed the blows "minor," the Supreme Court viewed the extent of Hudson's injuries as no basis to dismiss his claims and ruled in Hudson's favor by reversing the court of appeals.

DUE PROCESS COMPLAINTS

Due process complaints are brought under the Fourteenth and the Fifth Amendments and are based on procedural fairness. Most of the time disciplinary action in prison is taken on the word of the guard or the administrator, and the inmate has little opportunity to challenge the charges. Rules are often vague or not formally written out. Disrespect toward a guard tends to be defined by the guards themselves.

The Supreme Court, however, has affirmed that procedural fairness should be used in some institutional decisions. In *Wolff v. McDonnell* (418 U.S. 539, 1974), the Supreme Court declared that a Nebraska law providing for sentences to be shortened for good behavior created a "liberty interest." Thus, if an inmate met the requirements, prison officials could not deprive him of the shortened sentence without due process, according to the Fourteenth Amendment. The Court asserted

...that due process required that prisoners in procedure resulting in loss of good-time or in imposition of solitary confinement be afforded advance written notice of claimed violation, written statement of fact findings, and the right to call witnesses and present documentary evidence where such would not be unduly hazardous to institutional safety or correctional goals....

A prisoner is not wholly stripped of constitutional protections and though prison disciplinary proceedings do not imply the full panoply of rights due a defendant, such proceedings must be governed by a mutual accommodation between institutional needs and generally applicable constitutional requirements.

However, the inmate at a procedural hearing does not have a right to have counsel (lawyer, advisor) in the proceedings. Silence at a hearing can be used against the inmate because it is a disciplinary hearing, not a criminal proceeding. If incriminating testimony by an inmate could be used in later criminal proceedings, then he must be offered immunity if forced to testify (*Baxter v. Palmigiano*, 425 U.S. 208, 1975).

At the Metropolitan Correctional Center (MCC), a federally operated short-term custodial facility in New

York City designed mainly for pretrial detainees, inmates challenged the constitutionality of the facility's conditions. As this was a pretrial detention center, the challenge was brought under the due process clause of the Fifth Amendment. The District Court and the Court of Appeals found for the inmates, but the Supreme Court disagreed in *Bell v. Wolfish* (441 U.S. 520, 1979). Chief Justice William Rehnquist argued that:

> While confining a given number of people in a given amount of space in such a manner as to cause them to endure genuine deprivations and hardship over an extended period of time might raise serious questions under the Due Process Clause as to whether those conditions amounted to punishment, nothing even approaching such hardship is shown by this record.

> Detainees are required to spend only seven or eight hours in their room, during most or all of which they presumably are sleeping. The rooms provide more than adequate space for sleeping.... While "double bunking" may have taxed some of the equipment or particular facilities in certain of the common areas, ... this does not mean that the conditions at the MCC failed to meet the standards required by the Constitution. Our conclusion in this regard is further buttressed by the detainees' length of stay (most are released in 60 days).

The Court also ruled in *Bell* that the administrator could constitutionally prohibit inmates from receiving books that were not mailed directly from publishers, book clubs, or bookstores, and stop the delivery of packages of food and personal items from outside the institution. The administrator could also have body-cavity searches of inmates following contact visits with persons from the outside and require the detainees to remain outside their rooms during inspection.

EARLY RELEASE

Two cases decided in the late 1990s pertained to prisons releasing inmates early to relieve overcrowding and then later revoking their release status. Beginning in 1983 the Florida legislature enacted a series of laws authorizing the awarding of early release credits to prison inmates when the state prison population exceeded predetermined levels. In 1986 Kenneth Lynce received a 22-year prison sentence on a charge of attempted murder. In 1992 he was released based on the determination that he had accumulated five different types of early release credits totaling 5,668 days, including 1,860 days of "provisional credits" awarded as a result of prison overcrowding.

Shortly thereafter the state attorney general issued an opinion interpreting a 1992 statute as having retroactively canceled all provisional credits awarded to inmates convicted of murder and attempted murder. Lynce was rearrested and returned to custody. He filed a habeas corpus petition alleging that the retroactive cancellation of provisional credits violated the *ex post facto* clause of the Constitution.

The Supreme Court agreed with Lynce. In *Lynce v. Mathis* (65 LW 4131, 1997), the Court ruled that to fall within the *ex post facto* prohibition a law must be "retrospective" and "disadvantage the offender affected by it" *Weaver v. Graham* (450 U.S. 24, 29, 1981). The 1992 statute was clearly retrospective and disadvantaged Lynce by increasing his punishment.

The second case concerned Oklahoma's Preparole Conditional Supervision Program, which took effect whenever the state prisons became overcrowded and could authorize the conditional release of prisoners before their sentences expired. The Pardon and Parole Board determined who could participate in the program. An inmate was eligible for preparole after serving only 15 percent of a sentence, and was eligible for parole after one-third of the sentence had elapsed.

Ernest Harper was released under the preparole program. After he spent five apparently uneventful months outside prison, the governor denied him preparole. He was returned to prison without a hearing and on less than five hours' notice.

Despite Harper's claim that his reincarceration deprived him of liberty without due process in violation of the Fourteenth Amendment, the Oklahoma Court of Criminal Appeals and the Federal District Court denied him habeas corpus relief. The corrections department argued that the court had ruled that a hearing was not necessary to transfer a prisoner from a low-security prison to a higher-security one and that was what they were doing in this case.

The Tenth Circuit Court of Appeals, however, held that the preparole program was sufficiently like parole and a program participant was entitled to procedural protections. In *Leroy L. Young v. Ernest Eugene Harper* (65 LW 4197, 1997), the Supreme Court upheld the decision of the Tenth Circuit Court. It ruled that Oklahoma had violated Harper's due process rights by sending him back to prison without giving him a hearing to show that he had not met the conditions of the program.

THE COURT GOES BACK TO BASICS

In 1995 the Supreme Court made it harder for prisoners to bring constitutional suits to challenge due process rights. In a 5–4 decision in the case of *Sandin v. Conner* (515 U.S. 472), the majority asserted that it was frustrated with the number of due process cases, some of which, it felt, clogged the judiciary with unwarranted complaints such as claiming a "liberty interest" in not being transferred to a cell with an electrical outlet for a TV set.

Sandin concerned an inmate in Hawaii who was not allowed to call witnesses at a disciplinary hearing for misconduct that had placed him in solitary for 30 days. The Court of Appeals of the Ninth Circuit had held in 1993 that the inmate, Demont Conner, had a "liberty interest," allowing him a range of procedural protections in remaining free from solitary confinement. The Supreme Court overruled the Court of Appeals, stating that the inmate had no "liberty interest." Due process protections play a role only if the state's action has infringed on some separate, substantive right that the inmate possesses. For example, Wolff's loss of good time credit was a substantive right that he possessed. The punishment Conner had received "was within the range of confinement to be normally expected" since he was serving 30 years-to-life for a number of crimes, including murder.

"States may create liberty interests which are protected by the due process clause," but these will be limited to actions that "impose atypical and significant hardship on the inmate in relation to the ordinary incidents of prison life." Being put in solitary confinement in a prison where most inmates are limited to their cells most of the day anyway is not a liberty-interest issue. Because there was no liberty interest involved, how the hearing was handled was irrelevant.

Based on this ruling, the Court held that a federal court should consider a complaint to be a potential violation of a prisoner's due process rights only when prison staff imposed "atypical and significant hardship on the inmate." Mismanaged disciplinary hearings or temporary placement in solitary were just "ordinary incidents of prison and life and should not be considered violations of the Constitution."

Chief Justice Rehnquist asserted that past Supreme Court decisions have "led to the involvement of Federal courts in the day-to-day management of prisons, often squandering judicial resources with little offsetting benefit to anyone." Judges should allow prison administrators the flexibility to fine tune the ordinary incidents of prison life.

This decision continues the more conservative trend of the Supreme Court. Before the 1960s prisoners had few rights. A climate of reform beginning in the 1960s brought about a rash of cases that extended prisoners' rights over time. The pendulum has swung back since the 1980s in tandem with a rising rate of crime. A more conservative approach has led to more judicial restraint as the courts sought to balance the constitutional rights of the prisoners with the security interests of the correctional administrators.

THE INNOCENCE PROTECTION ACT

Not yet enacted into law as of mid-2003, the Innocence Protection Act, introduced in Congress by Senators Patrick Leahy (D-VT), Dorothy Smith (R-OR), and Susan Collins (R-ME) early in 2000 as Senate Bill 486, represents a potentially important step in the protection of prisoners' rights because it would provide prisoners convicted in capital cases access to post-conviction DNA testing. DNA testing has emerged as a powerful tool capable of establishing beyond doubt the innocence (but not the guilt) of a person in cases where organic matter from the perpetrator of a crime (blood, skin, semen, etc.) has been obtained by law-enforcement and these can be matched to DNA samples taken from an accused, indeed from a convicted, person.

All cells in the human body contain identical genetic material so that any particle of material taken from the body can be used to extract the person's deoxyribonucleic acid (DNA). DNA is made up of pairs of specific chemical bases arranged in sequence for the purpose of coding for proteins; DNA, however, also contains variable sequences the purpose of which is still not fully understood. Special enzymes can be used by the forensic technologist to isolate the same specific segments of the DNA from any two samples. DNA from two people can thus be compared. There is sufficient variability in the DNA of two people so that the same sequences, taken from the same places within the genetic material, are extremely unlikely to match unless the samples come from the same person. Guilt, however, cannot be established with certainty because an infinitesimal chance exists that two people *may* have exactly the same sequence of bases. DNA testing is thus used to establish innocence, which can be done with certainty.

According to Senator Leahy (Hearing on "Protecting the Innocent: Proposals to Reform the Death Penalty," Senate Judiciary Committee, June 18, 2002) as of mid-2002 101 persons had been exonerated of a capital crime by the use of post-conviction DNA testing.

Passage of S. 486 (pending as of July 2003), of which a House version has also been introduced by Representatives Bill Delahunt (D-MA) and Ray LaHood (R-IL), would empower prisoners convicted of a federal crime to apply to the courts for DNA testing to prove their innocence. Under the current version of the bill, the U.S. Department of Justice would also make grants to states to enable them to improve their procedures for defending those charged with capital offenses.

IMPORTANT NAMES AND ADDRESSES

American Bar Association
740 15th Street, NW
Washington, DC 20005-1019
(202) 662-1010
FAX: (202) 662-1032
URL: http://www.abanet.org

American Civil Liberties Union
Foundation (ACLU)
National Prison Project
733 15th Street, NW, Suite 620
Washington, DC 20005
(202) 393-4930
FAX: (202) 393-4931

American Correctional Association
4380 Forbes Blvd.
Lanham, MD 20706-4322
(301) 918-1800
FAX: (301) 918-1900
(800) 222-5646
URL: http://www.aca.org/index.asp

American Jail Association
1135 Professional Court
Hagerstown, MD 21740-5853
(301) 790-3930
FAX: (301) 790-2941
(800) 222-5646
E-mail: aja@corrections.com
URL: http://www.corrections.com/aja

Amnesty International USA
National Office
322 8th Ave.
New York, NY 10001
(212) 807-8400
FAX: (212) 627-1451
URL: http://www.amnestyusa.org/

Bureau of Justice Statistics
810 7th Street, NW
Washington, DC 20531
(202) 307-0765

FAX: (202) 307-5846
(800) 732-3277
E-mail: askbjs@ojp.usboj.gov
URL: http://www.ojp.usdoj.gov/bjs

Campaign for an Effective Crime Policy
1015 18th Street, NW, Suite 300
Washington, DC 200036
(202) 223-7770
FAX: (202) 223-8537
E-mail: info@hudsondc.org
URL: http://www.crimepolicy.org

Criminal Justice Institute, Inc.
213 Court Street, Suite 606
Middletown, CT 06457
(860) 704-6400
FAX: (860) 704-6420
E-mail: cji@cji-inc.com
URL: http://www.cji-inc.com

Families Against Mandatory Minimums
1612 K Street, NW, Suite 700
Washington, DC 20006
(202) 822-6700
FAX: (202) 822-6704
E-mail: famm@famm.org
URL: http://www.famm.org/index2.htm

Federal Bureau of Investigation
935 Pennsylvania Ave., NW
Washington, DC 20535-0001
(202) 324-3000
FAX: (202) 324-4705
URL: http://www.fbi.gov

Federal Bureau of Prisons
320 1st Street, NW
Washington, DC 20534
(202) 307-3198
FAX: (202) 514-6620
URL: http://www.bop.gov

Federal Judicial Center
1 Columbus Circle, NE
Washington, DC 20002-8003
(202) 502-4000
FAX: (202) 502-4099
URL: http://www.fjc.gov

Justice Research and Statistics
Association
777 North Capitol Street, NE, Suite 801
Washington, DC 20002
(202) 842-9330
FAX: (202) 842-9329
E-mail: cjinfo@jrsa.org
URL: http://www.jrsa.org

Juvenile Justice and Delinquency
Prevention
810 7th Street, NW
Washington, DC 20531
(202) 307-5911
FAX: (202) 307-2093
E-mail: askjj@ncjrs.org
URL: http://www.ojjdp.ncjrs.org

NAACP Legal Defense and Educational
Fund
1444 I Street, NW, 10th Floor
Washington, DC 20005
(202) 682-1300
NY Office: (212) 219-1900
FAX: (202) 682-1312

National Center on Institutions and
Alternatives
7222 Ambassador Road
Baltimore, MD 21244
(410) 265-1490
FAX: (410) 597-9656
URL: http://www.ncianet.org

National Conference of State Legislatures
7700 East 1st Place
Denver, CO 80230

(303) 364-7700
FAX: (303) 364-7800
URL: http://www.ncsl.org

National Council on Crime and Delinquency
1970 Broadway, Suite 500
Oakland, CA 94612
(510) 208-0500
FAX: (510) 208-0511
URL: http://www.nccd-crc.org

National Criminal Justice Association
720 7th Street, NW, 3rd Floor
Washington, DC 20001-3716
(202) 628-8550
FAX: (202) 628-0080
E-mail: info@ncja.org
URL: http://www.ncja.org

National Criminal Justice Reference Service
P.O. Box 6000
Rockville, MD 20849-6000

(301) 519-5500
(800) 851-3420
URL: http://www.ncjrs.org

National Institute of Justice
810 7th Street, NW
Washington, DC 20531
(202) 307-2942
FAX: (202) 307-6394
(800) 851-3420
E-mail: askncjrs@ncjrs.org
URL: http://www.ojp.usdoj.gov/nij

National Legal Aid and Defender Association
1140 Connecticut Ave., NW, Suite 900
Washington, DC 20036
(202) 452-0620
FAX: (202) 872-1031
E-mail: info@nlada.org
URL: http://www.nlada.org

The Sentencing Project
154 10th Street, NW, Suite 1000
Washington, DC 20004
(202) 628-0871
FAX: (202) 628-1091
E-mail: staff@sentencingproject.org
URL: http://www.sentencingproject.org

U.S. Parole Commission
5550 Friendship Blvd., Suite 420
Chevy Chase, MD 20815-7286
(301) 492-5990
FAX: (301) 492-6694
URL: http://www.usdoj.gov/uspc

U.S. Sentencing Commission
1 Columbus Circle, NE
Washington, DC 20002-8002
(202) 502-4500
URL: http://www.ussc.gov

RESOURCES

The Bureau of Justice Statistics (BJS) of the U.S. Department of Justice is a major source of data and information concerning crime, sentencing, and inmates. *Correctional Populations in the United States, 1997* (2000) summarizes information on inmates in the nation's jails and prisons. Other valuable BJS publications include: *Truth in Sentencing in State Prisons* (1999); *Felony Sentences in State Courts 1998* (2001); *Prison and Jail Inmates at Midyear 2002* (2003); *Capital Punishment, 2001* (2003); *Prisoners in 2001* (2002); *Education and Correctional Population* (2003); *Juveniles in Adult Prisons and Jails: A National Assessment* (2000); *HIV in Prisons 2000* (2002); *Prior Abuse Reported by Inmates and Probationers* (1999); *Mental Health Treatment in State Prisons, 2000* (2001); *Compendium of Federal Justice Statistics, 1998* (2000); *Health Treatment of Inmates and Probationers* (1999); *Incarcerated Parents and Their Children* (2000); *Women Offenders* (2000); *Trends in State Parole, 1990–2000* (2001); *Reentry Trends in the United States* (2002); *Probation and Parole in the United States, 2001* (2002); *Jails in Indian Country, 2001* (2002); *Immigration Offenders in the Federal Criminal Justice System, 2000* (2002), and *Drug Use, Testing and Treatment in Jails* (2000). The BJS also produced the *Sourcebook of Criminal Justice Statistics 2001* (2002), with the Hindelang Criminal Justice Research Center, State University of New York, Albany.

The National Institute of Justice (NIJ) researches criminal issues and publishes *The National Institute of Justice Journal,* whose article "Can Telemedicine Reduce Spending and Improve Prisoner Health Care?" (April 1999) was cited in this publication. Another NIJ publication used in this publication is *Research in Brief,* "Three Strikes and You're Out: A Review of State Legislation" (1997).

The Federal Bureau of Investigation's *Crime in the United States—2001* (2002) provides the latest arrest statistics and crime rates and is an essential resource for those interested in studying crime across the country.

The U.S. government's Office of Juvenile Justice and Delinquency Prevention (OJJDP), an excellent resource on juvenile justice, produced *Juvenile Offenders and Victims: 1999 National Report* (1999); *Juvenile Arrests 2000* (2002); *Juvenile Offenders in Residential Placement: 1997–1999* (2002); *Juvenile Residential Facility Census, 2000: Selected Findings* (2002), and *OJJDP Statistical Briefing Book* (2002).

Information Plus thanks the U.S. Census Bureau for numerous population studies, including *Profile of the Foreign-Born Population in the United States: 2000* (2001) as well as information contained in the *Statistical Abstract of the United States: 2002* (2003).

Other sources include: *The Impact of "Three Strikes and You're Out" Laws: What We Have Learned* (1996) from the Campaign for an Effective Crime Policy (Washington, D.C.); *The Case for Shorter Prison Terms: The Illinois Experience* (1994) from the National Council on Crime and Delinquency (San Francisco); and *Sexual Misconduct in Prisons: Laws, Remedies and Incidence* (2000), published by the National Institute of Corrections, Longmont, Colorado. Information Plus is also thankful for the valuable data presented in the United States Sentencing Commission's publication *2002 Federal Sentencing Guideline Manual* (2002). Also very useful were the data from the Central Intelligence Agency's *World Factbook 2002,* published in 2003.

INDEX

Page references with the letter t following them indicate the presence of a table. The letter f indicates a figure. If more than one table or figure appears on a particular page, the exact item number for the table or figure being referenced is provided.

I

Idaho
  incarceration rates, 26
  percentage change in prison
    population, 7
  ratio of parolees to population, 73
Illegal Immigration Reform and
  Immigration Responsibility Act of
  1996, 95
Illinois
  first juvenile court, 5
  minimum age authorized for application
    of death penalty, 64
Immigrant population, 94-97
  detainees under INS jurisdiction, 95*t*
  detainees under INS jurisdiction on
    selected days, 96(*t*10.4)
  illegal entry to the United States, 95
  increase in population, 94-95
  percentage of total population, 94*f*
  persons referred to U.S. attorneys for
    suspected immigration offenses, 95*f*
  rates of confinement in the United
    States, 91
Immigration Act of 1990, 95
Immigration and Nationality Act of 1965, 94
Immigration and Naturalization Service,
  See INS
*Immigration Offenders in the Federal
  Criminal Justice System, 2000,* 95
Immigration Reform and Control Act of
  1986, 95
Incarceration rates, 7, 25-26, 37
  by year, 16
  increase in federal and state prisons, 25
  increase in incarceration rates of
    women, 26
  per capita expenditures, 12(*f*.2.6)
  reasons for increase, 7
  selected states, 26
  United States compared to other, selected
    countries, 25
  weapons violations, 7
Indian Civil Rights Act of 1968, 94
Indian country
  American Indians and Alaska Natives
    under tribal jurisdiction, 94
  crimes relegated to federal
    jurisdiction, 92-93
  jail inmates and jail capacity, 94*t*
Indiana, 64
Inmates, *See* Juveniles; Prisoners; Women
Innocence Protection Act, 111
INS (Immigration and Naturalization
  Service), 95
Intensive Probation Supervision, 89-90
Intermittent incarceration, *See* Weekend
  sentences; Work programs

Isolation, *See* Eighth Amendment cases

J

Jackson v. Georgia (1972), 97
Jail industries, 23-24, 33-35
Jails, 15-24
  average daily population, by age and
    gender, 16(*t*3.3)
  capacity, 17, 21
  capacity and occupancy, 18
  capacity and percent of capacity
    occupied, 18(*t*3.5)
  distinction between jails and prisons, 15
  employees' characteristics, 21-22
  increase in number of federal and private
    jails, 21-22
  inmates, characteristics of, 19(*t*3.8)
  medieval, 1
  number of prisoners held in jail and
    incarceration rates, by year, 16(*t*3.2)
  occupancy as percent of
    capacity, 18(*t*3.6)
  persons under supervision, by
    confinement status and type of
    program, 20(*t*3.11)
  population, by size of jail
    jurisdiction, 17-18
  selected characteristics, 22(*t*3.14)
Johnson v. Avery (1969), 102
Johnson, Lyndon B., 4
Judiciary Act of 1789, 101
Justice Assistance Act of 1984, 23
Justice system expenditures per capita, 10*t*
Justification for punishment by
  imprisonment, 1
Juvenile boot camps, *See* Boot camps
*Juvenile Boot Camps: Cost and
  Effectiveness vs. Residential
  Facilities,* 65
Juvenile Court Act of 1899, 5, 55
Juvenile courts, 55-56
Juvenile Delinquency Prevention and
  Control Act of 1968, 56
Juvenile Justice and Delinquency Prevention
  Act of 1974, 6
*Juvenile Offenders and Victims: 1999
  National Report,* 56
Juveniles, 5-6
  in adult prisons and jails, 19(*t*3.9)
  arrest rates by offense and
    race/ethnicity, 59*t*
  arrest rates, by gender, 58(*f*7.4)
  arrest trends compared to those of adult
    population, 58
  arrested for Property Crime Index
    offenses, 57(*f*7.2)
  arrested for Violent Crime Index
    violations, 58(*f*7.3)

  average daily number incarcerated in
    local jails, 16(*t*3.3)
  changes in laws governing, by
    state, 56(*t*7.3)
  confined to jails and prisons, 59(*f*7.6)
  disposition of juveniles arrested, 58
  increase in incarceration rates, 57
  increase in inmate population, 16
  increase in numbers being tried as
    adults, 55
  increase in population in residential
    facilities, 61
  minimum age authorized for death
    penalty, 63-64
  minimum age authorized for death
    penalty, by state, 64*t*
  number of beds in residential placement
    facilities, by state, 62*t*
  offenders in residential placement, by
    offense, 60, 60(*t*7.6), 61
  offense profile of juveniles, by placement
    status, 63*t*
  oldest age for original juvenile court
    jurisdiction in delinquency
    matters, 55*t*
  oldest age over which juvenile court may
    retain jurisdiction, 56(*t*7.2)
  percent distribution of juveniles taken
    into police custody, 59(*f*7.5)
  percent of population,
    1980-2000, 57*t*
  prison population, 58
  proportion of U.S. total
    population, 57(*f*7.1)
  rehabilitation, 56
  residential facilities, by state, 61*t*
  in residential placement facilities, by
    legal status, 62
  in residential placement facilities, by
    race/ethnicity, 64*f*
  in residential placement, 60
  segregation from adult prison
    population, 5-6
  sentenced as adults, 65
  state definitions by age, 55
  substance abuse and treatment, 59-60
Juveniles in Adult Prisons and Jails, 59

K

Kansas, 64
Kentucky, 27, 64
King County (WA), 18
Kinnison, Abdullah v. (1985), 104
Koch Crime Institute, 65

L

LaHood, Ray, 111
Latin America, 95